Praise for Scrolling Forward

"*Scrolling Forward* . . . changed the way I relate to the world around me. . . . This book changed the way I think—and, more importantly, the way I feel—about written language, which is to say it changed the way I think and feel about time and text, mortality and materiality, meaning and being."

—from the foreword by Ruth Ozeki,
author of *A Tale for the Time Being*

"A masterpiece. Insightful, penetrating, and beautifully written. [Levy] takes us on a personal journey th⸮ eals the essence of documents, their pr⸮ nd their spiritual roles, roles that are noticed. . . . This book will speak to a ⸮ etter understand how we create meani⸮

—John See⸮ ⸮m, former director of Xerox Palo Alto
Research Center, coauthor of *The Social Life of Information*

"A fascinating and original personal mediation and cultural exploration . . . This book will change forever the way you regard the written word."

—Deborah Tannen, author of
You Just Don't Understand

"A nuanced, sympathetic, and endlessly fascinating portrait of our most ubiquitous servant and companion: the document . . . Levy's discussion goes far beyond the usual hype and techno-mystique to focus on the deepest questions of human communication and meaning. That he manages to bring all this off with warmth and good humor is not the least of the gifts this book offers."

—Norman Fischer, author of *The Strugglers* and
former abbot of the San Francisco Zen Center

"Absorbing . . . [Levy] is both adept in new technologies of writing and steeped in traditional ones . . . Refreshing to anyone weary of the platitudes of high-tech hyperbole and indignant old guard nostalgia."
—Geoffrey Nunberg, commentator on *Fresh Air* and editor of the *American Heritage Dictionary* and *The Future of the Book*

"Fascinating . . . Levy provides a rich context—personal, historical, philosophical, spiritual—for understanding these humble artifacts of human thought and human sharing."
—David Weinberger, NPR commentator and author of *Too Big to Know*

"Questions about how books and libraries will fare in the digital age . . . are elevated to exquisite and philosophical explanations of how we humans find meaning in life."
—Deanna Marcum, former president of the Council on Library and Information Resources

"Readers will never look at a deli receipt in the same way after finishing this gripping discussion of written forms. . . . [Levy's] assessment of how documents work and what they say about our culture and values is a worthy one."
—*Publishers Weekly*

"Levy offers a vigorous, philosophical, and intellectually stimulating interpretative overview of [documents] evolution and impact on culture. . . . As he considers the vagaries of digital technologies versus our craving for order, he expresses unexpectedly poetic insights into our carried-in-the-genes sense that there is a 'sacred quality' to reading, even in the age of multitasking."
—*Booklist*

SCROLLING FORWARD

Also by David M. Levy

Mindful Tech: How to Bring Balance to Our Digital Lives

SCROLLING FORWARD

MAKING SENSE OF DOCUMENTS
IN THE DIGITAL AGE

SECOND EDITION

by

David M. Levy

With a New Preface by the Author

Foreword by Ruth Ozeki

ARCADE PUBLISHING • NEW YORK

Second Edition

New York: September 11 photograph by Larry Towell/Magnum Photos.

"The House Was Quiet and the World Was Calm" from The Collected Poems of Wallace Stevens, copyright © 1954 by Wallace Stevens. Used by permission of Alfred A. Knopf, a division of Random House, Inc.

Mercury Villager SUV ad courtesy of Ford Motor Company

"The Annunciation, with Saint Emidius" painting by Carlo Crivelli, used by permission of the National Gallery Picture Library, London

Arcade Publishing books may be purchased in bulk at special discounts for sales promotion, corporate gifts, fund-raising, or educational purposes. Special editions can also be created to specifications. For details, contact the Special Sales Department, Arcade Publishing, 307 West 36th Street, 11th Floor, New York, NY 10018 or arcade@skyhorsepublishing.com.

Arcade Publishing® is a registered trademark of Skyhorse Publishing, Inc.®, a Delaware corporation.

Visit our website at www.arcadepub.com.
Visit the author's website at www.davidmlevy.net.
Visit Ruth Ozeki's website at www.ruthozeki.com.

10 9 8 7 6 5 4 3 2 1

Library of Congress Cataloging-in-Publication Data is available on file.

Cover design by Owen Corrigan
Cover photo: Thinkstock

Print ISBN: 978-1-62872-327-4
Ebook ISBN: 978-1-62872-698-5

Printed in the United States of America

For Zari

באהבה רבה

Why should I wish to see God better than this day?
I see something of God each hour of the twenty-four,
    and each moment then,
In the faces of men and women I see God,
    and in my own face in the glass,
I find letters from God dropt in the street,
    and every one is sign'd by God's name,
And I leave them where they are,
    for I know that wheresoe'er I go,
Others will punctually come for ever and ever.

—Walt Whitman, "Song of Myself"
as reproduced in the Peter Pauper edition of *Leaves of Grass*

Contents

Foreword

I F YOU ARE READING THIS foreword—and for the sake of this exercise, I'm going to assume that you are indeed reading it and not washing the dishes or watching a ball game on TV or checking your email—then you are holding a book in your hands. It might not be the kind of book your grandparents learned to read when they were little. They might not even recognize your device as a book. But for the sake of our discussion, let's agree to call this thing you're reading a book, regardless of whether it has an on/off switch or whether you're reading it on a screen or on pages made of paper, which you must operate by turning rather than swiping because they can tear.

This book you're holding is called *Scrolling Forward: Making Sense of Documents in the Digital Age*, and it's a book that changed the way I relate to the world around me. That's saying a lot. Few books have such a profound and lasting effect on a life, and as a result, this is one of my favorite books, which is also saying a lot because I read a lot of books. So you're holding it, and I'm holding it, and while we are holding the same book, I think we can agree that they are different books, too.

My copy of the book comprises 212 pages, bound between soft covers, containing some 75,000 or so words, not including the handwritten ones that I've scribbled in the margins over the past decade, which wind sinuously up and around the edges of the pages, occasionally trespassing into a column of underlined print or spilling excitedly into the gutter or onto an adjacent page, peppered with exclamation points and threaded with arrows. Your book does not contain my delighted marginalia, although it might contain other jottings if you happen to be rereading your old copy of the book, as I am, or if perhaps you purchased a secondhand edition, previously owned by a reader as besotted as I.[1]

However, if your book is the new and long-awaited 2016 reprint by Arcade Publishing, its pages are no doubt still pristine and free of user annotation. I'm fairly certain they won't remain that way for long. I'm fairly certain that by the time you finish reading it, your copy will be as replete with your thoughts, ideas, and exclamatory musings as my copy is with mine.[2]

When I say that *Scrolling Forward* changed the way I relate to the world, I'm not indulging in hyperbole or rhetorical excess. I'm simply stating a fact. This book changed the way I think—and, more importantly, the way I *feel*—about written language, which is to say it changed the way I think and feel about time and text, mortality and materiality, meaning and being. But I think some explanation is in order here, because this unassuming book is so much more than it appears to be at first glance.

Scrolling Forward sets itself a modest-seeming task, to examine the significance of written documents at a pivotal moment in the evolution of writing technology, and indeed it starts with a meditation on an ordinary cash register receipt. But in David Levy's hands, this mundane receipt for a tuna fish sandwich, a bag of chips, and a bottle of water unfolds like magical origami into something myriad and multifaceted, taking us back into early history, forward into our future, and deep

---

1 Of course, if you are indeed reading an old copy of the book, you are also not reading this foreword, which I've been asked to write for the new 2016 reprint edition by Arcade Publishing, and which is not included in previous editions . . . in which case this entire discussion is moot.

2 If you are reading a library book, you may have to claim you lost it and just pay the fine.

into the existential questions of what it means to be human. With his background in computer science, as well as his training in the physical arts of calligraphy and bookmaking, Levy is a consummate conjurer and guide as he moves us to consider the history and evolution of documents, and the human needs they serve: a Walt Whitman poem and our need for self-expression; bureaucratic documentation, the IRS, and our need for control; letters, postcards, email, and our need for connection; libraries, reading, and the economics of attention. He makes visible the invisible and animates the quotidian stuff of everyday life. He takes familiar things and makes them new and strange, which is what magic, art, poetry, and philosophy should do.

So, this wise, thoughtful, and thought-provoking book both moved me and woke me up. It changed the way I approach my own art making, which is the writing of fiction, and as I read it, I felt irresistibly drawn to respond. Books are like that. They are conversations between minds across time, and I wanted to be a part of this particular conversation and to meet this book where it lives, on the page. And so I did,[3] and so I continue to do, which is another way of saying that this book has inspired me and my own work in profound and mysterious ways.

I hope this book will inspire you, too. I hope it will wake you up, open your eyes, and move you to notice things you might not have noticed. I hope it will change the way you think and feel about life, language, and the myriad things of the world that surround you. I'm sure it will. Just holding this book in my hands again, after so many years, gives me a feeling of imminent excitement. Perhaps you are feeling this, too.

Ruth Ozeki
Whaletown, British Columbia

---

3 My recent novel, *A Tale for the Time Being*, was inspired by *Scrolling Forward*, and the one I'm working on right now will be, too.

Preface to the 2016 Edition

I FIRST SAW THE WORLD WIDE Web on Thursday, August 13, 1992, at 10:00 a.m. I know the date and time with this precision, because I still have a copy of the email message announcing that Tim Berners-Lee would give a presentation at the Xerox Palo Alto Research Center (PARC), the high-tech think tank where I was a researcher.

```
Date:Thursday, August 13, 1992
Time:10:00 am
Place:CSL Commons (35-2230)

What:World-Wide Web - The Universe of Information
Who:Tim Berners-Lee, CERN
```

The W3 initiative ties together many varying information systems into a homogeneous browsable, searchable web. By combining a hypertext user interface with index queries, the data model allows almost any existing information system to be represented in the web. The simple intuitive user interface gives the impression of a seamless continuum, when data is in fact furnished by FTP, Gopher, NNTP and WAIS in addition to native W3 servers.

A practical collaboration rather than research project, W3 has seen success as a distributed information system, and will in the future extend to collaborative authoring and multi-format document delivery.

The talk will outline the techniques used, describe methods of making data available on the "web," and describe the various browsers available for different platforms, and future directions.

On the day I was introduced to the Web, it was still relatively unknown. It would take several more years before the Web would explode onto the larger scene. Neither Netscape Navigator nor Microsoft Explorer had yet been developed; nor had their noncommercial antecedent, the Mosaic Web browser. Consequently, Berners-Lee was able only to give a fairly primitive demo, showing off the basic linking facility without the benefit of a sophisticated user interface. Using a computer in the conference room at PARC, he downloaded and displayed several documents stored on a computer in Switzerland.

Only a handful of researchers were present for Berners-Lee's demonstration in the beanbag room at PARC that morning. I still vividly remember my first impression of the Web. I was distinctly unimpressed. Nor did I detect much enthusiasm from my colleagues. From a research perspective, there was nothing particularly novel here. Two previously existing technologies—hypertext and the Internet—were being combined in a fairly straightforward manner, making it possible to follow links from one computer to another. What's more, the hypertext capabilities being shown off weren't all that impressive, at least as measured by the standards of the hypertext research of the time. I basically dismissed what I had seen as uninteresting and inconsequential. "Big deal," I thought to myself as I walked out of the room.

This story never made it into the first edition of *Scrolling Forward*. But over the years, I have told it many times in a number of speaking engagements. Here's proof that you should never trust my predictions, I tell my audience. (Fortunately, I'm not in the business of picking stocks or forecasting technological trends.) But, I go on to say, there is another, larger point to be made from this story. Yes, we can certainly say that I'd been shown the future and had failed to grasp it; from where we stand now, this seems an obvious enough conclusion. But what we were seeing that August day was a nascent technology or set of technologies. The Web—what we now think of as the Web—did not yet exist. For those rudimentary technologies on display to *become* the Web would require the accumulation of a significant amount of content; and the tools and materials yet to be realized would have to be taken up into people's lives in ways that really mattered to them. That this would happen at all, let alone at such a rapid pace, was not foreseeable. That it would look and feel like the Web as we currently know it was hardly fore-ordained. And none of this was simply inherent in the technology.

I wrote most of *Scrolling Forward* during the dot-com boom, when the World Wide Web and the Internet were being recognized as a remarkable new global information and communication platform. The bust following the boom was inevitable, and that's when *Scrolling Forward* appeared in print. During the boom, everything being written about the digital world was being reviewed (or so it seemed), but once the bubble burst, critics and the news outlets they represented lost interest in the topic, and *Scrolling Forward* received little critical attention in the mainstream press. The two exceptions were a book review in the *Los Angeles Times* and brief mention in the *New Yorker*.

But I was never interested in writing just for the moment. Rather than analyzing particular technologies or predicting new developments, I was interested in trying to locate digital developments in the larger sweep of history and in the age-old human search for stability and meaning. To the extent that I succeeded, the book remains relevant more than a decade after it first appeared. (Of course you, the reader, will be the ultimate judge of that.)

My primary aim was to understand the ways in which digital developments were novel—perhaps even revolutionary—and the ways in which they represented a gradual evolution from the past. I wanted to avoid the two standard and, to my mind, uninteresting extremes: the utopian view celebrating digital things as the answer to life's problems and the dystopian or Luddite view decrying the loss of a happier and healthier world. My way in was to examine the nature of documents—written forms of all kinds—and to see how the emergence of digital documents was in some ways continuous with the evolution of paper documents (and those created out of other tangible materials) and how in other ways it represented a break with the past. In a nutshell, this is the story the book tried to tell:

Our written forms, whatever their medium, are "talking things." They are bits of the material world that we imbue with the power to speak and act for us. They are surrogates for us, little sorcerer's apprentices we send out into the world to do our bidding. And what exactly do they do for us? In one sense, anything and everything— that's the power and beauty of them. A cash register receipt can serve as a witness to a financial transaction, a book of poetry can proclaim the words of the poet, a Facebook post or a tweet can inform our friends of our current status and whereabouts. But in another sense (or so this story goes) all of these functions can be understood as attempts to create and maintain a stable and meaningful world: to create stable, functioning organizations through bureaucratic records; to maintain personal, even intimate, relations among humans through letters and postcards, and now, social media; to sanction and circulate public knowledge through print and now digital publications.

This story provides an answer of sorts to the question: what's old and what's new? What's old—thousands of years old, in fact—is the use of written forms to make and maintain a meaningful world, a meaningful life. That's just what literate cultures do. What's new is the medium (from the Latin word meaning "middle"), this digital stuff out of which we've been busy creating new genres (new kinds of written forms) to do our bidding. When I was writing *Scrolling Forward*, blogs did not yet exist, nor did Facebook, nor Twitter. (And if readers are still finding their way to this book ten years hence, there will be many more new formats and genres that I can't begin to imagine today.) But even in these unimagined and unpredicted developments, we can see both what is new (new genres, new surrogates, new social functions) and also what is old (the ever-ongoing emergence of new kinds of talking things to serve the social, political, and commercial needs of the times).

Scrolling Forward, of course, is itself a document, a talking thing that speaks in a particular voice and from a particular vantage point. In preparing this new edition, I have decided not to alter the original text. There are occasional errors: on page 190, for example, I call the Mercury Villager a sport utility vehicle when in fact it is a minivan. Some of the examples are obviously dated, but at the same time they take us back—usefully, I hope—to a time when the Web was young. Several elements of the present edition are new: this preface; Ruth Ozeki's foreword, for which I am extremely grateful; and the index, which was prepared for the first edition but never included.

❁ ❁ ❁

The publication of *Scrolling Forward* was the summation of work I had been doing for more than a decade. What have I been up to since? I will mention two directions: the creation and teaching of a course based on *Scrolling Forward*, and an ongoing investigation into the possibility of achieving greater contemplative balance.

First, the teaching: I began my association with the University of Washington's Information School in the summer of 2000. (For that first academic year, 2000–2001, I was a visiting professor at the iSchool, and the next year accepted a full-time permanent position.) During that first year, Mike Eisenberg, then the dean of the school, suggested that I create a course based on *Scrolling Forward*, which was then largely completed but not yet published. He proposed a title: "The History of Recorded Information"—not a title I would have chosen myself but one I was willing to use.

As I began to mull over what such a course might contain and how it should be structured, I was introduced to Sandra Kroupa, the Book Arts & Rare Book Curator at the University Libraries. Chatting in my little office, one building away from the main library, we quickly discovered our shared loved of books and of the Arts and Crafts movement. I broached the subject of the course with her and invited her to participate in the creation and teaching of it. Thus began what has been a wonderfully fruitful collaboration of nearly fifteen years.

We first taught the course in the spring quarter, 2001, and we have taught it yearly ever since. The course has three main units, which address the nature of bureaucratic documents, the handwritten letter and the genres that have emerged from it, and the history of the book. Complementing these intellectual investigations, and crucial to our conception of the course from the very beginning, are a number of hands-on, experiential elements. A library bookbinder teaches students to make a simple book (a codex), folding the paper, sewing the sections, and creating a simple cover. Sandra teaches students the rudiments of descriptive bibliography (a traditional method of describing the structure of a printed book), and each student is given a historical book, most of them from the sixteenth and seventeenth centuries, to describe. She also shows students the basics of letterpress printing, demonstrating the process on a nineteenth-century Reliance iron handpress permanently installed in the Special Collections classroom, where the class regularly meets. I teach a session on the basics of calligraphy, giving students broad-edged pens and helping them see (and feel, through the movement of their hands and the contact between pen and paper) how the shapes of the Roman letters were first articulated by the hand and eye, and later reproduced in metal type, and still later on digital screens. Throughout the term, Sandra brings in relevant historical materials from Special Collections for students to handle and study.

Thus, in its structure and content, the course exemplifies a teaching principle that is quite dear to me: the blending of conceptual and experiential learning. Students learn about the shapes of letters by making them with a traditional tool. They don't just read about the history of books, they make one. And they hold historical books in their hands, discovering concretely how the traditional printing process regularly led to a number of printing and binding errors, making each copy of a printed edition unique.

And so, in the digital age, when material objects sometimes seem to be disappearing into the ether (now called the cloud), in this one course we continue to investigate and to celebrate the material artifact, not because there is anything wrong with digital materials but because there is something very right—sensual, instructive, enlivening—about the physical objects that for so long were such powerful conveyors of meaning and value, and that remain so. For a final project, students must choose an artifact (a document) or a collection to investigate. It can be something that has personal meaning (a letter or a book, for example, that has been passed down through the family) or that Sandra has helped them find in Special Collections. Their job is to investigate the artifact as a unique item but also to see it in its broader context, as an instance of a genre inhabiting a particular historical niche. They are also encouraged to bring themselves into the picture, talking about their response to and relationship with the artifact in question (much as I do in chapter 3, where I talk about my childhood copy of *Leaves of Grass*).

I love the papers students write about their chosen artifacts and collections. The students come alive when they've chosen something they really care about and when they're able to combine an intellectual investigation of form, content, and context with an account of their lived relationship to their object of study. Off and on for years I've thought about producing an edited collection of these essays.

At some point over these years of teaching, I discovered a book called *The Presence of the Past* by two academic historians, Roy Rosenzweig and David Thelen. Subtitled *Popular Uses of History in American Life*, it explores how ordinary people, rather than professional historians, relate to and make use of the past. One of their main discoveries is that people best connect with the past when they can find themselves in it. Discovering a personal connection makes the connection come alive:

"For most of the people who talked with us, the familial and intimate past, along with intimate uses of other pasts, matters most. They prefer the personal and firsthand because they feel at home with that past: they live with it, relive it, interpret and reinterpret it; they use it to define themselves, their place in their families, and their families' place in the *world* . . . In their desire to strip away layers of mediation, respondents trust eyewitnesses more than television or movies. They feel connected to the past in museums because authentic artifacts seem to transport them straight back to the times when history was being made. They feel unconnected to the past in history classrooms because they don't recognize themselves in the version of the past presented there. When asked to describe studying history in school, they most often use the words *dull* and *irrelevant*."[1]

In our course, Sandra and I have seen again and again, the presence of the artifact serves as a concrete bridge.

But *Scrolling Forward* was never just about the past, and neither is the course. Seeing the evolution of the letter, or of the myriad forms of bureaucratic documents, provides grounding for and helps illuminate the changes we are going through now, the new forms of intimate and social communication, such as Facebook or texting,

1 Roy Rosenzweig and David Thelen, *The Presence of the Past: Popular Uses of History in American Life* (New York: Columbia University Press, 1998), 12.

that continue to emerge and the way that business-oriented smart-phone apps exemplify the same principles of bureaucratic control that were central to the paper form.

What about the book, the codex? When I was writing *Scrolling Forward*, there was much debate about the future of the book, with predictions in some quarters of its imminent demise. Today, of course, the book is far from dead, although it has undergone some real changes. E-readers and tablets have established themselves as much-valued alternatives to reading on paper. For now at least, these are truly alternatives to, not replacements for, the printed, bound volume. What's more, the format of the digital book still largely reflects, and for the most part mimics, the paper book, with static pages and illustrations. (Yes of course, there are useful additions, such as the search function and live links to auxiliary material, but these haven't significantly altered the look or functionality of the book.) Curiously, it is the newspaper, as it has moved from paper to digital format, that has undergone a much greater transformation, incorporating video, reader's comments, and more. Whether the book will ultimately follow this trajectory is not for me to say—and given my opening story, you wouldn't want to trust my predictions on this score. Nor would I venture to say what will happen to the publishing industry, which seems to be in perpetual crisis.

What I do find most exciting in the world of the book, however, is a movement that I probably would have missed had I not been collaborating with Sandra over these years. In her more than forty years at the University of Washington Libraries, Sandra has amassed one of the great collections of modern book arts in the United States. The phrase "modern book arts" encompasses a variety of initiatives, including the modern letterpress movement (printing and binding fine, traditional-looking books); altered books; experimental writing; visual, conceptual and sculptural work; and graphic novels, comics, and zines. While Sandra collects in all these areas, she has a particular passion for what I will call innovative books. These are physical artifacts that play upon, adapt, or expand upon the traditional form and content of the book. There is a great upwelling of creativity being displayed in this area.

What seems to be happening is this: Digital materials have now proven themselves to be powerful and highly valued alternatives to paper and print. The book is no longer the only, or even the primary, vehicle for the packaging and distribution of "public" ideas. The author or the artist now has greater choice in the selection of a format. Choosing the book as one's vehicle represents a creative choice rather than a foregone conclusion, and the creator is free to play with form and content in highly original ways, as the University of Washington Libraries' collection so vividly demonstrates. It appears that we have not so much been liberated *from the book* (as celebrators of the death of the book once said) as liberated *to play with it*. Leaving aside the economics of book publishing and the uncertainties about future publishing models and revenue sources, I would suggest that this is actually a great time for books and book lovers, given the choice of modes (paper and digital) and the playful experimentation in the art world.

❅ ❅ ❅

Teaching this course once a year has kept me reflecting on the nature and transformation of written forms, and it has allowed me to witness ongoing changes in genres, technologies, and social practices through the eyes of my students as well as my own. But my primary focus has been elsewhere: For two decades I have been attending to, and concerned about, the acceleration of life, the growing sense of information overload, and the dangers inherent in a life lived entirely in the fast lane. These concerns make their appearance briefly in *Scrolling Forward*: In chapter 6, I raise the possibility that our digital technologies, while promising to connect us, are actually also contributing to the fragmentation and disconnection of our lives. And in chapter 11, the concluding chapter, I suggest that the challenge ahead is to achieve greater balance—not simply responding to the economic imperatives to work faster and harder but remaining open to more intimate, contemplative ways of living.

My interest in the contemplative dimension of life stretches way back. My decision to study calligraphy and bookbinding after finishing my PhD in computer science (described in the original preface of this book) was in part a search for more contemplative ways of living. I saw the world of craft as an alternative to the speedy, striving, fragmented world of digital pursuits (pursuits that both excited and exhausted me). As I put it in an essay for a calligraphy exhibition catalogue, published in 1995, craftwork calls for "a quality of attention, a kind of measured concentration, that can only be found by clearing a reflective, almost sacred, space." Works created in this way, I added, "ask for a quieter, more reflective reception. They call us to states of concentrated awareness that we are most likely to have encountered in places of worship or in libraries. Both in their making and in their reception and use, these artifacts embody a different rhythm of life—one that is slower, more measured, more grounded."[2]

Returning from London to Silicon Valley in the early 1980s, I first framed the challenge of finding balance in personal terms: Could I, in my own daily life, maintain a quieter, more contemplative attitude while living a fast-paced, Silicon Valley life? I took up a meditation practice (which I have now sustained, and which has sustained me, for a number of years), and came to realize that my calligraphy training had actually been my first contemplative practice, helping me to integrate mind and body and to achieve states of greater concentration. And in the early 1990s, I began to realize that questions of balance could (and probably should) be taken on as research

---

2 David M. Levy, "Slouching toward Cyberspace: The Place of the Lettering Arts in a Digital Era," in *Codes and Messages: Lettering Today*, ed. Ewan Clayton (London: British Crafts Council, 1995), 30.

questions as well as a personal quest. The first article I wrote on this subject, "I'm Not Here Right Now to Take Your Call: Technology and the Politics of Absence,"[3] published in 1995, asked if the new digital technologies of connection (then including cell phones and email) might equally be tools of disconnection (the question I later posed in *Scrolling Forward*).

But it was only when I moved to the University of Washington, around the time that *Scrolling Forward* was published, that I began to devote much of my professional attention to the challenge of achieving contemplative balance. And I have largely pursued two directions. One has involved asking why life is accelerating and what role digital technologies have played in this speedup. The other has explored how we might use our digital tools, and live our digital lives, in more contemplative ways. (Readers wanting to learn more about both of these directions should consult my website, davidmlevy.net, where they will find articles I have written, videos of some of my talks, and press stories about this work. They may also want to read my new book, *Mindful Tech: How to Bring Balance to Our Digital Lives*.[4])

More than a decade after *Scrolling Forward* first appeared, I still believe what I wrote in the conclusion:

"What we're most in need of, I believe, is balance. Depersonalized, disenchanted ways of being have increasingly come to dominate our lives. Melvil Dewey—obsessive, controlling, making order, and fearing death—is the symbol of our times. We see too little of Whitman—expansive, accepting, lingering, celebrating—even though he lives in us

3 David M. Levy, "I'm Not Here Right Now to Take Your Call: Technology and the Politics of Absence," in *Proceedings of the Oksnoen Symposium*, ed. Elin Ronby Pedersen and Lucy Suchman (Oksnoen Symposium 1995, Oksnoen, Norway, 1995), 61–66.

4 David M. Levy, *Mindful Tech: How to Bring Balance to Our Digital Lives* (New Haven and London: Yale University Press, 2016).

too. Ironically, though, to see this imbalance, and to stand a chance of correcting it, we need the very qualities of time, attention, and reflection that are so sorely lacking. It is almost as if the condition of modern life conspires to deprive us of that which would allow us to make the necessary adjustments." (198–199)

In the years since I wrote these words, our lives have only become faster and more overloaded. Ironically, perhaps, I find hope in this fact. For the intensification of our "more-faster-better" lives has made the lack of balance that much more visible. And along with this continuing speedup, the contemplative response—not just the longing for quiet and simplicity and reflective time, but the investigation of methods for achieving them—has also grown stronger.

***

Scrolling Forward first appeared in October 2001, just weeks after 9/11. The night before the tragedy, on September 10, 2001, my wife and I had arrived in Seattle in preparation for my taking up a faculty position at the University of Washington. My cell phone rang the morning of September 11; it was my sister saying, "Mom and Dad are okay, but the World Trade Center has been destroyed." My parents lived four blocks from Ground Zero.

Around the country and the world, so many of us grieved these events and tried to make sense of them. For me, a New Yorker by birth, it was hard to be so far away and not to have more intimate contact with my parents or my city. The news media, and the *New York Times* in particular, were my main sources of information and connection.

Within days of the tragedy, I began to notice a curious phenomenon: a regular thread of the reporting focused on documents—what I came to think of as "the documents of 9/11." The earliest stories were about how documents "rained upon the city" as the documen-

xxx • PREFACE TO THE 2016 EDITION

tary contents of the Twin Towers were blown out across the New York–New Jersey region. In those first weeks, the *New York Times* reported on the "storm of paper work"[5] and *The New Yorker* on "the airborne detritus of commerce" that blanketed the city.[6] Following these reports came another wave of stories describing the missing posters that began to appear. The *Times* explicitly marked this shift when it observed: "The first wave of paper rained upon the city from the World Trade Center like death's disembodied proxy. As if in answer, a second wave rose up from the photo albums and word processors of thousands of desperate families." At first the posters represented hope—that loved ones might still be alive. It wasn't long, however, before the posters were transmuted into memorials to those now believed to have died. And as these posters were rained upon, and blown about, some news stories noted, "it seemed . . . as if the tragedy had happened all over again."[7] Yet another wave of stories arose as letters laced with anthrax were discovered. Suddenly, the normally-invisible process by which the post office sorts and delivers the mail was front-page news.

Two weeks after the tragedy I flew to New York, and on the first day that traffic was permitted below Canal Street, I took a cab down to my parents' apartment, just east of City Hall and south of the Brooklyn Bridge. From all the windows of my parents' apartment, you could previously see both of the towers looming above you. And on visits over the years—this wasn't the apartment where I'd grown up—as I was falling asleep I'd sometimes wonder whether the towers would hit the apartment building if they ever fell in our direction.

Over the next few days, I wandered the streets of the city,

---

5 Francis X. Clines, "Before & After: Voices in the Wind; A New Form of Grieving Evolves Over Last Goodbyes," *New York Times*, n.d.

6 "September 11, 2001," *The New Yorker*, September 24, 2001, 61.

7 Amy Waldman, "A Nation Challenged: The Fliers; Posters of the Missing Now Speak of Losses," *New York Times*, September 29, 2001.

always one of my favorite activities. And in my wanderings, I came across a remarkable exhibition that had emerged in response to the tragedy. Called "Here is New York," the exhibition was set up in a vacant storefront on Prince Street, where photographers — both professionals and ordinary camera-wielding citizens — were invited to display their images of 9/11. There was a table inside the gallery where people could submit their images, and those that were accepted were scanned in, formatted, printed, and displayed on the gallery walls, or hung from ceiling. The organizers of the exhibit referred to it as a "democracy of photographs."

Walking around the gallery, I discovered that many of the images mounted on the walls were of documents: A color photograph of the Twin Towers lying face up in the rubble. A couple sitting on the grass in a park reading the *New York Daily News*, its headline proclaiming, in large capital letters, THE EARTH FELL ON TOP OF ME. A crumpled up newspaper abandoned in an alleyway. A charred ledger book lying open in the World Trade Center rubble.

Over the next few months, it wasn't unusual to find not just stories about ordinary documents but images of them as well appearing in the *New York Times*, both in the print edition and the online version. Photographs appeared showing a to-do list, a handwritten note, a personal check, a page from a manual detailing emergency evacuation procedures, and a family photo of three young children. A story published on December 20, 2001, described a letter that was being mailed from New Hampshire to California and happened to be on one of the jets that crashed into the World Trade Center. The color image of the torn but still legible envelope, which was recovered in Manhattan and mailed back to the sender by a Good Samaritan, appeared on the front page of the B section of that day's paper.[8]

What struck me about all these newspaper reports and images

---

8 Pam Belluck, "A Nation Challenged: Aftermath; One Letter's Odyssey Helps Mend a Wound," *New York Times*, December 20, 2001.

was that they weren't only elements of the documentary record: they were *about* documents. Reporters and photographers had chosen to tell some of the story of 9/11 by focusing on the written forms intimately associated with the destruction of the towers and the people working in them. In one sense, it was obvious why: the masses of documents scattered across the greater New York region were a highly visible dimension of the tragedy. But what I also saw, having spent years trying to understand the nature of documents, was how these documents had come both to embody and to symbolize the destruction of human lives and human order that had just taken place. For these documents, these talking things, had in very real ways been agents of order and stability as they made their way through the bureaucratic pathways within the two towers, and their loss could both give concrete evidence of and symbolize the great loss—not only of lives and routines but of our collective sense of meaning and order—that had just taken place.

Of all the textual descriptions and images that I collected during this period, the one that has stayed with me most forcefully is the photograph of a man picking up a single, singed piece of paper. It was taken by Larry Towell, a commercial photographer, and was later published in a book, *New York September 11.*[9] In the black-and-white photograph, the man, dressed in a sports jacket and an open-neck dress shirt, is standing in the middle of the street, facing toward the camera, and is intently staring at the piece of paper he's just picked up from the ground. Papers and other forms of detritus are scattered across the street; behind him, to our left, you can see a number of people walking in the opposite direction, away from him.

It took me years to identify the site of this photograph in lower Manhattan. It is John Street, between Nassau and William Streets.

---

9 Magnum Photographers, *New York: September 11* (New York: powerHouse Books, 2002).

(The building immediately above the reader's head is the John Street Church, at 44 John Street, which calls itself "The Oldest Methodist Congregation in America.") Which means that the reader at the center of the photo is facing *toward* the site of the World Trade Center, while everyone else, understandably enough, is walking away from it. Why did this unidentified man pick up a single piece of paper? What was it about it, among all the other objects on the street, that caught his attention? And why is he starring at it so intently?

We will probably never know, but I like to imagine that he is trying to make sense of what has just happened. The seemingly safe, secure, and stable world has just exploded, in ways that he, and we, could never have imagined. It is shocking and it is terrifying—and it is also mysterious, this crazy world that eludes our ability to control or even understand. As he stares at this piece of paper, I imagine that this man is looking at, and through, one of the material objects that both symbolizes and facilitates our ongoing search for a stable and meaningful life. For he holds in his hands, touchable but ultimately ungraspable, a concrete manifestation of the greater mystery of life, one more "letter from God dropt in the street."

Preface to the Original Edition

IN 1981, TWO YEARS AFTER FINISHING A Ph.D. in computer science at Stanford University, I went to London to study calligraphy and bookbinding. My intention was clear: to leave the world of high tech and immerse myself in a traditional craft. To those around me, this seemed at best impractical and at worst just plain stupid. Why would someone throw away a hard-earned degree, a ticket to success? And for what purpose — to study what? I remember one conversation with an uncle, who tried to persuade me to make my fortune first and pursue my hobbies later.

It wasn't hard to understand these reactions. To most people, calligraphy must seem a minor craft at best, the moral equivalent of macramé — hardly worthy of serious, let alone full-time, study. It represents a quaint and dusty past, a medieval world of monks with cowls and quills. Whereas computer science is the craft of the new priestly class, and pays accordingly. What could possibly tempt one to abandon the shiny new for the shabby old?

In fact, the discontinuity wasn't as great as it seemed. As an undergraduate, I had been passionately interested in language and literature as well as computers. I was aware of, and fascinated by, boundary issues between disciplines: C. P. Snow's *Two Cultures* had introduced me to the rift between the sciences and the arts, and Jorge Luis Borges, the Argentine essayist and storyteller, to the playful interaction of fact and fiction. After college, I entered a doctoral program in artificial intelligence (AI), hoping to explore questions at the intersection of language, mind, and technology.

It didn't take long to discover that neither AI nor computer science offered the richness of perspective I longed for. (With hindsight it seems foolish to have sought it where I did.) Both disciplines seemed ungrounded to me, lacking cultural and historical perspective. My early graduate studies of language centered around analyzing the syntax and semantics of sentences like "John hit Mary." From the sublime to the misogynistic — how much further from poetry and literature could you get? The philosopher Hubert Dreyfus had just written *What Computers Can't Do,* a strong attack on AI claiming that its conception of intelligence — and indeed its very understanding of human thought and action — was fundamentally wrong. In those days it wasn't acceptable to acknowledge you'd even read the book. I wasn't very happy.

Partly as an antidote, I began to study calligraphy, taking evening classes in San Francisco. This was actually a return to a childhood interest. I had first been exposed to the craft by my fourth-grade teacher, Mr. Unterberger, a wonderful man with a great love of books and stories. Once the required work — spelling and arithmetic — was out of the way, he would sit on the edge of his desk and talk with us about books, not just their content but their physical properties: paper and margins and typefaces. At some point he handed out Speedball pens and India ink and encouraged us to make calligraphic letters, composed of thick and thin strokes. I was hooked, and for years afterward I continued to draw letters, although with little understanding of how the broad-edged pen actually worked.

While I was a graduate student, two significant developments were happening in the world of computers. In my department at Stanford, Donald Knuth was developing the computer typesetting system TeX and the typeface design tool MetaFont; and at Xerox PARC, the high-tech think tank where I was a research intern, the personal computer was being invented, along with powerful tools for doing computer-based typography and graphic design. These were major steps in the invention of digital documents and digital document technologies. I wasn't involved in either effort, other than as a user of the technologies being created. (I wrote my dissertation on an Alto computer using the Bravo editor, precursors of the Macintosh and Microsoft Word, respectively.)

On completion of my doctorate, I decided to study calligraphy full-time. This was both a move *toward* the richness of expression and opportunity I felt the craft offered and a move *away* from the (for me) stultifying narrowness of computer work. In the fall of 1981 I entered the one full-time calligraphy program I had found in the English-speaking world, a program in Calligraphy and Bookbinding at Digby Stuart College in London, established by Ann Camp. Immersing myself in these studies, I began to find some of the extra dimension lacking in my academic work: a sense of history and culture, the freedom to play with visual language, and permission to explore a broad range of literary texts. (My main project for the first year was the design and execution of a calligraphic work based on the climax of Borges's story "The Aleph.") Our studies stressed historical understanding as the basis for sound design and grounded innovation. The visual and the historical went hand-in-hand. And the craft itself, the handwork, was a counterweight to the highly intellectualized, abstracted work of graduate school. It was a pleasure to train my hands to *make things* that carried meaning — in virtue of their linguistic content, as well as their form and their place in history and culture.

Calligraphy had been revived in England around the turn of the twentieth century as part of the Arts and Crafts Movement, which arose as a protest against the dehumanizing effects of industrialization and bureaucratization. The initial protests had come from the workers, the so-called Luddites, beginning in Nottingham in 1811. Today the term Luddite has come to mean anyone who is (or is perceived to be) anti-technology. But the original Luddites weren't lodging a general protest against machines or industrialization; they were unhappy with certain specific effects of mechanization on the textile industry, notably lower wages and the poor quality of goods. Initially they vented their anger at the machines, not at people.

But unhappiness with the culture of the machine soon spread to the educated classes as well. In 1829 the historian Thomas Carlyle wrote an influential essay, "Signs of the Times," in which he protested against the ways people were becoming "mechanical in head and heart, as well as in hand."[1] Later in the century, John Ruskin, the eminent English art critic, was equally vehement in his condemnation of machines. The problem, he said, was not so much with the machines themselves as with the effects they had on their products and on the human beings who used them. "It is . . . possible and even usual," he wrote in *The Seven Lamps of Architecture,* published in 1849, "for men to sink into machines themselves, so that even hand work has all the character of mechanization."[2]

With Ruskin as its standard bearer, the Arts and Crafts Movement arose in England in the last decades of the nineteenth century. Where the industrial ethos championed the mass production of machine-made artifacts, the artisans of this new movement advocated the crafting of individual, custom-designed and handmade artifacts for particular clients. Where industrial methods stressed speed, efficiency, and quantity, the craft ethos emphasized deliberate craftwork and quality. These values were applied to a succession of products, among them furniture, architecture, pottery, textiles, and metalwork.

It was through this movement, too, that calligraphy was revived, when the architect W. R. Lethaby asked a young man, Edward Johnston, to teach a course on the subject at the Central School of Art and Design in London. Johnston had no prior experience in the subject — no one did. Quill pens were still in use at the time, although they were being increasingly supplanted by steel. For many centuries prior to the invention of the printing press, the quill, cut with a broad or flat edge rather than a point, had been the principal tool for manuscript and book production. Following the ascension of print, its use had gradually declined — especially for the purposes of the mass production of texts — and the art of writing, the masterful use of a broad-edged tool to make "beautiful writing," had essentially been lost.

Johnston, an intense and introspective young man who had dropped out of medical school for reasons of health, began by studying medieval manuscripts in the British Museum, trying to work out how they had been made. In partnership with his students at the Central School, over the next two decades he gradually recovered the main techniques — cutting quills, preparing vellum (calfskin), gilding (laying gold), mixing ink, and, of course, writing with a broad-edged pen. My teacher, Ann Camp, had studied with Irene Wellington, perhaps the best of Johnston's students.

In my studies in London, I too learned to cut and use quills, to prepare vellum for writing, to lay gold. I learned the basics of book-binding: how to fold paper (much more involved than you might think), how to sew book pages together, how to cover books with cloth and leather bindings. I studied historical letterforms, read extensively in the history of writing, looked at lots of art. But mostly I did calligraphy: I spent endless hours with quill or pen in hand, writing, designing, experimenting. It wasn't unusual for me to spend the entire weekend at my drawing table, lost in explorations of form and meaning, in the tactile pleasures of laying ink on paper, in the knotty but earthy problems of visual design.

At the end of those two years, I wasn't sure what to do next. Throughout my studies I had done computer consulting work on the side as a means of supporting myself. I happened to be doing computer work in California the summer of 1983, the summer following my second year in London. As it turned out, that August the International Typographic Association was sponsoring a Working Seminar on Digital Typography at Stanford. Digital typography (the use of computers to typeset documents and to design typefaces for display on computer screens and on paper) was in its infancy then. The organizer of the seminar urged me to attend. From his point of view, I must have seemed an ideal candidate, with training in both computers and calligraphy. But I was hesitant: I had scrupulously kept my craft work distinct from my computer work, afraid that the latter and its high-tech values might contaminate the former. He persevered, though, and I enrolled.

And how right he was. The ATypI seminar profoundly affected my thinking. I found myself amid a very interesting and wide-ranging group of speakers and attendees, among them calligraphers, typographers, computer scientists, graphic designers, and historians. Sometime around the middle of the conference I had an epiphany: *The computer is the writing tool of the future*. On the face of it, this is hardly an earth-shattering insight. For me, though, it required a significant leap in both my intellectual and emotional life. I had been programming and using computers for nearly twenty years, and had been educated to view the computer primarily as a very powerful calculating device or, in the tradition of AI, as an artificial mind. It was therefore something of a leap for me to see it as a tool in the lineage of the quill, the pen, the printing press, and the typewriter. But once so located, it acquired a historical and cultural context — a past *and* a future. The epiphany seemed to signal that I was ready to bring together the two worlds I had so assiduously kept apart.

Less than a year later I was offered a full-time research position at Xerox PARC. I jumped at the chance to explore my epiphany. I wanted to see what could be said about the computer as a writing tool — how it was like or unlike prior writing technologies. I also wanted to understand what could be said about the products of writing, the written forms or documents, produced by computers, in contrast with those produced on paper, with pens and pencils, typewriters and printing presses. And so I returned to PARC with a direction, if not a clear agenda or research program. I was back in the world of high tech — at the high temple of technology, no less — but with a very different outlook from the one I had held in my graduate-student days. I was no longer concerned with artificial minds, but with tools that enable natural minds to express themselves, and with artifacts that carry and preserve cultural achievements. I was no longer afraid that computer work would contaminate calligraphy, but was instead hopeful that calligraphy might contaminate computers. My idea was not literally to bring calligraphy into the computer age, or even to design digital type based on a calligraphic understanding of letterforms, as some have done, but instead somehow to carry the *spirit* of calligraphy — some of its worldview and values — into the thinking about documents in the age of computers.

I had been back at PARC for less two years when something happened at Xerox that lent further support to my efforts. Most people associate Xerox with photocopying, and with good reason. In 1947

Xerox (then called the Haloid Corporation) acquired rights to xerography from its inventor, Chester Carlson. With the protection afforded by its patent on xerography, Xerox prospered. In 1970 it created the Palo Alto Research Center, setting it far from its core business units in Rochester, New York. PARC was given a mandate to think bold new thoughts. And that's just what it did. Within five years a team of researchers had invented the personal computer and invented or adapted virtually all the supporting hardware and software that have become the mainstay of the personal computer industry. These included raster screens, the mouse, laser printers, and software for producing text and graphics documents that looked the same on the screen as when they were printed on paper. By 1975, when I first came to PARC, these devices were in regular use by everyone at PARC. It was obvious to all that we had seen the future and it was us.

But it was less obvious to Xerox executives three thousand miles away. Geographically and organizationally separated from the rest of Xerox, PARC had gained the autonomy and perspective that enabled it to innovate; but this isolation also made communication with the rest of the corporation — especially of radically new ideas — that much more difficult. It wasn't obvious to executives focused on the photocopier business what the market would be for these new inventions, or why Xerox should care. In fact, at that time no such market existed. Over the next ten years, Xerox tried and failed to make a business of personal computers; many of the PARC inventions found their way to other companies, including Apple and Microsoft.

By the mid-1980s, though, one thing was clear to Xerox's top management: its heartland business would shortly be affected by the new computer technologies. The development of low-cost scanners and printers meant that a personal computer could, in effect, be turned into a copier; the computer market was probably going to merge with and overtake the copier market. A concerted effort was undertaken to develop a new vision and identity for Xerox, one that would capitalize on its strength in photocopying and its public identification with this technology.

I had been back at PARC for less than two years when Xerox announced that it intended to move beyond its image as a "photocopier company" to become a "document company." Through the successful introduction of the photocopier, Xerox strategists reasoned, it had revolutionized the handling of paper documents in the office. And through the invention of the personal computer and its associated technologies, it had revolutionized — had practically invented — the handling of digital documents as well. By taking documents as its explicit focus — a notion big enough to encompass both of these developments — it now saw an opportunity to fashion an identity and an agenda for the future. That was the intuition, at any rate, and attempts to articulate it, both inside PARC and across the corporation, precipitated a conversation that lasted for years. What are documents, anyway? Does it make sense to extend the notion to digital materials, and if so, on what basis? Why does it even matter, and why should anyone care?

The Palo Alto Research Center, it turned out, was an ideal place to investigate such questions. The idea behind documents is a very big one, spanning art and science, the academy and industry, mind and body, technology and people, past and future. PARC was itself, intellectually, a very big place, sitting on the boundary between academic and corporate life and bringing together physical scientists, computer scientists, linguists, anthropologists, psychologists, artists, and the occasional philosopher. "The boundary," Paul Tillich once said, "is the best place for acquiring knowledge." Sitting on the boundary between multiple disciplines and worldviews, PARC was the perfect place to investigate an idea too big to be located in a single discipline or to be defined by a single approach.

When I returned to PARC in 1984, I brought with me several kinds of knowledge that have proved invaluable in my quest to understand documents. As a computer scientist, I was conversant with digital developments — in ways only a practitioner can be. As a student of calligraphy, I had developed some fluency with the tools and techniques of earlier crafts, had cultivated a sense of visual design, and had acquired some feeling for history and for the unfolding of document technologies in historical time. But it was only at PARC that I began to learn methods and approaches for studying explicitly how people *use* technologies. Close collaboration with PARC's small group of anthropologists over more than a decade nurtured my sense of the subtle interplay between technology and human practice. Both my computer and my calligraphy studies had essentially been technical enterprises: they were focused first and foremost on artifacts — on computer programs in the first case and on handwritten documents in the second. An awareness of people and their patterns of use was present, but only distantly so. My exposure to anthropology, however, began to turn this way of seeing upside down, making people and their activities the central focus, and locating artifacts in the flow of ongoing human work.

These are some of the personal and historical forces that have been at play for me as I have pursued an understanding of documents. It was only as I was drafting the final chapter of this book that I became aware of another major influence on this work. Nearly thirty years ago, I delivered a controversial commencement address at my college graduation. It was 1971 and the country was in turmoil. The Vietnam War, racial unrest, and the recent assassinations of Martin Luther King and Robert Kennedy had created a poisoned, oppositional climate. At my college's graduation ceremony the previous year, the valedictorian had spoken out against the war, urging graduates to flee to Canada to avoid the draft. The administration wanted no more of such behavior. They put a fifteen-minute limit on the speech I was to deliver.

In my address, I began by describing an incident that had happened to me several months before. I had gone to bed after a long evening of studying, and had been awakened in the middle of the night by terrible, literally gut-wrenching, stomach pains. Suddenly afraid that I might die, I looked over at my desk where my books were neatly stacked from the evening's work. In the light of my impending death, they seemed absolutely meaningless — no more than "black ink on white paper," I told the five thousand people seated on the lawn in front of the college library.

Since that time, I went on, I had found it hard to live. Where was the meaning in life? I had considered suicide, but been unwilling to commit it. I then proceeded to ask a series of questions guaranteed to upset one constituency in the audience after another. Could rich parents tell me how money made their lives worthwhile? Could alumni tell me how their (hallowed) undergraduate experience made their lives worthwhile? Could students please tell me how their studies made their lives worthwhile? I concluded by asking those with answers to write me a letter. I even supplied my parents' mailing address. (Afterward a friend approached me and asked if this had been a pun — giving the "valedictory address.")

I had never intended the speech to travel beyond my immediate academic community. But a friend of mine, unbeknownst to me, was a stringer for *The New York Times*. He had alerted them to the subject of my speech, and a *Times* reporter was in the audience that day. He interviewed me afterward. What did I intend to do now? he asked. I'd like to be a bartender, I replied. Naturally this made it into the article. Through his reporting, my story made it onto the wire services. Stories with titles like "Valedictorian Despairs" began appearing in newspapers and on the radio all around the country. Paul Harvey, the syndicated commentator, did a short radio piece. Art Buchwald, the political humorist, wrote a column following on the *New York Times* article. The gist was, didn't I know that bartenders need to listen to *other people's* problems, not tell them *theirs*?

Letters poured in, not only from those in attendance but from people all over the country. Some were quite hostile — and with good reason. One alumnus accused me of spoiling the party — "pissing in the champagne," he called it. But many others offered deeply heartfelt responses. Some were remarkable gifts. The further the speech traveled geographically and socially from its original audience, the more its complexities disappeared. The anger and frustration in the questions, the partly taunting "in your face" quality, dropped away. What remained was the cry for meaning of a lonely, despairing individual — "the voice of one crying in the wilderness."

The speech had actually been a mixture of truth and fiction. I had been awakened several months earlier by terrible stomach pains, and had indeed been afraid that I might die. But when the incident was over, I had felt great relief, an appreciation for the life I had been given, not the despair I reported. Still, the questions were genuine and the anger and unhappiness behind them were genuine, too. I was mad at society and at the elitism of my school. I was unhappy with my life (and detested being told again and again that my undergraduate years were the best years of my life). I *was* searching for meaning.

For months prior to this, I had been struggling to write an appropriately deep and wise speech. Then, one night, the words I eventually spoke at the commencement emerged in the course of a half hour, as if being dictated to me. During this period I had been rereading Dostoyevsky's "Notes from Underground," a novella in which the protagonist, a bitter, resentful man, tells the world the truth it doesn't want to hear. The title, literally translated from the Russian, is "Notes from Under the Floorboards." The image is that of a bug, a cockroach, who dares to speak out from the underbelly (or the underfoot) of society. It was his voice, in effect, that was speaking in my address. Without the use of the first-person singular, it wouldn't have had the same immediacy and power. The four paragraphs that emerged took exactly fifteen minutes to deliver.

The speech was bold and naïve . . . and stupid. It was a product of its time and of my own confusion. Once it was out of the box, though, there was no putting it back. I rode out the ripples — my fifteen minutes of fame — and they slowly died down. I did my best to eliminate further publicity. *Time* and *Newsweek* approached me to do stories. They wanted to include material from the letters I had been sent. I refused them access to the letters, and no stories appeared.

It was only as I was working on the concluding chapter of this book that I realized how much my work of the preceding years, and how much the content of this book, are responses to that youthful address and the circumstances surrounding it. Thirty years ago, in my first real occasion for public communication, I was struggling not only with the great questions of life but with the forms and mechanisms of public address. Perhaps my single strongest memory of that day was the moment I took the podium. In the pause before I began speaking, and in the fifteen minutes during which I spoke, I was aware of the power of speech.

Words that had come to me weeks earlier and had been written down, polished, rehearsed, typed up, and carried to the podium had been transformed into spoken utterances. These utterances, delivered in a communal, ceremonial setting, put into motion a whole cascade of events involving other written forms. These included the letters mailed to me, numbering in the hundreds, the *New York Times* article, the AP and UPI stories, and the subsequent articles in newspapers around the country. Through these responses of various kinds, I experienced the power of speaking out publicly. But I also experienced the loss of power that was equally involved, as my words were appropriated and interpreted in new settings. It had never been completely straightforward who the "I" was who was speaking in my address. (Perhaps it never is.) As my words and the reports of them traveled, further dimensions of personhood and identity were attached to me — "valedictorian," "despairing individual," "lost soul." It was all much more complex than I could ever have guessed when, sitting at my desk in my dorm room, I had written out those four paragraphs.

Although the speech wasn't literally *about* documents, written forms had also played an important rhetorical part in it. The books neatly stacked on my desk had symbolized many things at once. To the audience it would have been immediately, and perhaps largely unconsciously, apparent that they represented the long Western tradition of study and learning, and the values embedded in these. To me personally, books were a source of delight, and the locus of my daily routines of reading and study. To suggest that those books — and not only those particular books, but *all* books and the practices and values they symbolized — were without significance was at once to deny the very traditions that formed the background for the graduation ceremony and that provided grounding for my own sense of self.

I have learned a few things in the intervening years. At least I hope so. Although I am still angry about society's hypocrisies, I am more aware of the moral complexities we face every day (and more aware of my own hypocrisy). Little in life is black and white — even black ink on white paper has many more shades than might at first appear. I am aware that righteous anger and self-righteous anger are dangerously close — and that, indeed, the latter can masquerade as the former. I am also aware that people don't react well to being taunted with the deep, and possibly unanswerable, questions of life. People really only listen to love letters, says Thich Nhat Hanh, the Vietnamese Buddhist peace activist and poet. Besides, life is hard enough without the occasions for genuine celebration being pissed on.

I have also spent these many years investigating the nature of written forms. Whereas thirty years ago, books and other kinds of documents were *vehicles* of study for me, they have become the *objects* of my study. I can't say I ever really thought that books were merely black ink on white paper — I had, after all, loved them deeply since childhood. But I have spent many years trying to say just what they are, and trying to assess the significance of the movement from ink and paper to pixels and screens. It is to this story — a love letter to documents — that I now turn.

Acknowledgments

Every book is the product of an immense effort. This book would never have been begun, and could not have been completed, without the support, encouragement, and involvement of many people.

I owe an immense debt to my (now former) colleagues at Xerox PARC, with whom and from whom I learned so much about documents, work practice and life. Brian Smith, Geoff Nunberg, Lucy Suchman, John Seely Brown, Dan Brotsky, Cathy Marshall, Richard Southall, and Ken Olson were wonderful co-conspirators in the quest to make sense of documents. The members of the Work Practice and Technology Area (WPT) — Jeanette Blomberg, Gitti Jordan, Susan Newman, Julian Orr, Lucy Suchman, and Randy Trigg — gently tutored me in matters anthropological and taught me how a research group could operate democratically and compassionately.

Thanks too to the many people who read portions of this manuscript in various stages of its development: Allyson Carlyle, Ewan Clayton, Paul Duguid, Margaret Hedstrom, Carl Lagoze, Marc Lesser, Cathy Marshall, Andreas Paepcke, Richard Southall, Lucy Suchman, Nancy Van House, David Weinberger, Zari Weiss, and Alice Wilder-Hall (who also provided editorial assistance).

Many thanks to my agent, Eileen Cope, for her encouragement and tireless efforts; to my editor and publisher, Dick Seaver, for his patient and gentle stewardship; to Greg Comer for his patience and meticulous attention to detail; and to Peter Finkelstein, Jack Lawrence, Jim Neafsey, and Paul Roy for their masterful coaching.

I must also thank the two institutions that supported me during the researching and writing of this book: Xerox PARC and the Information School of the University of Washington. I am grateful to John

Seely Brown (former director of PARC) and to Mike Eisenberg (dean of the Information School) for providing the space, literally and figuratively, in which the work could be done.

Finally, I have no adequate words to thank two people — Ewan Clayton and Zari Weiss — for their efforts in support of this book and their contributions to it. If selfless giving is a condition of entry into the world to come, they are both assured palaces in heaven.

SCROLLING FORWARD

Introduction:

The Universe Is Expanding

Toward the beginning of Woody Allen's 1977 movie *Annie Hall,* little Woody (called Alvy in the movie) is sitting in the doctor's office with his mother. "What seems to be the problem?" the doctor asks. "Well," his mother says with evident frustration, "he's depressed. It's something he read." "The universe is expanding," Alvy says, morosely slumped on the couch. "The universe is everything, and if it's expanding, someday it will break apart and that will be the end of everything." "He's even stopped doing his homework," his mother continues, with a look of total disgust. "What's the point?" Alvy counters. "What has the universe got to do with it?" his mother explodes. "You're here in Brooklyn. Brooklyn is not expanding!"

What makes this little scene so funny, like so much of Woody Allen's humor, is the juxtaposition of the mundane and seemingly trivial with the cosmic and existential. It has the quality of a Kafka parable, or perhaps a Zen koan. Is the universe expanding or isn't it? In a sense they're both right, little Alvy and his mother. The mother can see concretely that Brooklyn isn't expanding. Its streets, tenements, shops, and the rhythm of daily life are just the same as they've always been. But Alvy is right, too. Whether or not the universe is really expanding (after all, it's a scientific theory), the anxiety he's feeling is real enough. Such anxiety can directly affect his ability to function — to do his homework, or anything else for that matter.

But today Alvy is right in another sense as well — and in a way his mother couldn't have foreseen in 1952, or whenever this scene is supposed to have taken place. Brooklyn *is* expanding. The Brooklyn

Botanic Garden is on the Web, where you can take a virtual tour of its gardens from just about any spot on the planet. The Brooklyn Museum is on the Web, too, as is the Brooklyn Academy of Music. And the same technologies that have made this expansion possible are changing the way children do their homework: how they do research, how and what they read, how they write reports and communicate with one another. There is understandably a great deal of excitement about these developments. But there is anxiety, too. Many of us, along with Alvy, are somewhat disoriented by all these changes to our patterns of communication, and specifically to our various written forms — unsure how big and how destabilizing these changes will ultimately prove to be. This confusion is understandable when you consider the pervasiveness and importance of written forms in our lives.

How pervasive? Well, just look around.

If you are sitting on an airplane at the moment, in the seat pocket in front of you are the in-flight magazine, the advertising supplement, and the safety instructions card. Above you are little signs indicating seating rows and numbers, as well as the no-smoking and fasten-your-seatbelt signs. A video monitor may be playing a safety video or a recently released movie. Your briefcase or pocketbook is filled with many more written things: the latest book you're reading, your calendar, driver's license, credit cards, money, checkbook, receipts, and photographs. Your laptop probably holds current e-mail, spreadsheets, memos, and reports.

If, instead, you are at home, you're likely to be surrounded by some combination of books, magazines, newspapers, letters, bills, hanging pictures, junk mail, and stacks of videos. Have a look at the refrigerator. For many of us, it's a collection point for an odd assortment of current and near-current materials — school play announcements, kids' drawings, receipts and raffle tickets, and shopping lists.

If you are standing in line at the moment, say at the bank or the post office, you might notice the many signs and placards posted on walls and even hanging from the ceiling, as well as the stacks of forms (deposit slips, change-of-address forms, loan application forms) waiting to be filled out.

And even if you are reading these words in a car, you are no less surrounded by written forms — road signs and billboard advertisements, car license plates, bumper stickers, as well as the jumble of maps and other written matter by your side.

Day and night, no matter where we are, written forms are constantly calling out to us, vying for our attention: *Buy this, Don't walk here, Sign on the dotted line, I just wanted to say hi, You may already have won one million dollars, President Signs Healthcare Bill, This product contains 50% of the minimum daily requirement, I saw the best minds of my generation destroyed by madness. . . .*

Most activities in our day are subtly or blatantly mediated by writing. Try making a purchase without being able to handle money or sign your name to a credit-card receipt. Try driving without being able to recognize road signs. Try finding a job that doesn't require some minimal — but still substantial — level of literacy. Try making any sense of our culture without an ability to decipher the barrage of advertising images and slogans on billboards, TV, and video. This is of course what it is to live in a highly literate society, a society permeated by signs of all kinds, by all manner of written, drawn, printed, painted, etched, photographed, neoned, and copied symbols.

Yet despite the constant immersion in this sea of written forms, few of us — until recently, at least — have stopped to reflect on them or on their significance. And this is probably just as it should be. The philosopher Martin Heidegger is famous for showing how a hammer becomes an extension of the person using it. While it is being used, the hammer loses its status as a separate object, a thing to be measured, observed, or studied. It disappears into the work of hammering and building. So too do written forms disappear into the fabric of daily life. The road map, the telephone book, the business card, the advertising flyer on the windshield — these are instruments to be used, not objects to be studied. The point of all those years of schooling, you might say, was exactly to cause this to happen. It was to make us so conversant with reading and writing that those acts would become automatic and the materials on which they operated would disappear into the flow of life.

But things don't lose their importance just because they drop from sight. On the contrary, some of the most significant aspects of life disappear from view for long stretches of time. What is the most miraculous thing in life? asks the great Indian epic, the Mahabharata. That each of us is surrounded by death, yet we still hold to the belief that we won't die. Even when things have become invisible — whether it is the fact of death or the endless varieties of written forms around us — there may still be times and reasons to bring them to light, to open them up to inspection and reflection. Heidegger notes that the hammer returns to the foreground of awareness when it breaks and needs to be repaired.

We are living through a time when our written forms are being stressed and stretched, possibly to the breaking point. Our carefully cultivated habits of reading and writing are being disturbed by new technologies and practices. Instead of a pad of tickets, the meter maid now carries a handheld device that is connected to a central database. In hundreds if not thousands of libraries around the country, OPACs — online public access catalogs — have now replaced the familiar card catalogs. Millions of people now maintain their personal calendars on palmtop computers, periodically synchronizing them with the calendars on their desktop machines, bypassing paper altogether. E-mail, a digital offshoot of the letter and the memo, has found a place in both the home and the office. In a few short years the World Wide Web has been densely populated with advertisements, academic papers, flight schedules, pornography, news articles, recipes, personal musings and rantings — materials that had a familiar, and in some ways comforting, form and place in the world of paper.

It is clearly a time to reflect. Many people have begun to do just that, and there are many more questions than answers. Is paper about to disappear? What is the future of the book and of publishing? What will happen to libraries, to copyright, to education? And alongside these "big picture" questions, perhaps even woven through them, are much more personal ones. What does all this mean *for me*? What does it mean for my livelihood, my sense of self, my place in the world? How am I to cope with all this change? When will it settle down, if ever, and what is the shape of things to come? What exactly is going on here?

This book is a reflection on the nature of documents. I will be aiming to say what documents are, what they are for, and how they work. And at a time when many people are wondering how to make sense of the newer, digital forms, I will be offering a view of them that shows how they are like our earlier written forms — those on paper, for example — and, to some extent, how they differ. By pointing up how documents are implicated in the current sense of disorder and disarray, both on an institutional and a personal level, I hope to contribute to our understanding of what's actually going on in these tumultuous and confusing times.

Unlike so much of what is being written today, then, my real focus is on the present. This might seem odd when so often these days we turn to visionaries and futurists, hoping they will illuminate the road ahead. We want them to show us the future, and thus perhaps assuage our fears. But in my experience, we have a hard enough time seeing what is right in front of us. We are so often caught up in our own projections that we miss what's happening most immediately and directly. One of the strategies we often use to *avoid* the present is to plan, imagine, fantasize, and project. Not that those activities are bad — in fact, they are crucial — but they need to be balanced by clear-sighted impressions of *what is*.

One of the best sources of information about the present is our own experience. During this time of transition, I think it is essential that we, each of us, draw on this resource to the fullest extent. It is attractive and perhaps too easy to give ourselves over to experts, who claim to know more than we do. Of course, I too am writing as an expert, but with a difference, I hope. Yes, I will be painting a picture of what is going on, drawing on my research, my thinking, and my experience. But I am less interested in persuading you that I am right than in encouraging you to think things through for yourself and from your own experience. To the extent that my ways of looking provide you with useful tools for doing this, I will have succeeded.

It is worth saying something about the word *document,* which will figure so prominently in the pages ahead. There are several other terms that cover some of the same territory, which I will sometimes use, including *writing, written form,* and *text.* Each has its own history and its own biases. *Writing* and *written form* tend to suggest alphabetic materials and therefore leave out (or downplay) photographs, drawings, paintings, maps, and other nonverbal forms of expression. The word *text* in addition often seems to suggest something abstract and disembodied, and misses the sense of concreteness and physical presence that is so central to the story I have to tell.

The word *document* has its problems, too. Most notably, it is often used to designate the kinds of materials that have traditionally appeared on paper, such as legal contracts (e.g., wills) and identity papers (e.g., passports). This is much narrower than the use I intend, which is broad enough to include not only things written on paper but videotapes, films, audiotapes, and all manner of digital materials, including text files, spreadsheets, and Web pages. Still, there are several reasons why I am inclined to use the word *document.* First and perhaps least important, I have used it for a number of years in exactly this way, and it is the term of choice in the academic and business settings I frequent. More important, the word does seem to be expanding its meaning within certain circles, especially among computer users. Finally, *document* has an etymology that is at once both useful and pleasing: it comes from the Latin *docere,* which means "to teach."

So, in the end, this is a book not about the word *document* but about a class of cultural artifacts and the central idea that underlies them in all their myriad forms. Documents have much to teach us, I believe, if we will only listen.

1

Meditation on a Receipt

Wʜᴀᴛ ᴄᴀɴ ᴅᴏᴄᴜᴍᴇɴᴛꜱ ᴛᴇᴀᴄʜ ᴜꜱ? Let's begin by looking at one, close up. The one I have in mind is a cash register receipt, a small strip of paper, 1¾ inches in width and approximately 4¼ inches in length, marked in light blue ink. At the top it reads "Steve's Deli & Catering." Immediately below is a sequence of numbers, 10-29-97, and near the bottom is a decimal value, 5.85. From the look of it, someone bought something from Steve's Deli on October 29, 1997, and paid $5.85 for it.

This might seem like an odd place to begin a discussion of documents. Why not begin with a more magnificent specimen, perhaps something beautiful, such as the Book of Kells? Or something more reverently ancient, a Sumerian clay tablet or the Rosetta stone? Or something with an aura of power about it, the U.S. Constitution or an international treaty? This little receipt is so plain and ordinary, so manifestly uninteresting. There are millions and billions of receipts just like it. Every financial transaction at the supermarket, the newsstand, the florist, the drugstore, produces one. You can see people's attitude toward them in the way they're handled. They are often left on the counter — refused or even handed back with a vague air of displeasure. (I can't be bothered with this.) Or they are stuck away in a grocery bag or stuffed in one's pocket or purse, only to be discarded later. Surely receipts like this are the bottom of the bin.

A receipt for the purchase of a tuna-fish sandwich, a bag of chips, and a bottle of water

But this is exactly the point. If we are going to see into the nature of documents, we would do well to deal directly with the most abundant and ordinary of them. It is easy enough to be transported to heights of ecstasy by the most magnificent specimens. Indeed, we may be spellbound by their beauty and power. The bigger challenge is to look closely and respectfully at the lowest and homeliest of them. And should we find beauty, depth, and power in *these,* we will surely have accomplished something.

This little receipt is a historical document. Although hardly of the magnitude — or the permanence — of the Rosetta stone, it is a snapshot of something that happened at another time and place.

Embedded in it physically, through the absorption of blue dye into processed tree pulp, is the record of a moment when someone (in fact it was me) bought a tuna sandwich, a bag of chips, and a bottle of water in a deli on El Camino Real in Burlingame, California.

The receipt is historical in another sense as well. If it serves as a reminder of a minor transaction in late October 1997, it simultaneously carries within its form the memory of thousands of years of human struggle and development. That receipts like this one are so readily printed and so casually tossed away is due in large measure to the availability of cheap, high-quality paper. This wasn't always so.

Paper was invented in China in the second century C.E. and made its way to Europe in the twelfth century, carried by Arab traders. We tend to think that brilliant new inventions explode onto the scene and are immediately embraced by all (making fortunes in stock for the founders of companies that produce them). But that isn't usually the way it works. There is more typically a slow process of diffusion and adaptation, and this is certainly what happened with paper.

People have always made writing surfaces from the natural materials immediately around them. Some, like clay, require little preparation to be usable. Others, most notably papyrus and animal skins, need to be manufactured. Papyrus, from which the word *paper* is derived, is a rush or grasslike plant that grows in the Nile river delta. To make a writing surface, the plant is sliced lengthwise into long strips. These strips are laid in rows and allowed to dry in the sun, resulting in a highly durable surface that will accept marks on one side.

The process of turning animal skins into writing surfaces is more extensive: it involves raising the animals, skinning them and removing the hair, then stretching and sanding the skins. But the resulting product can be marked on both sides, and while papyrus can only be cultivated in limited regions of the world, livestock is raised in most climates as a source of food and clothing as well. The resulting surface can be remarkably thin, smooth, soft, and pliable. It is also extremely durable: pieces of vellum (from the same Latin root that gives us *veal*) have survived, with their marks intact, for a thousand years or more.

Medieval monasteries typically had to maintain extensive herds — for food, of course, as well as books. The invention of paper provided a vegetarian alternative that could be made locally. Instead of killing and skinning animals, plant fibers could be mashed into a pulp, spread out in thin layers, and dried. With proper treatment the resulting surfaces could accept forms written with a quill or brush.

The main advantage of medieval paper over animal skins was its lower price. Paper was actually more fragile and had a rougher surface than animal skins. It didn't accept inks and pigments nearly as well, and was harder to correct. It wasn't until the fourteen or fifteenth century, several hundred years after its introduction into Europe, that paper began to supplant animal skins. Initially this was due to its improved quality and availability. But with the invention of the printing press in the middle of the fifteenth century, which produced better results on paper than on most skins, the demand for paper increased dramatically.[1]

In those first centuries after the papermaking process was introduced into Europe, and indeed for many centuries afterward, rags provided the primary raw material for the making of paper. We might think of this as an early form of recycling. Once clothing, made of cotton, linen, and hemp, had served its useful lifetime, it was collected by the "ragman" as the first step in the papermaking process. (So important were clothes fibers to papermaking that in seventeenth-century England a law was passed mandating that the dead be buried in wool, which was unsuitable for making paper.)[2] The availability of rags placed limits on the quantity of paper that could be produced. Periodic shortages of rags produced crises in book production.

The search began for an alternative to rags. Although the use of wood was first suggested in the eighteenth century,[3] it wasn't until the middle of the nineteenth century — not so very long ago — that techniques for making paper from wood pulp became commercially viable. With the invention of the steam engine as a cheap and reliable source of power, it was finally possible to produce large, continuous rolls of inexpensive paper. It thus became possible to make lots of cheap, expendable documents, like the receipt we're currently examining. Looking closely, you can indeed see that this receipt was torn from a continuous roll. The ragged upper edge gives evidence of the sudden gesture of the wrist and hand that separated it from the mother roll.

So much for the paper it's printed on. What makes this a document rather than a mere scrap of paper is its symbolic or representational power. Its little blue marks allow it to tell a story. From the time of the cave paintings at least, human beings have been working out how to depict, name, and describe events and objects in such a way that they could be called to mind — re-called or re-presented — at a later time and place. That this receipt is able to tell its tale so succinctly and efficiently is the result of thousands of years of developments in written forms.

Each of the shapes has its own history, its own story. Let's start with the capital letters. These come to us most directly from Roman times, adapted from earlier Etruscan and Greek letterforms. Two thousand years ago, the Romans had a twenty-three-letter alphabet (lacking only our *J, V,* and *W*), the forms written just as we see them on this receipt. Which means that all the capital letters — *A, C, D, E, G, I, L, N, Q, R, S, T* — appearing on this receipt would have been immediately recognizable to our Roman ancestors.

Not so the lowercase letters. These didn't begin to develop until the third century C.E. The Roman capitals had been written slowly; they were often carved in stone — a deliberate and painstaking process. (We call them capitals — from the Latin *capitalis* for "head" — because they were often incised at the head or top of monumental columns.) But as these forms were written more quickly — with quills on vellum rather than with brushes and chisels on stone — the shapes became rounder and simpler. The uncial alphabet, which made its appearance in the third century C.E., has a very mixed look to our modern eyes. While most of the forms look decidedly uppercase, a small number of others have a distinctly lowercase feel to them, including *a, d, h, m,* and *q.*[4] It was during Charlemagne's so-called Carolingian renaissance in the eighth century — an intense period of spiritual and literary exploration during which handwriting was refined and reformed — that the lowercase letters as we know them finally emerged in a clear and beautiful form.

(The terms *lowercase* and *uppercase* are actually derived from printing practice. The compositor or typesetter kept his pieces of metal type in bins or "cases." The small letters were traditionally kept in the case below the one holding the capital letters; thus the small letters were in the lower case, the big letters in the upper case. Strictly speaking, it is anachronistic to call letterforms of the eighth century lowercase. More accurate terms would be *minuscule,* meaning small, for lowercase and *majuscule,* meaning big, for uppercase.)

At any rate, by the eighth century, more or less, all the letter shapes needed to make this receipt had come into existence. But they functioned quite differently at that time than they do now. The capitals and the lowercase letters formed essentially separate scripts or "hands." A text, or portions of a text, would be written in one script or the other. It wasn't until the Renaissance that the practice of mixing capitals with lowercase letters within a single word (e.g., to begin a sentence or write a proper name) began to emerge. This seems to have been an outgrowth of the use of versals — large illuminated letters — to start a page or a new section of a text. Thus, although the forms of the letters appearing on this receipt are quite old, stretching back a thousand years or more, the manner of combination, as seen in the word "Steve's," is much more recent.

Yet letterforms play a fairly minor part in the receipt we've been examining. Instead, this receipt is mainly filled with numbers — or numerals to be more exact — and with good reason: it is a financial record, a kind of accounting document, and in this respect it harks back to the earliest days of writing. Archaeological evidence indicates that counting and accounting were some of the first uses of writing. Many of the Mesopotamian cuneiform tablets dug up in Iraq and Iran are administrative records: lists of tribute received, rations distributed, payments made. One scholar, the anthropologist Denise Schmandt-Besserat, even theorizes that writing was a direct outgrowth of counting and accounting practices conducted within increasingly complex, urban societies.[5]

Numerals have at least as long a history as letters. The familiar forms appearing on this receipt are of relatively recent origin. Like paper, they seem to have been brought to Europe through Muslim conquest and settlement. (Whereas paper came originally from China, the numerals originated in India.) Like the adoption of paper in Europe, the diffusion of the numerals was a slow process, lasting centuries. The most radical of the numerals, zero, took a slower course than the others. Although the numerals had made their way to Spain by the tenth century, zero wasn't in common use until the eleventh or twelfth century. There is a certain logic to the delay, since the Arabic numerals were serving as a replacement for the earlier Roman numerals, which lacked a zero. It must have taken quite a while for educational and commercial practices to adjust to this strange new symbol, a mark signifying nothing, a presence signaling an absence. (Still, how strange to think that the use of zero in the West is only a thousand years old.) Decimal notation is even more recent; the decimal point was first used at the end of the fifteenth century.

The decimal point is just one of the nonalphabetic, nonnumeric symbols appearing on the receipt. I count five of them in all — the decimal point or period, the hyphen or dash, the asterisk, the apostrophe, and the ampersand. All but the last of these are punctuation marks (from the Latin *punctus* or "point"). They are secondary signifiers — meta-symbols, you might say — that have been developed over the millennia to make reading easier and to help resolve potential ambiguities. Early writing used few such devices; indeed, in a style called *scriptio continua* (continuous writing), words were strung together without any visual indication of the divisions between them. At a later stage, dots or points were added to mark the boundaries of words. This was finally replaced by the convention we use today, that of separating words spatially. This convention didn't become the norm until the twelfth century. It took quite a while then for space — the absence of a mark — to come to serve as punctuation. Perhaps it is only accidental that it made its appearance at about the same time as zero, the absence of all quantity.

But space functions as more than punctuation in this sense. It is the single greatest resource for the writer, at once the most blatantly obvious and the most invisible resource on the page. Written marks, after all, are only discernible against an unmarked background. The shape of a single letter, a capital B for example, is equally made up of its negative spaces (the holes that make up its two bowls) and the empty space that forms its outside borders. If we think of the receipt as a planet and the blue marks as its continents, then most of its expanse, like our planet, is ocean.

To see the receipt in this way is to locate it in time. It is to see the receipt as the product of endless developments and innovations, small and large, stretching back over many centuries and reaching across many regions of the globe. As George Kubler has put it in *The Shape of Time:* "Everything made now is either a replica or a variant of something made a little time ago and so on back without break to the first morning of human time."[6] To see the receipt in this way is therefore to give it a past, but it is also to give it a future, a future that is necessarily uncertain and unknown, at best dimly and imperfectly glimpsed.

This receipt stands at a particularly interesting, and perhaps challenging, moment in time. The paper on which it's printed has acquired a political and, indeed, even a moral resonance. The seemingly endless availability of cheap paper, which took so many centuries to achieve, has permitted us to be cavalier about its use and mindless about its disposal. In recent decades, the association between the use of paper and the depletion of the planet's natural resources has come into focus, raising great concerns about sustainability and our collective long-term welfare. It has become increasingly difficult to see little pieces of paper like this one as disposable in the ways we once did.

It is worth noting that not all cultures have been quite so cavalier about their written records. In a book written in 1938, Chiang Yee speaks movingly of the traditional Chinese attitude toward written forms (an attitude that surely cannot have survived the revolution):

> Affection for the written word is instilled from childhood in the Chinese heart. We are taught never to tear up a sheet of writing, nor to misuse any paper with writing upon it, even if it is of no further practical use. In every district of a Chinese city, and even in the smallest village, there is a little pagoda built for the burning of waste paper bearing writing. This we call *Hsi-Tzu-T'a* — Pagoda of Compassionating the Characters. For we respect characters so highly that we cannot bear them to be trampled under foot or thrown away into some distasteful place. It is a common sight to see old men with baskets of plaited bamboo on their backs, gathering up this kind of waste paper from the streets and roads for burning in the *Hsi-Tzu-T'a*. You may be sure these old men do not act only on an impulse of tidiness! There may be people nowadays who think them foolish; but we cannot bring ourselves to abandon our deep-rooted traditional habits. Newspapers, books, every kind of printed matter are poured out on all sides and in increasing quantity, but still the old reverence for the written word prevails.[7]

(To this day, Jewish law dictates that all materials on which the Divine Name are written are to be handled respectfully, and they are to be buried when their useful lifetime is over.)

It is likely that future generations of receipts will have a very different look and feel. Digital receipts are already being created, part of a more general movement toward digital commerce. This very receipt may already carry the seeds of change within it: it may actually have a digital component to it, and if so it is something of a hybrid, a hermaphrodite. Although we can't tell just by looking at it, this receipt was probably produced using a digital cash register, a computer incorporating a printer and a cash drawer. If so, a digital record of my tuna-fish-chips-and-water transaction was being created as the sales clerk punched the cash register keys; and from this the paper version we see before us was printed. Viewed in this light, the receipt is an evolutionary creature like the famed coelacanth, a fish with leglike fins marking the point at which sea creatures first began to venture onto land.

Still, we are missing a crucial perspective on the receipt — perhaps *the* most crucial. Although we have begun to locate it in the sweep of time, we have yet to see it in its own cultural time and place. We need to see it not so much in relation to events in the distant past or an unknown future, but in relation to its immediate surroundings. Within its local circumstances, what kind of thing is it? What work is it doing, and why is it doing it?

The first thing to notice is that the receipt is telling a story of sorts. It is admittedly a highly selective one, not likely to win any prizes for literature. Why would anyone bother to tell it? The answer is, of course, to be found in the way financial transactions are orchestrated in our culture. The receipt is meant to function as "proof of purchase," as evidence that an exchange of money for goods actually took place. Coming into being at the very time and place the food was prepared and the goods were delivered, the receipt serves as witness to these facts. Its job is to tell its story in future situations, at other times and places — to play a role in other activities. It may be used, for example, to return or exchange the items purchased, when requesting reimbursement of the cost of the purchase (when submitting a travel expense report, say), or as a way of documenting expenses for tax purposes.

One could imagine a person performing such a service, someone who had witnessed the purchase and could testify to the facts when called upon to do so. Indeed, as M. T. Clanchy observes in his book *From Memory to Written Record*,[8] in England up until the thirteenth century, people were required to witness and thereby validate financial and legal transactions. To transfer a piece of property (real estate) from one person to another, the donor would speak his intentions aloud in the presence of witnesses, at the same time handing over a symbolic object, say a knife or a small piece of earth, from the land being transferred. Should there be a dispute, the witnesses to the event would be required to testify. By the end of the thirteenth century, however, a written document could serve as both the statement of intent and as witness to the facts of the matter.

Although we don't quite hear it this way, witnesses are people who have their wits about them. The root of the word *wit* is the Old English *witan,* meaning "to know," as well as the Latin *videre* and the Greek *idein,* "to see." The dictionary defines *wits* as "mental abilities, or powers of intelligent observation, keen perception." Etymologically, then, a witness is someone who is not only present at some event, but who intelligently exercises his or her powers of observation.

What would it take, then, for a person to do the work this receipt is being asked to do? Such a person, first of all, would have to be present at the exchange of food for money. He or she would have to remember the transaction and be available to testify to it at some future time, possibly on multiple occasions. If I were ever audited, for example, and had claimed this meal as a business expense, I would bring this person along to vouch for my story. (The word *vouch* is from the Middle English *vouchen,* meaning to summon to court — in other words, to act as a witness and a guarantor.) But in testifying to the event, this person would need to express his testimony in terms that were useful to the proceedings. To say, "Well, I saw this guy come into the deli and leave about fifteen minutes later," might be just right if the police were trying to determine my whereabouts, but it would be useless in establishing the specifics of the financial transaction that took place during that time. Finally, in addition to speaking truthfully and relevantly, the witness would have to appear credible; he would need to look and sound like someone who could be trusted, who could be counted on to speak truthfully and relevantly. The IRS auditor might not look favorably on someone who dressed and spoke as if he had spent the previous ten years on Skid Row.

But it would be hard to imagine building a global system of commercial exchange like the one we have now, with billions of transactions taking place each day, if human beings were required to stand around in grocery stores, gas stations, and bookstores to witness the transactions taking place there, to remember them, and to testify to them at any time of day or night. Fortunately for global capitalism, we've figured out how to delegate this responsibility to small, marked pieces of paper (and now, increasingly, to invisible codes sent between computers). We've figured out how to get them to remember and report back what they've witnessed, to speak succinctly and accurately, and to do so in a credible manner.

But how is our little receipt able to accomplish this rather remarkable feat? The answer can't be found *in* the receipt itself — or in the receipt *alone*. To find it, you have to broaden your gaze and look at the way the receipt is situated, or embedded, in a huge web of human practices and knowledge distributed through space and time.

Let's start by noticing that the receipt has a conventional form. The thin strip of paper, the column of numbers in blocky fixed-width characters, the logo at the top all serve to identify it *as* a cash register receipt. It wears its identity on its sleeve, for all to see. What's more, this conventional form carries a conventional content (the cost of items purchased, sales tax, totals, cash back, and so on). Nowhere on the receipt, however, does it actually state that this *is* a receipt, that this is a record of an exchange of goods for money, that "4.25" stands for the cost of an item and ".75" for another — nor does it explain any number of other facts that are immediately available to us. It doesn't have to. It can simply rely on the fact that we, literate members of the culture, have already acquired the skills needed to recognize receipts *as* receipts and to use them as such.

Behind the scenes, however, a huge amount of invisible work (invisible from the perspective of this little receipt) is constantly being done to support the receipt in its apparently effortless work. There's the work of the cash register manufacturers, for example, continuing to produce machines that can record purchases and spew out receipts that obey the conventional formats. There's the work of the paper manufacturers producing paper rolls of the right consistency and price. There's the work of graphic artists and designers making the typefaces and the logos that appear on the receipts. There's the work of shop employees training other shop employees to operate the cash registers, so they can push the right keys, change rolls of paper, and so on. All this and more is happening, just to make sure that receipts will be produced that conform to cultural expectations. And as for their ordinary, everyday use, that's where we customers come into the picture. For without our having learned to recognize and use receipts, thereby tacitly agreeing to uphold their conventions, the system couldn't possibly work.

Collectively, then, we conspire to help this receipt do its job. And when everything is working just right (which happens, amazingly, most of the time), a little piece of paper can emerge from a cash register in a deli, it can be torn off the roll and placed in a brown paper bag, and that piece of paper will count as a credible witness to the financial facts of a particular transaction.

But to say all this is almost to neglect the important work that the receipt itself is doing. Its job is to keep itself together, to maintain its form, content, identity, and stability. If it is to serve as proof of purchase, what was first witnessed in the deli must still be available days, weeks, months, and perhaps even years later, and in situations very unlike the one in which it first arose. A human witness would be asked to tell his story at a later time, and possibly to repeat it multiple times. The receipt does this too, achieving repeatability through fixity. By holding its little blue marks fixed, it does its best to ensure that the story conveyed by these marks will be repeatedly available.

Cheap ink, cheap paper, simple, unadorned numerals and letterforms — these qualities suggest something quite humble, insignificant, and generally unremarkable. And yet there is something remarkable about the receipt's ability to preserve or freeze some aspect of the world. The world, after all, is characterized by ever-ongoing change, motion, and transformation. Our bodies are changing all the time. Our thoughts are an endless parade of memories, dreams, and reflections. Our physical and social environment is constantly in motion as well, in ways both great and small. But over many millennia, in the midst of and in response to the reality of this ongoing flux, human beings have figured out how to shape and freeze bits of the material world for a wide range of purposes. *Homo faber,* human being as maker, has learned how to make tools and artifacts of all kinds — hammers and knives and tables and bowls — that maintain their shape and function. Writing is essentially the marrying of this ability to fix or preserve with the ability to symbolize or represent. It is the creation of stable artifacts and the affixing of meaningful marks to them.

Flimsy and inconsequential though it may outwardly seem, the receipt is actually quite powerful. Gazing at a massive dam as it holds forth against the huge forces of a river, can we doubt that we are witnessing a marvelous feat of engineering, a triumph of human ingenuity over nature? Yet what this receipt does is no less remarkable and no less powerful, even if it is less immediately apparent, for it is holding forth against the ravages of time. One might even say *heroically holding forth.* Since ancient times, books have been considered vehicles of immortality because they were capable of preserving literary works — and thereby their authors' souls. The word *hero* is from the same Indo-European root, *ser-*, as the word *preserve.* A hero is someone who preserves and protects others. A document — be it a book or a cash register receipt — is something that preserves someone's thoughts or ideas, or some bit of information that would otherwise be carried away by the river of time. Although the content of this receipt is obviously less outwardly noble, less artistic, than a copy of one of Plato's dialogues or one of Shakespeare's plays, it partakes of the same basic technologies and practices of preservation that have allowed these works to live on through the ages.

It may seem strange to place small, trivial, invisible documents like this one alongside the great ones, and to speak of them in the same breath, but this is exactly what we must do if we are to see the entire class of documents, all of them, as a single species; and if we are to see their shared properties and their joint work in the world.

2

What Are Documents?

A FEW YEARS AGO, a short article titled "What's a Document?" appeared in *Wired* magazine. Written by David Weinberger, then a vice-president of the Open Text Corporation and now a business consultant, it begins with the provocative question, "Have you noticed that the word *document* doesn't mean much these days?" Here is the article in its entirety:

> Have you noticed that the word *document* doesn't mean much these days? It covers everything from a text-only wordprocessing file to a spreadsheet to a Java-soaked interactive Web page.
>
> It didn't used to be like this. A document was a piece of paper — such as a will or passport — with an official role in our legal system.
>
> But when the makers of wordprocessors looked for something to call their special kind of files, they imported *document*. As multi-media entered what used to be text-only files, the word stretched to the point of meaninglessness. Just try to make sense of the file types Windows 95 puts into the Document menu entry.
>
> The fact that we can't even say what a document is anymore indicates the profundity of the change we are undergoing in how we interact with information and, ultimately, our world.[1]

Weinberger is making several claims here. Once upon a time, he says, *document* meant something: a document was something on paper that had an official or institutional role to play. And he is right about this, at least according to the dictionary. *The Random House Dictionary* defines a document as "a written or printed paper furnishing information or evidence, as a passport, deed, bill of sale, bill of lading, etc.; a legal or official paper." *The American Heritage Dictionary* calls a document "a written or printed paper that bears the original, official, or legal form of something and can be used to furnish decisive evidence or information." The word *document,* according to these sources, has something to do with writing, paper, and evidence.

Weinberger also claims that *document* is now being used to name things that lie outside this scope. Here too he is right. These days people regularly refer to various kinds of digital materials — text files, multimedia presentations, and Web pages — as documents. All of these materials fall outside the scope of the standard dictionary definitions. None is on paper; only some are "written" (that is, alphabetic or textual); and few if any function primarily as evidence.

From these two points, he then makes his most substantial claim, that new uses of *document* stretch the definition to the point of incoherence. But does this necessarily follow? Weinberger's point, it seems to me, is about more than just a word: it's about the status of a cultural category. We once had a notion of written things, and it was coherent, it made sense. But now we've thrown other things into that category, things like text files and multimedia presentations and Web pages, and the grouping no longer makes sense. The reason we can't say what belongs is that there's no longer a rationale for putting all these things in the same bag. It's like those children's games where you're shown a room filled with objects and asked, "What's wrong with this picture?" What's wrong with this picture is that multimedia presentations don't *belong* with legal contracts; spreadsheets don't *belong* with passports.

This might seem like a minor question, one best left to lexicographers or philosophers. Except that Weinberger believes there is a connection between the loss of this once-meaningful category and some of the big changes now taking place in the world. The disruption to our notion of documents is consequential, he seems to say, it really matters. "The fact that we can't even say what a document is anymore," his last sentence reads, "indicates the profundity of the change we are undergoing in how we interact with information and, ultimately, our world."

I am certainly in accord with Weinberger on this last point. But I take issue with his main claim. We *can* say what a document is. Doing this, however, requires a somewhat different approach from that which dictionaries take. It requires going beyond word usage. It does require looking at the relevant technologies, but in such a way that we aren't fixated on them, that we don't fetishize them. Most of all, it requires immersing ourselves in the social roles these technologies play.

What are documents? They are, quite simply, talking things. They are bits of the material world — clay, stone, animal skin, plant fiber, sand — that we've imbued with the ability to speak. One of the earliest characterizations of documents comes in Genesis, and curiously, it is a description of human beings, not of written forms. "God formed Adam from the dust of the earth, and blew into his nostrils the breath of life, and Adam became a living soul." In Hebrew, the name Adam is a pun, a play on the Hebrew word *adamah,* meaning "earth." Adam is literally an earthling, and this meaning is directly preserved in the word *human,* from the Latin *humus,* earth. (If this account of our lowly origins makes us feel humble, it should, since the word *humble* is from the same Latin root. To be humble is to be close to the earth.)

The first human, according to the biblical account, was made by mixing breath with earth. But this is also how we make documents. Writing is the act of breathing our breath into the dust of the earth (not literally our breath, of course, but something very much akin to it: our speaking voice). While this act doesn't literally bring the inert material to life, it does infuse it with an identity, a soul, you might say. (The Hebrew word *neshamah* means both breath and soul.) Or, to put this another way, writing is an act of ventriloquism, of throwing the voice into an inanimate object. Ventriloquism, the dictionary says, is "the art of speaking in such a manner that the voice does not appear to come from the speaker but from another source." If this is a trick, it is nonetheless one we begin teaching our children at a very early age.

For many centuries Jewish scholars and mystics have explored this story of Adam's creation, searching out its hidden meanings and making more explicit the connections between earth, writing, and life. Some of this speculation has come down to us in the form of legends or folktales about the creation of a Golem, an artificial man. In the most popular version of these, Judah Loew, a sixteenth-century scholar living in Prague, is said to have created a Golem to be his servant. Having shaped it from the dust of the earth, he brought it to life by inscribing the Hebrew word *emet* (truth) on its forehead. But the Golem ran amok and Loew was forced to destroy it, which he did by erasing the first letter of the word *emet,* leaving the Hebrew word *met* (dead). The Golem then crumbled, returning to the dust from which it was formed.

As literate members of a literate society, we are completely immersed in a world filled with these creatures, these talking Golems. We are so used to living with them in all their myriad forms that we've become inured, or blinded, to them. Under such circumstances, it's hard to see them for the remarkable, even magical, beings they are. Somehow, we must see them afresh, with children's, or aliens', eyes. The literary critic George Steiner relates how the medieval scholar Erasmus, "walking home on a foul night, glimpsed a tiny fragment of print in the mire. He bent down, seized upon it and lifted it to a flickering light with a cry of thankful joy."[2] Writing in 1923, the anthropologist Lucien Lévy-Bruhl observed that the native peoples he was studying treated writing as magical, and "even when the native appears to have learnt what writing is, even if he can read and write, he never loses the feeling that a mystical force is at work."[3] It is easy, with Lévy-Bruhl, to see this as an example of "primitive thinking," the perspective of uneducated and unsophisticated natives. It is harder to hold on to a sense of wonder.

Yet, without question, language is a wondrous achievement. Speech is something we assume to be uniquely human. For medieval

Jewish philosophers, the Hebrew word *ha-medaber* — literally "the one who speaks" — was synonymous with "human being."[4] In recent decades, attempts have been made to determine whether chimpanzees or dolphins might possess some rudimentary degree of language skills. Understanding the process of human language acquisition is a challenge that draws researchers on. ("Language is a virus from outer space," says William S. Burroughs.) Our inheritance from the Golem legends includes a fascination with robots, in both science and science fiction. Myths and fairy tales are filled with stories of talking animals and inanimate objects that can speak. There is active speculation about the possibility that intelligent, and presumably communicative, beings may exist elsewhere in the universe.

But why look elsewhere? For here, right under our noses, too close and intimate to be seen clearly, are creatures that share with us the ability to speak. And we have created them. Some of them — books in particular — aspire to nobility and long life. Others, such as cash register receipts and personal notes, typically have a less exalted status and a shorter useful lifetime. But all of them are bits of the material world we have taught to talk. Surely this is a remarkable feat.

An awareness of written forms as talking things has ancient roots. If it is subtly embedded in Genesis, it is much more explicitly made in Plato's *Phaedrus,* which has an extended reflection on the nature of writing. Written forms may speak, Socrates observes, but they are dumb. Indeed, writing has some of the same disadvantages as painting. Painting may produce very realistic images, but they are representations, and not the real things. If you query one of them, it is unable to respond. "The same holds true of written words: you might suppose that they understand what they are saying, but if you ask them what they mean by anything they simply return the same answer over and over again."

This is a crucial point. For Plato, it shows up the limits of writing. Written forms are pale shadows of their human counterparts. They are incapable of dialogue, the Socratic path to wisdom. This seems true enough, but it fails to acknowledge what is truly powerful about documents. For it is precisely in their ability to "return the same answer over and over again" that the utility of documents is made manifest. The brilliance of writing is the discovery of a way to make artifacts talk, coupled with the ability to hold that talk fixed — to keep it the same. The result is a talking thing, capable of repeatedly delivering up the same story at different points in time and space. This is something that documents do well and that people, by and large, don't. It's not that we are incapable of performing in such a manner. A messenger, after all, can deliver a singing telegram to multiple hotel rooms. But it is not of our essence to do so. Yet it is exactly of the essence of documents, a defining characteristic.

But at the same time that Plato underestimates the importance of sameness, he also exaggerates it. Once something has been engraved in stone, literally or figuratively, it is easy to imagine that it will last, that it will stay the same, *forever*. Alas, nothing, at least in the material world, is so destined. Stone, vellum, and paper all weather, though admittedly at different rates; words change their meaning; and interpretations vary depending on time, place, and many other factors. Does this mean that documents can't actually achieve fixity or repeatability? Not quite. It just means that they can't do it forever, for all people, for all purposes. If it is a partial victory, it is still a remarkable achievement.

Looking at documents this way sets up a strong parallel between documents and people. Both in their own ways are talking things. This is hardly an accidental parallel. Documents are exactly those things we create to speak *for us,* on our behalf and in our absence. It is a common enough situation, when one person stands in for and speaks for another. Lawyers and agents — press agents, literary agents — do this for a living. Lovers in some of our most famous love stories send their confidants to do the talking for them. Documents do this too, they speak for us in order to act for us, to take on jobs or roles.

The sociologist Bruno Latour uses the term *delegation* for this process of handing off jobs or tasks to others. He is interested in how we delegate responsibility not just to other people but to inanimate objects. He gives the example of a door. Suppose we lived in a world with walls but no doors, he begins a thought-experiment.[5] Whenever we wanted to enter a room, we'd have to break a hole in a wall with a pickax. And if we then wanted to close up the wall, for privacy or to protect ourselves from the cold, we'd have to reconstruct the part of the wall we'd just demolished. A door is clearly a much more workable idea, an object to which we can delegate the task of covering and uncovering the hole.

But the door doesn't do the whole job. There is a division of labor, a contract, between the door and its human users. The door will agree to seal and unseal the hole in the wall if we will agree to push it open and closed. The door thus assumes certain responsibilities, but in return it asks something of the people who use it. People must know how to open and close the door — they must not only have such competences (including the skill and the strength to perform these acts), but they must exercise them. In this sense, the process of delegation is reciprocal: the door delegates to us as much as we delegate to it. Of course the job of opening and closing the door can itself be delegated: to a person we call a doorman. And this task too can be delegated to an inanimate object: to a sensor and motor that automatically opens and shuts the door. The division of responsibility between humans and other humans, and between humans and objects, can be shifted.

Through examples of this kind, Latour paints a picture of a world realized through the ongoing interactions of human and nonhuman actors. We humans may make artifacts and delegate certain tasks to them, but they in turn shape our behavior, in effect delegating to us as well. It may seem odd to anthropomorphize objects in this way, to ascribe agency and intention to them. For my part, I understand this as a strategy aimed at pointing up certain truths about the social dimension of life and the sociality of artifacts. The artifacts around us, Latour seems to be saying, are more than just lumps of matter. They are bits of the material world that we have molded and shaped to participate with *us* — in our world, in the human lifeworld.

Documents are exactly those artifacts to which we delegate the task of speaking for us. Each kind of document, each genre, is specialized to do a certain kind of job — to carry a certain kind of information and to operate within a particular realm of human activity. Receipts are designed to witness financial transactions, handwritten notes to carry a message from one person to another, books to transmit stories and verse and knowledge deemed publicly significant. It's useful to think of genres by analogy with human jobs. The doorman's job is to open and close the entry door of a building. He typically wears a uniform, which signals his role, quickly establishing expectations about what we can and can't (or should and shouldn't) do in relation to him, what forms of service we can reasonably expect, and the nature of the dialogue we are likely to engage in with him. Of course, understanding the doorman's role requires knowing a lot more than that he's paid to open and close one particular door. His job is embedded in a rich set of cultural distinctions: between hotels and more-permanent dwelling places; between high-class apartment buildings and others; between tenants, guests, and employees; and so on. If we understand these distinctions, it's largely because we, like the doorman, are immersed in the culture from which they spring.

Each document genre, too, has a uniform that signals something about the role it's meant to play. A receipt looks like . . . a receipt. A newspaper has a telltale size and shape and an easily recognizable visual structure consisting of columns of tightly packed text separated by larger headlines. A passport has its own distinctive size and shape — an official look about itself — and, internally, a characteristic visual rhythm made up of passport photo, signatures, colored stamps and seals. A pulp romance novel, a travel guidebook, and a college textbook all have highly distinctive looks as well, in terms of their shapes, cover designs, and inside typography. In each of these cases the uniform is distinctive enough to be discernible at some distance.

And rapid identification is important. Once we know a document's genre, we more or less know what it is and how to use it, since we know what its job is. We have a basis for interpreting what it's saying. (If I come across a piece of writing that begins, "The President must die," it makes all the difference in the world whether it is the first line of a thriller or an excerpt from John Hinckley's journal.) All this knowledge of form, function, use, and interpretation has been established by many years of schooling and living. To be literate is not just to be able to read and write, literally, but to be able to traffic in the many genres that surround us. Most of us may have already forgotten it, but it took considerable effort to learn how to use a checkbook, to read a job announcement, to write a résumé, to fill out a job application. (And the people who, for lack of schooling or experience, are weak in these skills are at a severe disadvantage.) But this is really no different from the work we've had to do to understand the social roles and responsibilities, the jobs, of the many kinds of human workers with whom we constantly interact — doormen, policemen, flight attendants, and so on.

No document, no genre, is an island. Our little strip of cheap paper with blue symbols makes its mark in the world in virtue of being something with social meaning and value. To be a receipt is to be connected to cash registers, sellers, buyers, products, expense reports, the IRS, and so on. If these connections are severed — puff! — the receipt, as a receipt, is no more. It returns to the (saw)dust of the earth. It's a curious thing about documents: you can't see them if you don't look at them; but you also can't see them if you look *only* at them, ignoring the surroundings in which they operate.

To delegate to others is of course to exercise some measure of power and control over them. You get someone, or something, to do *your* bidding. But it also inevitably involves a loss of control. Someone else, an autonomous actor, now takes over, who will surely do things differently than you would — and perhaps not up to your standards. Indeed, the Golem legend can be read as a parable on the problems of delegation. You just can't get good help anymore. It's probably no accident that of the many versions of the legend, the one that retains the greatest currency has the Golem going berserk. This is the version that is continually retold — in the sorcerer's apprentice in Disney's classic film *Fantasia,* as well as in countless retellings of *Frankenstein.*

Few documents actually go berserk. But in endless ways they manage to escape the chains of their creators. Once these creatures go out into the world, they live a life that is at least partly independent of their creators' concerns. (Think of my valedictory address.) They can be endlessly interpreted and reinterpreted, reused, subverted, and coopted for other purposes. Over the centuries the Bible has been used to argue both for and against many positions; in the nineteenth century it was invoked both in defense of and in opposition to slavery. Delegation, like so much of life, is at once powerful, complex, and *partial*.

But the question arises: Shouldn't we say that all artifacts speak? Don't all the things around us have a story to tell? Each was created at a certain time and place. It comes out of a certain community, exemplifies a certain style and design aesthetic. It has been subject to wear and tear, has perhaps been broken and repaired; it bears evidence of the passage of time. A Shaker cabinet has much to tell us about Shaker life and living. Its simple, spare design and careful construction arise from, and give voice to, a steady, quiet, and reverential attitude toward life. A house — any house — speaks not only of the era in which it was built, but of the lives that have been lived in it. Cars have much to tell us about their owners, about how they see themselves and the kind of image they wish to present to the world. Does this mean that all artifacts — cabinets, houses, and cars — are documents?

Actually, no. For although documents speak in these same ways, it's not what they are primarily about. Unlike cabinets and houses and cars, documents are representational artifacts. As with crystal balls, we peer into and through them. Documents are made to carry and offer up very particular kinds of stories and in very particular ways. Perhaps the simplest instance of such a representational stance is the knife or piece of turf, mentioned in chapter 1, which would have been given as evidence of the transfer of property in medieval times. The knife was meant to stand for, to bear witness to, and to call to mind the declaration through which property was transferred from one owner to another. This is an extremely limited case of the kind of talk documents exhibit. The knife as an undifferentiated whole is meant to stand for the fact of property transfer, and it is only in the context of particular witnesses and their memories that one can have any idea what the knife is saying — or that it has anything to say at all. Documents talk much more powerfully and broadly when their representational abilities are more fully articulated.

The most obvious case of such further articulation is written language — the use of alphabetic or other symbolic marks to create composites that correspond more or less directly to human utterances. But it is not only through alphabetic and textual representations that documents can be said to speak. There are many other "written" forms, especially if we allow the root meaning of the word *writing* — "to score or incise on a surface" — to be heard. Maps, diagrams, pictures, photographs, and all manner of other conventional and well-articulated, nonverbal representations will count as well. It might seem slightly odd to say that a Mathew Brady photograph of Lincoln or a map of the New York subway system *speaks*. But certainly these forms stand in for us too, they tell stories, they represent.

To say that documents speak is perhaps to indulge in a certain poetic license, which might be avoided by simply saying that they represent or communicate and leaving it at that. But to do this would be to lose the elegant and suggestive parallel between documents and people. Like all parallels, this one is incomplete and inexact. If it is useful, however, it will not be because documents and people are exactly the same, but because their similarities and their differences are illuminating, because the partial parallel sheds light on what documents are, and perhaps also on what we humans are.

Traditionally, this parallel has been conceived of as a distinction in language — between spoken and written language, or between orality and literacy. When we humans speak directly, with our voices alone, our words are evanescent. Yet when we speak through writing, our words acquire a degree of fixity. (*Verba volent, littera scripta manet,* the ancient maxim states: words are fleeting, written letters remain.) There is a long history of speculation about the relationship between these two modes of communication. For much of the twentieth century, beginning with Ferdinand de Saussure, linguists have taken writing to be a straightforward derivative of speech and undeserving of sustained attention. As recently as the 1960s, the linguist Otto Jespersen declared that "language is primarily speech" and the written word only a poor substitute for the spoken word.[6] Earlier in the century, another linguist, Leonard Bloomfield, was even more blunt: "Language is basically speech, and writing is of no theoretical interest."[7] If these linguists were disdainful and dismissive of written language, they were also oblivious of its nonverbal forms — or at least so uninterested as to withhold any commentary whatsoever.

This attitude has been changing, if slowly. Within linguistics, Geoffrey Sampson's *Writing Systems,* published in 1985, was one of the first books to take written forms as an object of study in their own right.[8] About the same time, another British linguist, Roy Harris, decried the "tyranny of the alphabet over our modern ways of thinking about the relation between the spoken and the written word."[9] Operating in different disciplinary orbits, others have ventured further. In a book first published in 1968, the philosopher Nelson Goodman explored the properties of text, painting, diagrams, and musical notation as examples of "languages of art."[10] And in his Panizzi lectures, given at the British Library in 1985, the bibliographer D. F. McKenzie argued for a "sociology of texts" that would broaden its horizons to include not only books, but maps, film and TV, and, in his most audacious example, natural landscape, when it fulfills a narrative function.[11]

Michael Buckland, a professor of library and information science at the University of California, Berkeley, has described how the European documentalists in the first half of the twentieth century argued about what could and could not be a document.[12] (The documentation movement, the predecessor to today's information science, aimed to organize scientific and technical publications.) Suzanne Briet, for example, a French librarian and documentalist, declared that "a document is evidence in support of a fact" and is "any physical or symbolic sign, preserved or recorded, intended to represent, to reconstruct, or to demonstrate a physical or conceptual phenomenon."[13] Briet's most unusual example was that of an antelope. In the wild, she claimed, it isn't a document, but once captured and placed in a zoo, it becomes evidence and is thus transformed into a document.

In all of this, a movement can be discerned toward greater inclusiveness: from a preoccupation with spoken forms alone to the inclusion of written forms; from the verbal or textual alone to other sign systems; from printed, bound books alone to other media and technologies. Surely one of the forces at work here is the computer, bringing together previously separated forms in a single medium. It isn't only David Weinberger who is being led to reflect on and rework previously stable categories and boundaries.

Although all these attempts to make sense of documents are intriguing, from my perspective they work too hard: they fail to see what is most obvious and in plain sight. The simple fact is, we humans have found a way to delegate the ability to speak to inanimate objects, and have become deeply dependent on them for an endless array of services. But if I say that documents are talking things, I don't so much mean this as an ironclad definition, as a means of drawing a tight boundary around a set of objects; I mean it as an orientation, as a way of seeing. Adopting this perspective has one immediate payoff: it gets us away from a narrow and overly exclusive focus on the details of particular technologies. Discussions of documents tend to begin with the technology — talk of clay tablets, the alphabet, the invention of paper and the printing press. While historical treatments of technology are certainly useful, they risk hiding as much as they reveal, for they tend to overemphasize the technological particulars and to mask the nature and workings of the creatures made from and with these technologies. We may miss the documents for the wood pulp.

But if we don't insist on defining documents with respect to particular technologies, such as paper, then we have greater latitude to embrace, and to make sense of, other technological constellations as equally documentlike. Take something like audiotape, for example. This doesn't fit comfortably under the standard dictionary definition. Indeed, it clearly fails to meet two of the three dictionary properties: it isn't on paper and it doesn't involve writing. (Depending on the circumstances, an audiotape recording may or may not count as evidence.) But an audiotape recording *is* most definitely a talking thing. And it does achieve sameness of talk: by playing the tape over and over, we can hear the same thing again and again.

Writing, narrowly defined, is the inscribing of communicative marks in a surface. Visible symbols have traditionally been scratched or carved into a hard surface, such as stone, or puddled onto a smooth surface, such as animal skin or paper. The success of this kind of writing has been dependent on the durability, the fixity, of the resulting forms. But audiotape works differently. Certainly it works by fixing marks (representations of sound) in a medium. But these marks aren't directly available to us: we can't hear them or see them directly. So there needs to be another device (an audiotape player) to generate the sounds we *can* actually hear. These sounds, just like spoken, unrecorded speech, are evanescent. Once you've played a recording of Dr. Martin Luther King saying, "I have a dream," that particular performance — the acoustic signal that just rang in your ears — is gone forever. Yet these transient sounds are documentlike too; not because they are permanent, but because they are exactly repeatable. The audiotape can be played an indefinite number of times, and each time it "will return the same answer over and over again." A different technological means is being used to achieve the same ends.

For most of the five thousand years of writing history, all our techniques and technologies have been aimed at making visible marks stick to surfaces. It is only in the last hundred years that radically different mechanisms have been invented. Audio recording technologies, film, and videotape all achieve reproducibility of talk by making transient visual and auditory performances exactly repeatable. And now, thanks to computers, we are developing still other mechanisms and forms. These include "everything," as David Weinberger puts it, "from a text-only wordprocessing file to a spreadsheet to a Java-soaked interactive Web page."

Are these new forms really a breed apart, as David Weinberger argues? Not really — certainly not to the extent that he suggests. Are text files and spreadsheets and Web pages talking things? Of course they are. They speak through text and sound, through still and moving images — the same basic communicative repertoire we had before computers appeared on the scene. The fact that these signs and symbols are being realized in technically novel ways — Java, HTML, global Internet connections, and so on — is a red herring. We are simply learning to throw our voice into new materials.

But there is also good reason to be confused about all this — and not just because the technologies involved are opaque to all but the most technically sophisticated. It's confusing because the genres now online are a mishmash of old and new, and because they're currently unstable. Some, like academic conference papers or online newspapers, have been relatively straightforwardly imported from paper. Others, like e-mail, while still displaying their offline roots, have been around long enough to take on novel features, but not long enough to fully stabilize. Still others don't have clear identities, and hover uneasily between parody, experimental art, and just plain weirdness.

Another question must be addressed: If digital materials are talking things, do they, can they, ensure the sameness or repeatability of their talk? The answer would seem to be no, if you accept the claims of certain hypertext enthusiasts and high-tech visionaries. For such people, digital technologies have sounded the death knell for the fixed text. Because it is so easy to edit digital materials, there will no longer be a final, stable version. Because it is straightforward to produce "print-on-demand" materials that have been customized for individual readers, editions will soon consist of single copies rather than the print runs of thousands to which we have become so accustomed, effectively doing away with the notion of an edition. And as we increasingly produce hypertext webs in which there is no determinate reading order, there will no longer be any guarantee that two people, approaching the same work, will read the same text. The transience of materials on the World Wide Web — where the average lifetime of a Web page is measured in days — would seem to offer the final truth of these assertions.

There is an inherent difference between paper and digital technologies as communicative substrates: where paper documents are *fixed,* digital materials are *fluid.* This is the essence of the claim being made. One of its clearest articulations can be found in Jay David Bolter's book *Writing Space: The Computer, Hypertext, and the History of Writing.* Published in 1991, before the Web exploded onto the scene, his book nonetheless manages to capture the sense of movement and change that seems to typify the Web. "Electronic text," Bolter says,

> is the first text in which the elements of meaning, of structure, and of visual display are fundamentally unstable. Unlike the printing press or the medieval codex, the computer does not require that any aspect of writing be determined in advance for the whole life of the text. This restlessness is inherent in a technology that records information by collecting for fractions of a second evanescent electrons at tiny junctions of silicon and metal. All information, all data, in the computer world is a kind of controlled movement, and so the natural inclination of computer writing is to change, to grow, and finally to disappear.[14]

Attractive and popular though it may be, this understanding of the difference between paper and digital forms is, quite simply, wrong. What it fails to grasp is that paper documents, and indeed all documents — are static *and* changing, fixed *and* fluid. It also fails to see the importance of fixity in the digital world. There is a reason why text and graphics editors have a Save button, after all. And if digital materials at the moment are highly impermanent, this is increasingly seen as a problem, with libraries and other institutions working hard to guarantee the survival of these materials into the future.

Bolter is quite right, however, in suggesting that digital information is "a kind of controlled movement." But the same is true for paper documents. Look at any document — a cash register receipt, a book, a laundry list, a greeting card — and you will see the ways in which it is moving and changing and the ways in which it isn't. Its effectiveness depends exactly on its engaging in a *controlled* movement: holding certain things fixed, allowing other things to change. The success of any genre, or of a particular instance of any genre, comes in its pattern or rhythm of fixity and fluidity: what information it holds fixed, when it can be changed and by whom. Different genres, to be sure, will exhibit different rhythms: a shopping list may come into existence for a brief period of time and may change often during its useful lifetime; a published volume may exist for decades and undergo relatively little change during that time.

What the death-of-fixity arguments miss is the significance of communicative stability. The ability to keep talk fixed, to guarantee its repeatability, is a basic building block of human culture. Putting talk into stable, external forms allows it to be shared, to be held in common. (The root of the word *communicate*, as well as of the words *community* and *communion*, is the Latin *communis*, meaning "common.") Just as the stability of the earth allows us to build stable structures on top of it, so written forms provide stable reference points that help us orient ourselves in social space.

It is no accident that all our social institutions — including science, law and government, religion, education and the arts, commerce and administration — rely on the stabilizing power of documents to accomplish their ends. In the form of books and journal articles, documents are carriers of scientific knowledge. As sacred scripture, they are the central artifacts around which many religious traditions have been organized. As written statutes, charters, and contracts, they play a crucial role in constructing and regulating lawful behavior. As works of literature, paintings, and drawings, they are the tangible products of artistic practice. As textbooks and student notes, they are crucial instruments around which learning practices are organized. As receipts and accounts, memos and forms, they are critical ingredients in the way commerce, and indeed all bureaucratic conduct, is organized. In each of these cases the ability to hold talk fixed — to provide communicative stability — is crucial.

It would be strange indeed if, in making talking things out of new materials, we were somehow to omit this crucial ingredient. Better to say that we are still working out how best to achieve fixity in the digital world, not that we are trying to abolish it — or, worse yet, that fixity is inherently absent from the new medium. Most of the digital forms we are now creating and using already possess this property, to whatever limited degree, and it is crucial to their success. CNN's main Web page displays a set of stories, much as does the front page of *The New York Times*. Certainly their Web page changes more quickly than the *Times* puts out new editions. But the page exhibits a kind of punctuated equilibrium (to borrow and abuse a phrase from evolutionary theory): it stays the same for periods of time, then undergoes change, then stays the same. It may well be true that digital documents will generally maintain their sameness for *shorter periods of time* than their paper counterparts, but this is a different matter.

Seeing documents in this way — as talking things, as beings exhibiting patterns of stasis and change — should only increase our respect for their significance and power. Each one is a surrogate, a little sorcerer's apprentice, to whom a piece of work has been delegated. Each one speaks out, tells its story, makes itself known. Small and insignificant though most are, when seen in aggregate they are hugely powerful, helping to make meaning and order. Of course, they don't do this work alone — they need our help as we need theirs. And at this stage in human societal development, the conduct of life would be unthinkable without them. Is it any wonder that changes in the technology for producing and using these things are sending ripples through our institutions and practices? Even through our sense of ourselves?

For if documents are surrogates for us, they are extensions of ourselves, parts of ourselves. The best and the worst of ourselves can be found in them: our loves and hates, our destructiveness and our altruism, our honesty and our deceptiveness. Which means that looking at documents gives us a way to see ourselves. We can look at each one, close up, to see its form and content. But to make sense of these properties, we need to look at its surrounding context, the activities in which the document plays a part. And if we pan back farther still, we can see the larger slice of life, the qualities and values, that a document reflects and supports. And in seeing these forms, meanings, activities, and values, we just may catch a glimpse, like a passing reflection in a store window, of who we are and who we long to be.

3

Leaves of Grass

Well before the World Wide Web came into existence, books had begun to migrate from paper to digital form. Today, many of the classic works of literature — works whose copyright protection has expired, such as *Crime and Punishment* and *Alice in Wonderland* — are freely available for downloading and printing. No one, however, is yet sure whether people will want to read online, how the online reading experience will differ from earlier, paper-based practices, or whether we should ultimately care. It may be too early for definitive answers to such questions, but it isn't too early to reflect on our own experience of particular works. So in just this spirit of concrete exploration, I want to have a look at one particular work, which began its life as a printed book and now can also be found on the Web.

The book I have in mind is Walt Whitman's *Leaves of Grass,* undoubtedly one of the great works of American literature. It is a work that was guaranteed to shock its first readers, in 1855, who encountered these opening lines:

> I celebrate myself,
> And what I assume you shall assume,
> For every atom belonging to me as good belongs to you.

I loafe and invite my soul,
I lean and loafe at my ease. . . . observing a spear of summer grass.

With this bold announcement, the author had clearly broken with poetic tradition. The lines were written in free verse, and their subject matter — the poet himself, his body, his sensual desires — violated the social and literary norms of the day. And who was he, anyway? To the extent that he had a presence in the public arena, it was as a hack journalist, the author of mediocre and often inflammatory prose. What's more, the man who published these lines at the age of thirty-five was still living at home and sleeping in the same bed with his feebleminded brother, George.

Ever since Whitman made this extraordinary appearance, scholars and critics have been at pains to explain how this third-rate writer could become a literary genius, capable of producing a poem that, for one commentator at least, ranks as "the greatest poem ever written by an American."[1] For some, the explanation is quite mundane. In *Walt Whitman: The Making of the Poet,* Paul Zweig traces Whitman's early experiments in form and content that prepared the ground for his surprising emergence.[2]

But for others, there is an air of the mystical about this emergence, which is in keeping with the prophetic tone and content of some of Whitman's poems. Malcolm Cowley, in his introduction to a reprint of the first edition of *Leaves of Grass,* argues that Whitman had had a powerful religious experience, a mystical insight into cosmic unity, in 1853 or 1854, just a year or two before he published the first edition of *Leaves of Grass.* "Such ecstasies," says Cowley, "consist in a rapt feeling of union or identity with God (or the Soul, or Mankind, or the Cosmos), a sense of ineffable joy leading to the conviction that the seer has been released from the limitations of space and time and has been granted a direct vision of truths impossible to express."[3] It was such an experience, according to Cowley, that laid the ground and supplied the energy for *Leaves of Grass.* Whitman is describing just such an experience in "Song of Myself," Cowley believes, when he says:

Swiftly arose and spread around me the peace and joy and
    knowledge that pass all the art and argument of the earth;
And I know that the hand of God is the elderhand of my own,
And I know that the spirit of God is the eldest brother of my own,
And that all the men ever born are also my brothers . . . and the
    women my sisters and lovers.[4]

In the end, no one can say with certainty whether these poems
emerged as the result of mundane experimentation or mystical
insight — or perhaps through a combination of the two. But it is
clear that the *subject matter* of these poems is at once both mundane
and mystical, and that the two are inseparable for Whitman. It is his
gift to see the transcendent in the ordinary and to speak to us in ways
that can invoke this awareness in us as well. The poet looks at the
smallest and most ordinary of things — a blade of grass, refuse in the
street — with an eye tuned to its fullness and mystery.

Why should I wish to see God better than this day?
I see something of God each hour of the twenty-four, and each
    moment then,
In the faces of men and women I see God, and in my own face in
    the glass;
I find letters from God dropped in the street, and every one is
    signed by God's name,
And I leave them where they are, for I know that others will
    punctually come forever and ever.

Unlike the earlier cash register receipt, there is nothing arbitrary
about my decision to write about this particular book. Of the books
that have shaped my life, none has been more important than *Leaves
of Grass*. I have been reading Walt Whitman's great nineteenth-
century work of poetry for close to forty years. But I should probably
say I have been reading *in it:* I have never actually traversed it cover-
to-cover; instead I have dipped into it over the years, finding poems
appropriate to my age and interests. In the first years, poems like "O
Captain! My Captain!" — with its conventional rhyme and meter,

and relatively straightforward subject matter — were most accessible to me. Early on, though, I was also drawn, however unconsciously, to the poet's exuberant voice, his wild declarations and untamed lists. When he turned his gaze on New York City, where I grew up, he assured me that the magical qualities I found there were known to others as well, and in other eras than my own. It was only in later years, as I matured, that his meditations on death, inseparable from his celebrations of life, began to speak to me.

But when I say this book is special, I mean not only the work of literature in some generic sense but one particular copy, which is before me now. For this is my childhood copy, a hardcover book given to me by my Uncle Jack when I was perhaps ten or twelve years old. There have of course been many editions of *Leaves of Grass*, and many more are sure to follow. A number are currently in print and easily available: the Modern Library edition in hardcover; and the Bantam Classic, the Penguin Classics, and the Wordsworth Poetry Library editions in paperback. I have copies of all of these, as well as copies of several older, out-of-print editions. While these are all useful to me in various ways — they help satisfy my interest in comparative study and lay scholarship — it is always my childhood copy to which I return for nourishment. It is this copy that I *read*.

But it is surely a sign of the times that *Leaves of Grass* is now available in yet another format, not just in another edition: it is on the Web. As I write, the opening lines of "Song of Myself" are visible in a Web browser running on my laptop. Placing both my childhood copy and this new online version side by side on my desk gives me a chance to reflect on them in relation to one another. What strikes me first is how vastly different they are in gestalt. They are both ostensibly doing the same piece of work, making Whitman's poems available to me, and they do this through essentially the same communicative mechanism, placing typographic letterforms on a flat surface. Yet they are markedly different in form and, what may come as more of a surprise, in content. Although each has its source, ultimately, in Whitman's creative spark, they are products of different choices made not only by Whitman but by any number of intermediaries who have had a hand in shaping what is before me now. It should hardly be surprising, then, if my experience of them is different as well.

My childhood copy comes from an illustrated edition produced by the Peter Pauper Press. The Peter Pauper Press was started by Peter Beilenson in the late 1920s in Mount Vernon, New York, and was taken over by his wife, Edna, after his death in 1962. It was known for books like mine, lovingly yet inexpensively prepared. They typically sold for one or two dollars. Peter Beilenson credited his wife with bringing an integrated sense of color and design to the books they produced, and this is evident enough in my copy of *Leaves of Grass*. The covers are bound in dark green paper as a background for repeating images of white and light green blades of grass. The top edges of the pages are tinted green, and the headbands — decorative stitching at the head and tail of the spine, which also provide structural support — have an alternating pattern of green and white thread.

The book's ten or so drawings — pastels printed in green ink — are by the Kansas artist John Steuart Curry, and were presumably commissioned for it. They are straightforward and, to my mind at least, unimaginative. The illustration for "Song of Myself" shows a barefoot man, in worker's clothes, leaning up against a tree while reading a book. All the drawings have a dreamy quality, suggesting that this is the product of an idle and harmless dreamer. Looking at them, you would never suspect that it might instead be the work of a prophet, or of a radical poet breaking with traditional forms, or of a sensualist living outside the bounds of normative sexuality. There is nothing here to offend — or, for that matter, to excite — anyone.

As for the text printed in this edition, it is based on Whitman's 1891 edition, the so-called deathbed edition. When reading Whitman, I've discovered, it helps to know something about the edition you have in hand. There can be substantial textual differences among editions, a good deal of which are due to the changes Whitman made over the years. During his lifetime, he published seven separate editions of *Leaves of Grass*: in 1855, 1856, 1860, 1867, 1872, 1876, and

SONG OF MYSELF

1. I CELEBRATE myself, and sing myself,
And what I assume you shall assume,
For every atom belonging to me as good belongs to you.

I loafe and invite my soul,
I lean and loafe at my ease observing a spear of summer grass.

My tongue, every atom of blood, form'd from this soil, this air,
Born here of parents born here from parents the same, and their parents
    the same,
I, now thirty-seven years old, in perfect health begin,
Hoping to cease not till death.

1891. The text of each edition differed in significant ways from its predecessors. The editions grew in size as Whitman added new poems. The first edition of 1855 had a mere twelve poems, while the final edition of 1891 had 383. But Whitman also deleted poems, reordered them, grouped them in different ways, gave them titles when first they had none, and sometimes changed them. He even tinkered with the words.

The opening lines of "Song of Myself" appear in the first edition as I've rendered them on the first page of this chapter. But in my childhood copy (see facing page), based on the 1891 edition, a new phrase, "and sing myself," has been added to the first line:

I celebrate myself, and sing myself,
And what I assume you shall assume,
For every atom belonging to me as good belongs to you.

In the first edition, "Song of Myself" appears first in the collection, but it is as yet untitled. In the next edition, a year later, it acquires a title, "A Poem of Walt Whitman, an American." This changes to "Walt Whitman" in the 1860 edition and ends up, in the 1891 edition, with the title "Song of Myself," which has since become its standard name.[5] The poem also changes its location, losing its position as our introduction to the poet. By the deathbed edition (and also in my childhood copy), it appears a good twenty poems into the work.

Changes of this kind are hardly atypical in works of literature. Indeed, they can be even more dramatic. Marianne Moore's "Poetry," for example, first published as a poem of thirty lines, later appeared in versions of thirteen, fifteen, and twenty-nine lines, ending up as a poem of only three lines.[6] Clearly, texts have lives: they change over time, they aren't fixed forever in stone. We can't see this if we only stare at one manifestation, one particular application of ink to paper. But if we broaden our gaze to encompass the larger sweep of history, we can see that works on paper exhibit the same "controlled movement" that Bolter wants to attribute to digital works. Of course, we are still within our rights to ask whether or how much such textual changes matter. And in the case of *Leaves of Grass* specifically, how significant is the addition of a phrase here, the modification of a line there?

For Malcolm Cowley, at least, the changes Whitman made to "Song of Myself" are substantial. He believes they reflect Whitman's changing relationship to the mystical experience that inspired the poem in the first place. When, in the first version of the opening line, Whitman declares,

I celebrate myself,

the self to which the poet is referring isn't Walter Whitman, the hack journalist still living at home, but "a dramatized or idealized figure" whose "distinguishing feature is that he has been granted a vision, as a result of which he has realized the potentialities latent in every American and indeed . . . in every living person."[7] So that when Whitman celebrates "myself," he is celebrating the divinity within each of us.

But in time, according to Cowley, Whitman was partly misled by his vision. He became inflated with it and began to confuse his small self with the divinity to which he had been given access. In time he also lost the acuity of that original vision. He continued to edit the poem, making seemingly small changes, which together reveal to Cowley a trail of increasing self-involvement and self-aggrandizement. The addition of the phrase "and sing myself" in the first line — which Cowley claims for Whitman would have meant "write a song about myself" — represents a loss of the immediacy of revelation. For now the poet is no longer witnessing and exclaiming, but self-consciously collecting material for his song. (This one observation would hardly make his case, but Cowley points to a number of other changes to support his thesis.)

Whether or not Cowley is right, surely Whitman's continuing revisions reflect a changing conception of the poems, an ongoing process of reinterpretation. Cowley is not alone in thinking that Whitman's changes represent a dimming of the original poetic insight, whatever its origin. "As he grew older," Stephen Mitchell says in the introduction to his own edited version of "Song of Myself," "his insight faded, and with it the vivacity of his words. Yet in each successive edition he kept tinkering with 'Song of Myself' and the other early poems — adding, deleting, revising. And while certain of these revisions are excellent, most of them are disastrous."[8]

My childhood copy is the product of Whitman's rethinking and reinterpreting, for better or worse. But it is equally the product of the Beilensons' hands, their design aesthetic, and their recasting of the poems as gentle, harmless reveries. To look at my copy in this way is therefore to see it as the product of many hands, and the embodiment of a number of interpretations, not all completely aligned. It is also to see it less as an isolated, static object than as a constituent in an ongoing process of literary production, revision, and renewal.

The online version of *Leaves of Grass* is another thread in this same process. That it is on the Web is due to the efforts of a man named Steven van Leeuwen. When van Leeuwen was a librarian at Columbia University, he began making digital copies of various literary works whose copyright protection had expired, calling this collection the Bartleby Library and himself its editor and publisher. It is an eclectic collection, apparently still growing, made up of works by Sherwood Anderson, T. S. Eliot, Theodore Roosevelt, and Gertrude Stein. In 1997, van Leeuwen moved the collection off Columbia's server, creating bartleby.com as an independent Web site.

Van Leeuwen's online *Leaves of Grass* is based on a print edition published in 1900 by David McKay. To create this digital copy, van Leeuwen scanned and OCRed the text of the poems (performed optical character recognition on digital images of the pages), coding the resulting text in HTML for display on the Web. The print edition includes images of Whitman and facsimiles of notes in his own handwriting. Van Leeuwen scanned these too, and when I first began examining the online version, they were available for viewing as bitmapped images, along with a scanned image of the title page of the 1900 edition.

As it happens, van Leeuwen's choice of this particular print edition has been somewhat controversial. The problem is that McKay based his edition loosely and unsystematically on Whitman's 1871 edition. In a review of Whitman materials on the Web, Charles Green makes the following points about McKay's edition, by way of criticizing van Leeuwen's choice of texts:

> The edition published by McKay in 1900 . . . is actually based upon an edition published by Whitman in 1871. What makes the text questionable . . . is that McKay took liberties with this unauthorized edition, shifting the placement of some poems, and omitting others. The . . . Bartleby Library's online text of *Leaves of Grass,* then, presents an arrangement that reflects neither Whitman's wishes in 1871, nor his final wishes. In fact, it presents a text different in arrangement than anything Whitman ever produced.[9]

McKay had known Whitman personally, and had printed and distributed earlier editions of his works, including the deathbed edition. In the preface to the 1900 edition, McKay refers to himself as Whitman's "most successful publisher." (He was evidently as capable of self-promotion as Whitman.) But in attempting to produce this new edition after the poet's death, he ran afoul of copyright. In the Library of Congress, I inspected a copy of this edition that had been owned by Thomas B. Harned, one of Whitman's literary executors. On the inside cover Harned has written: "When D. McKay was refused a renewal of his contract, he printed this edition of *Leaves of Grass,* using all matter where the copyright had expired." McKay himself acknowledges this, somewhat indirectly, in the preface when he says: "For any errors of commission I accept all responsibility; for those of omission (and there are a few), conditions which I could not control are alone responsible, a fact which time will yet correct."

Unable to use the text of the 1891 edition, which he himself had published, he resorted to the text of the 1871 edition, which no longer enjoyed copyright protection. To this base text he added other material: footnotes giving variant readings of words and phrases as they appeared in editions earlier than 1871; poems not found in these

CONTENTS   BIBLIOGRAPHIC RECORD

Walt Whitman (1819–1892). Leaves of Grass. 1900.

14. Walt Whitman

1

I CELEBRATE myself;
And what I assume you shall assume;
For every atom belonging to me, as good belongs to you.

I loafe and invite my Soul;
I lean and loafe at my ease, observing a spear of summer grass.   5

Houses and rooms are full of perfumes—the shelves are crowded with perfumes;
I breathe the fragrance myself, and know it and like it;
The distillation would intoxicate me also, but I shall not let it.

The atmosphere is not a perfume—it has no taste of the distillation—it is odorless;
It is for my mouth forever—I am in love with it;   10
I will go to the bank by the wood, and become undisguised and naked;
I am mad for it to be in contact with me.

2

The smoke of my own breath;
Echoes, ripples, buzz'd whispers, love-root, silk-thread, crotch and vine;
My respiration and inspiration, the beating of my heart, the passing of blood and air   15
through my lungs;
The sniff of green leaves and dry leaves, and of the shore, and dark-color'd sea-rocks,
and of hay in the barn;
The sound of the belch'd words of my voice, words loos'd to the eddies of the wind;

*The opening lines of "Song of Myself" as they appear in the Bartleby Library's
online edition of* Leaves of Grass.

earlier editions; and personal remembrances of his relationship with Whitman. In printing "Song of Myself," for example, he renders the first verse as:

> I celebrate myself;
> And what I assume you shall assume;
> For every atom belonging to me, as good belongs to you.

These lines reproduce the text of the first edition — with three exceptions: semicolons have been substituted for commas at the end of the first two lines, and a comma has been added in the middle of the third. McKay doesn't acknowledge these changes; he generally only notes variant words and phrases. It is perhaps more interesting that he fails to acknowledge the later addition of the phrase "and sing myself," a change he would have known only too well. To do so with a footnote, I'm guessing, would either have constituted a violation of copyright or would have forced him to make explicit his strategy for dodging it.

McKay renders the title of the poem as "Walt Whitman." He fails to note that the poem was untitled in the first edition, or that it had other titles in earlier and later editions. This is curious, since in the preface McKay says: "As Walt Whitman's publisher, I was frequently called upon to give information concerning poems whose headings had been changed. These have been noted, and in the alphabetical list at the end of the volume all such titles appear, with reference to the present title." Not so, in this case.

These are just a few of the idiosyncrasies and inconsistencies in McKay's edition. To modern scholars, trained to produce painstakingly precise critical editions, this must be a nightmare, and seen as not just bad scholarship but a moral lapse. As far as I know, this was the first version of *Leaves of Grass* to appear on the Web, and if one imagines future generations taking this text as gospel, it isn't hard to understand the reaction of the scholarly community.[10]

But, frankly, I am less shocked than *interested*. What strikes me most about this edition is the strong personal element throughout — the person of McKay as much as of Whitman. This is *McKay's* tribute to Whitman, as he makes clear in the preface:

> Walt Whitman was an [*sic*] unique character. As his most success-
> ful publisher I saw much of him, and learned to love his sweet
> and kindly nature. No one could enter the charmed circle of his
> friendship without feeling the mastery of his personality. This
> book, the work of my own hands, I give as a token of those
> never-to-be-forgotten days. To have met Whitman was a privi-
> lege, to have been his friend was an honor.

The illustrations make it all the clearer how much this book is *McKay's* testament to Whitman, a labor of love and ego that cele-brates and advertises the publisher's relationship with the poet (or, perhaps more to the point, the publisher's *perception* of his relation-ship with the poet). Included are photographs of Whitman at dif-ferent ages, several of them inscribed to the publisher. One of them shows an elderly, white-haired Whitman sitting in an ornate, straight-backed chair, holding a cane in his right hand, his left hand resting inside his jacket pocket. The inscription reads, "David McKay / from his friend / Walt Whitman." More than the words, I am struck by the placement of the photograph in the book. It appears on the left-hand page facing the title page, the same position in which, forty-five years earlier, a photograph of the unnamed author appeared in the first edition. Subtly and perhaps unconsciously, McKay seems to be claiming a greater part in the production of Whitman's work. And when you open the volume to the midpoint, there on facing pages are a note Whitman wrote to McKay and another inscribed photograph of the poet. At the balance point of the book, you find poet and publisher metaphorically embracing.

Van Leeuwen's digital rendering maintains this character, but in a somewhat diluted form. The poems, the preface, the illustrations are still there, but a transformation has taken place, the result of van Leeuwen's efforts, as well as of the medium in which he is working.

When I first came across this digital *Leaves of Grass,* I browsed through it, eager to get a feel for it. I quickly found the images, most of them located on a single Web page. Lovely as it was to find them, I was also left vaguely disoriented and discomfited, unable quite to grasp their place, literally and figuratively, in the overall design. They seemed to float oddly unanchored in (cyber)space. It was this discomfort that sent me in search of a print copy. In the end I found several: one in the Columbia University Library's rare-book room, a second in the Library of Congress, and a third in a used-book shop. It was only when I held the physical volume in my hand, when I turned the pages, when I felt as well as saw the location of the images, that I was able to grasp, quite literally, the full impact of McKay's design.

Without question, van Leeuwen, like David McKay and the Beilensons before him, has left his mark, but it is an indecisive one. In transposing McKay's design to the Web, he has partly dismantled it. Whereas the Beilensons might be accused of imposing a lukewarm interpretation on the poems, and McKay criticized for egotistical and sloppy work, still their products are coherently personal and intelligible. Van Leeuwen, by contrast, fails to understand that a new edition, digital or otherwise, is inevitably a new interpretation, and has made design decisions without a larger literary plan.

I should mention that van Leeuwen's *Leaves of Grass* has undergone a dramatic change since I began looking at it: all the facsimile materials from McKay's edition have disappeared. When I first noticed this, I sent e-mail to Van Leeuwen, asking him what had happened. He explained that so long as Columbia University was hosting his Bartleby Library for free, he hadn't needed to worry about the cost of online storage. But having gone independent, he was now forced to pay for it. "We've been forced to minimize the graphics for economic consideration," he said, expressing the hope that the images would return shortly. More than a year later, though, they still haven't reappeared. (It is tempting to see this loss as unique to the digital world, where commitments to sameness and preservation are partial at best.

But I would point out that the copy of McKay's 1900 edition that I found in a secondhand bookstore lacks the photographs at midpoint, presumably also the result of an economic decision — to issue a later, less costly printing.)

Clearly, the two copies of *Leaves of Grass* before me now are the product of significantly different historical processes. And the more I understand those processes, the better I can account for the differences in form and content, in illustration and interpretation, of the two copies. But no catalog of the relations between them will, in itself, predict or explain how I, or anyone else, for that matter, is likely to read and experience them. It is a question not just of the differences between the two copies, but of *which differences really matter*. And this can only be determined by real readers in real situations. If each edition and each copy of an edition has its own unique characteristics and its own life history, then surely so does each reader. Each act of reading will be a meeting of one particular reader with one particular copy.

So let's consider one real reader: me. I have a strong preference for the bound volume — and for my childhood copy, in particular — over the online edition. This should hardly be surprising. But why? Is it just a sentimental attachment to books, or is there something more?

In his book *The Gift: Imagination and the Erotic Life of Property*, Lewis Hyde explores the work of art as a participant in a system of gift exchange. The idea of gift exchange comes out of the early anthropological literature. Bronislaw Malinowski, in studying the people occupying a group of South Sea islands, had discovered that they engaged in an elaborate exchange of armshells and necklaces. They never kept or owned these prized objects; instead they were bound by tradition to pass them on, thus forming a circuit of gifts. For the outsiders who first observed such practices, it was evident, says E. E. Evans-Pritchard, a social anthropologist, "how much we [westerners] have lost, whatever we may otherwise gained, by the substitution of a rational economic system for a system in which exchange of goods was not a mechanical but a moral transaction, bringing about and maintaining human, personal relationships between individuals and groups."[11]

In his book, Hyde applies this notion to the work of art in the West, seeing the artist as someone who by nature lives in a gift economy but is forced to operate in a market economy (to sell his works) in order to "earn" a living. Hyde points to the different senses of gift involved in the production and circulation of works of art. The artist, having been granted certain talents and insights (one sense of gift), works from within a gifted state. (A gifted state, according to Hyde, is one in which the artist "is able to discern the connections inherent in his materials and . . . bring the work to life.")[12] What he then produces, the work of art, is itself a gift, which, when received by others, its audience, has the potential to put them, too, into a gifted state. Sometimes, says Hyde, "if we are awake, if the artist really was gifted, the work will induce a moment of grace, a communion, a period during which we too know the hidden coherence of our being and feel the fullness of our lives."[13]

As I see it, Whitman's gift is his vast embrace, his inclusive stance, which Alfred Kazin calls his "boundless affirmation":

> The whole world of existent phenomena is open to Whitman's general lovingness, which is boundless affirmation. Nothing may be excluded; nothing is higher or lower than anything else. He is the perfect democrat, in religion as in love and politics. There is no hierarchy in his determination to love everything and everyone in one full sweep."[14]

Whitman's embrace is broad enough to encompass both body and soul, heaven and hell. "I am the poet of the Body and I am the poet of the Soul," he declares in "Song of Myself" (in my childhood copy). "The pleasures of heaven are with me and the pains of hell are with me." He can embrace and celebrate death as much as life. "Has any one supposed it lucky to be born?" he asks in the same poem. "I hasten to inform him or her it is just as lucky to die, and I know it."

And, perhaps even more startling, good and bad are for him on an equal plane. "What is called good is perfect," he says in "To Think of Time," "and what is called bad is just as perfect."

Surely Whitman is speaking from a gifted state. For in reading him, I *feel* it. I feel raised up, held in his all-encompassing embrace, and reminded that I too am capable of it. His open, celebratory stance toward the world is available to me too. This is more than an intellectual experience, simply in my head: it is an experience of the whole body. My senses are heightened and my mood may shift, becoming lighter and more joyful. Sometimes, to increase this effect, I will read aloud, feeling the sounds vibrate in my body, much like when I listen to music. I liken this mode of reading to contemplation or meditation.

This mode of reading is supported and enhanced, I have found, by reading *Leaves of Grass* in book form, and even more so by reading my childhood copy. Why is this?

I would start by noting that Whitman designed his collection *as a book*. This was the main format available to him for distributing his poems, and he was steeped in the book, both as a member of the culture, as a reader, and as someone with particular professional skills and experience. As a young man, he was a printer's apprentice, and his primary work as an adult was as a journalist and newspaper editor. He obviously cared a great deal about how his book turned out, overseeing the printing of the seven editions produced during his lifetime, and possibly even setting some of the type for the first edition. He also designed the title embossed on the green leather cover of the first edition: leafy tendrils intertwined in the hand-drawn letters spelling out "Leaves of Grass." Given Whitman's embrace of bodies, of the material dimension of the world, it should hardly be surprising that he would care about the material condition of his poems.

And it is through his book, these "leaves of grass," that life and death, body and soul, his life and our lives are brought together. Indeed, for me at least, the leaves to which Whitman refers in his title are both the pages of the book and the plant matter from which those pages are made. Throughout the poems, grass functions as a symbol of both life and death, and of their relationship. In "Song of Myself" (my childhood copy) he says, "I guess the grass is itself a child, the produced babe of the vegetation," while later he refers to it as "the beautiful uncut hair of graves." His book is not only a celebration of this reality, the cycle of life and death, but a participant in it. The pages of the book, made from trees no longer living, embody the living voice of the invisible poet, made and kept visible through the magic of writing. And much as the poet has passed on, so too will the pages through which he sings crumble and return to the earth, fertilizing future generations of trees and grass — and poets.

The pages of the book, in other words, exemplify the very concerns of which the poet speaks, in effect amplifying his voice. When I hold the bound volume in my hands, I am aware — through sight, smell, and touch — of the organic process, the slow process of decay, it is undergoing. And this awareness is all the stronger when I read my copy of the Peter Pauper Press edition, which has been my companion all these years. So that when I hold it and read it, I am more in touch — quite literally — with myself, as I am in the moment, but also as I have been in decades past. And, perhaps most important, its signs of aging parallel and reflect my own. To read this poem in this very copy is therefore to be put more fully in contact with my own mortality and the mystery of my own life. This is possible because the book is a tightly integrated physical unity; it is a stable physical object capable of traveling with me through time.

Not so the online edition. If there is a stable, solid, physical object here, it is my laptop, which provides a portal through which I can view not only *Leaves of Grass,* but airline flight schedules, stock market quotes, movie reviews, and corporate e-mail. The text of the online edition is stable too, in the sense that the server on which the Bartleby Library is located can be expected reliably to deliver up the same text again and again (for some indefinite period of time, at any rate). But whereas text and physical object are inalienably united in the book, they have been pulled apart in the online edition. This has its advantages, to be sure. It means that digital representations of the text can be transported and realized (made visible and real) on any number of surfaces. But it also means that there is no particular and unique object that can be my companion and share my history.

I am not suggesting that we pull the plug on the online Whitman, nor am I making an argument for the inherent superiority of books over bytes, or for paper over digital materials. The observations I have offered are quite specific: to one particular work, to two particular copies of this work, to a particular mode of reading, and to one particular person at a particular stage in his life. To vary any of these conditions is likely to result in different preferences. Given a choice, I will choose to read my childhood copy over the online edition, but the online edition has its advantages too. The search capability is certainly superior to what I can do with the book's index and my limited ability to scan with my eyes. The illustrations in the online edition — sadly no longer available — are to my mind far more interesting and valuable than the tepid drawings in my childhood copy. In fact, I feel all the happier for having *both* the Beilenson and the McKay/van Leeuwen editions available to me. Does one have to win, and the other one lose?

If there is a lesson to be drawn from these observations, it is that in evaluating the relative merits of books and their online counterparts, we must look to *their* specific material conditions and to *ours*. We are living through an era in which information — conceived of as abstract, disembodied, and infinitely manipulable — is given pride of place and we are taken to be "information processors." Under such circumstances, documents — and, most unfortunately, books — come to be treated as information delivery vehicles: useful to the extent that they accurately deliver up their payload. To the extent that digital technologies can perform this particular task better (which typically means faster and cheaper), they are to be preferred.

In the end, I am not so interested in arguing for the superiority of one copy of *Leaves of Grass* over another, or for one technology over another. Rather, what interests me more is broadening the terms of our collective exploration. If we want to see more fully into the nature of our documents and their enabling technologies, then we may well need to see how form, content, and medium are not-to-be-fully-separated constituents in our lives and in the richness of our experience. And it is perhaps for this reason that I have chosen Whitman's book as the object of this chapter's reflection. He is a poet of embodied experience, and his great work is to be experienced through its various bodies and ours. He calls us back to the richness and diversity of our experience, which lies beyond simple generalizations or categorizations.

When I look at *Leaves of Grass* with the eyes of Whitman, what I see is an ongoing movement, which can be only arbitrarily dated to 1855, and which continues on, today and beyond. It is a movement of inspiration and revelation, realized in various material objects — books and manuscripts — as well as in acts of reading and writing organized around these objects. When I look specifically at these objects — these books and manuscripts — I see both their sameness and also their differences. For each one is an instance of *Leaves of Grass,* yet all of them are different in endless and ultimately uncategorizable ways. But it isn't just *Leaves of Grass* I see this way; it is receipts and handwritten notes and Web pages and videos — all of them, paper and digital forms alike, partaking of the dance of fixity and fluidity, of stasis and change.

4

The Dark Side of Documents

ALAS, ALL IS NOT BOUNDLESS AFFIRMATION, sweetness and light, in the realm of documents. A scene in Terry Gilliam's 1985 film *Brazil* plays on some of our worst nightmares about written forms. The movie depicts a highly bureaucratized, totalitarian state — part *1984,* part Kafka, part *Alice in Wonderland,* and part Monty Python. The most visible symbols of the state's intrusiveness and suffocating infrastructure are the ducts and pipes spilling out into every room. The film follows one man: Sam Lowry, played by Jonathan Pryce, a clerk in the Ministry of Education. It is the story of this Everyman's awakening to, and eventual destruction by, the state.

The scene opens with Lowry coming home to discover that his air conditioning is on the blink. He puts in a call to Central Services, which is intercepted by Harry Tuttle (Robert De Niro), a heating engineer wanted for his terrorist acts against the state. Lowry asks Tuttle why he doesn't work for Central Services. "I couldn't stand the paperwork," he replies. "Listen, this whole system of yours could be on fire and I couldn't even turn on a kitchen tap without filling out a 27b/6. Bloody paperwork." "I suppose one has to expect a certain amount," Lowry muses, half to himself. "Why?" Tuttle replies. "I came into this game for the action, the excitement. Go anywhere, travel light, get in, get out, wherever there's trouble, a man alone.

Now they've got the whole country sectioned off — can't make a move without a form."

A moment later, two looney engineers from Central Services show up at Lowry's door. He tries to get rid of them, telling them his air conditioner has fixed itself. They don't buy it, and push their way into his apartment. Just as they are about to discover Tuttle, Lowry calls out in desperation, "Have you got a 27b/6?" One of the men begins to shake uncontrollably. "Now look what you've done to him," the other man says, and begins to pull his co-worker back into the hall. "Sorry," says Lowry. "I'm a bit of a stickler for paperwork, you see. I mean, where would we be if we didn't stick to the correct procedures?"

Admittedly this scene is a parody, but it points to a very recognizable and unfortunate dimension of our lives. Who among us hasn't felt trapped in a tangle of paperwork and bureaucratic red tape, unable to make a move without a form? At such times we may well feel that we are caught in an airless, joyless world — a world in which every step must be documented and every action must conform to a logic that is not our own. It is fine to celebrate a single cash register receipt, but when you see it in the context of trillions of similar documents, the desire to celebrate may quickly disappear. A single snowflake may be beautiful, but aggregations of them make for avalanches. When you broaden the picture to include not just cash register receipts but the innumerable other forms of administrative, commercial, and bureaucratic documents, *Brazil's* dark vision doesn't seem so far off the mark.

Surely, though, the use of documents to administer human affairs, to regulate institutional and personal practices, is a good thing. They make it possible to keep the wheels of commerce, government, and industry rolling. How, then, can we make sense of this abusive side documents sometimes display? Is it simply a matter of scale, a mob mentality that arises when too many documents congregate in one place? Are some of them just bad eggs? Or is there something more to be understood about the way documents function in our lives?

Documents have been used for administrative purposes since the earliest days of writing. Indeed, writing, counting, and accounting have a close and ancient connection. While it is possible to do simple counting without external aids — just using one's fingers, for example — more-complex forms of counting and calculation have generally required additional tools. Tallies — notches or tick marks cut in bone to keep count — have been unearthed dating back ten thousand years and more. The use of pebbles is also quite ancient, and, like tick marks, it is a technique still in use today. Both tallies and pebbles can be thought of as primitive forms of writing, since they make use of simple surrogates — bones and pebbles — to tell stories about the world: how many sightings of the moon I've made or how many sheep are in my flock. And if Denise Schmandt-Besserat is right, full-blown written language may have arisen from such humble beginnings. She has developed an elaborate theory showing how simple clay "tokens" used to count agricultural and manufactured goods evolved into marks inscribed on clay tablets.[1]

Whether or not Schmandt-Besserat's thesis is right, there can be no doubt that writing and counting are intimately related. So too counting and accounting. Certainly the English words *counting* and *accounting* share the same etymological root: the Latin word *computare*. But long before English, or even Latin, was spoken, counting was an important administrative tool. The Bible tells how Joseph, through his ability to interpret dreams, gained favor with the Pharaoh. He correctly interpreted two of the Pharaoh's dreams as indicating that seven years of famine would follow seven years of abundant crops, and he set out to centralize the collection of foodstuffs and other provisions so they could be doled out in the approaching time of need. The Bible doesn't tell us how he kept track of the provisions in his storehouses — how he recorded the deposits made by the farmers during the years of plenty, or the quantities handed out during the famine — but he must surely have done so. A task of this complexity would have required careful bookkeeping. In this sense, the Joseph story is paradigmatic of the movement from a nomadic society to an agrarian one, and the bureaucratic methods that would necessarily have accompanied it.

Accounting is essentially a means of keeping track of your resources in order to exercise some measure of control over them. By keeping track of who has borrowed which of your books, you stand a chance of getting them back from your absentminded friends. By making "to-do" lists, you empower yourself to take certain courses of action. These are examples of personal accounting, all of them relatively innocuous and well-meaning. But in situations where some people have power over others — whether it is Joseph in relation to the Pharaoh's subjects or a boss over his or her employees — accounts can be highly charged, because they have to do with who has what, who owes what, and who ultimately gets to decide. Accounting, in other words, is about *accountability:* about who is accountable to whom for what. Accounting — and the acts of writing and record-keeping that are integral to it — is all to do with power.

I ran afoul of the IRS some years back because of an accounting error. The initial error was theirs, but I stupidly compounded it through inexperience with bureaucratic ways. According to their records, the IRS informed me, I hadn't filed a tax return for the year 1982. But I had. In my files I found a handwritten copy of the Form 1040 I had submitted for that year. I also located the canceled check, written to the IRS, in the exact amount of the taxes I owed.

This would be an easy enough problem to fix. I made a photocopy of both sides of the canceled check and sent it to the IRS. Sorry, they replied, we're still unable to find your return; and they asked me to resubmit it. I made a photocopy of my hand-copied return. And here is where I made my mistake: I had never signed or dated the handwritten copy of my tax form, since I had intended it only as an informational copy. But because I was now submitting an official tax return, I signed and dated the photocopy. The date I wrote was the date *in 1984* when I was resubmitting the return, not the date *in 1983* when I submitted the original return for the year 1982.

When next I heard from the IRS, they kindly informed me that since I had submitted my return a year late, I owed them interest. Never mind that the canceled check proved conclusively that I *had* paid my taxes on time. The bureaucratic machinery had seized on the newly submitted Form 1040 and seemed incapable of reasoning from the full set of records. I spoke to my father, a lawyer, and he offered to help me out. Over the next year he carried on a lengthy written correspondence, punctuated by occasional phone conversations, with IRS employees. (I still have the careful records he maintained: the typed letter, the handwritten memos, the postmarked envelopes, and photocopied forms.) Finally he reached a sympathetic ear. After listening patiently to the saga (and understanding its subtleties!), a well-meaning IRS employee counseled him: Listen, she said, we're not talking about a whole lot of money. Your son is better off just paying the interest and being done with it. Quite honestly, it will be nearly impossible to get the system to respond properly.

So in the end, I paid the interest. There was no question about where the truth lay; but there was also no question about where the *power* lay. For those of us who have lived with frustrating encounters of this kind, it is probably small comfort that others too have struggled with the bean counters, and for thousands of years. Roman emperors relied in large part on an efficient bureaucracy to maintain control over their far-flung empire. But as C. M. Kelly, a scholar at Cambridge University and the University of London, points out, this dependence on bureaucracy was a two-edged sword:

> While undoubtedly it allowed a more penetrating and detailed control over empire, bureaucracy also posed a serious threat to imperial power. At its simplest, the problem was one of delegation and independence. The efficient functioning of any bureaucracy requires the delegation of power in order to allow officials to take decisions in their own right. But, from an imperial point of view, delegation was also a dangerous and uncomfortable necessity. Too much delegation might so far remove emperors from the actual exercise of power that they could become the prisoners of an administrative system which monopolized and controlled important policy-making information.[2]

Evidently even those officially in charge are vulnerable to the force of bureaucratic logic.

Although bureaucracy has a long history, if we are to understand its force in our lives today, I suggest we look to relatively recent developments, for it is only over the last two hundred years that recognizably modern document forms and administrative practices have arisen. Modern bureaucracy — as lampooned in *Brazil* and manifested in my IRS story — is a product of the industrial revolution. It came into being as a means of creating and managing large-scale, distributed organizations (railroads, corporations, government offices) capable of responding to the conditions presented by an emerging industrial economy.

The Industrial Revolution began in England in the second half of the eighteenth century with the transformation of the textile industry. During this period, newly developed, mechanized methods of spinning and weaving were put into practice. Initially, running water powered the looms. But with James Watt's development of the steam engine in 1765, a whole new source of energy became available, one not directly dependent on the natural powers or rhythms of wind and water. The nineteenth century saw the application of steam power to all aspects of economic life: the mining of raw materials; the manufacturing of finished goods; and the distribution of raw materials and finished products via the railroads. A society based largely on agriculture reoriented itself for industrial production.

In the United States (the case I know best), signs of what James Beniger has called a "control crisis" began to emerge in the midnineteenth century. By the 1850s — to choose one example that Joseph would appreciate — networks of grain elevators and warehouses were being set up to store and transport wheat, corn, and cotton around the country. But shippers were having trouble keeping track of what was stored where, and what needed to be shipped to whom.[3] "Never before," says Beniger in *The Control Revolution,*

> had the processing of material flows threatened to exceed — in both volume and speed — the capacity of technology to contain them. Suddenly, owing to the harnessing of steam power, goods could be moved at the full speed of industrial production, night

and day under virtually any conditions, not only from town to town but across entire continents and around the world.

To do this, however, required a system of manufacturers and distributors, central and branch offices, transportation lines and terminals, containers and cars, that grew staggering in its complexity. Even the logistics of nineteenth-century armies, then the most difficult problem in processing and control, came to be dwarfed in complexity by the material economy. Just as the problem of control reached crisis proportions, however, a series of new technological and social solutions began to contain the problem.[4]

Through at least the first half of the nineteenth century, American institutions operated with limited administrative apparatus. If we were to go back to mid-nineteenth-century America, we might be surprised at how small and informally structured were even the most prominent of institutions. Government was much smaller, for example. In 1831, during Andrew Jackson's administration, the entire federal government was run by fewer than one thousand people. During that same period, the Bank of the United States was run by just three people.[5] Indeed, the American economy was dominated by small companies, owned and managed by one person or by a partnership.[6]

But these methods, which one writer in the 1890s called "the old slipshod way of our forefathers,"[7] were not adaptable — or at least were not adapted — to the demands of the new economy. The control crisis precipitated by rapid industrialization therefore initiated a search for new forms of organization and oversight. By the 1870s, JoAnne Yates explains in *Control Through Communication,* a new theory was being espoused that promoted a supposedly rational and impersonal approach to management. In this scheme, called systematic management, a business was organized as a hierarchy of departments. Workers' jobs were carefully defined, via job descriptions, and organizational knowledge was systematized as formal procedures. In essence, this new type of organization was modeled on the machine — many of the new management theorists were engineers — with workers seen as interchangeable parts performing scripted work within a formal organizational structure. One of the central concerns was efficiency, and "[o]nly by replacing individual idiosyncrasy with system, individual memory with organizational memory, and personal skills with firm-specified skills at all levels did the systematizers feel that they could achieve the current and future efficiency they sought."[8]

A central question in this new system was how exactly workers and their work could be coordinated and controlled. In earlier times this was accomplished mostly through face-to-face interaction. The owner of a factory might not be present onsite, but his foreman would. The foreman could physically oversee — and talk directly with — the men on the shop floor. This worked well when business was conducted at a single, relatively small site. But as larger, geographically distributed organizations came into being, it was no longer satisfactory. The problem was how to control workers' practices in larger, distributed organizations.

One of the first instances of this new form of organization was the railroad. Railroad stations and stationmasters were, of course, geographically distributed along the track, the central offices located elsewhere again. The need for precise coordination was made evident by a series of early railroad accidents. Initially, railroads ran in both directions on a single track. This meant that a slipup in scheduling could easily result in accidents. Company investigations following a series of collisions in 1841 on the Western Railroad between Worcester and West Stockbridge, Massachusetts, pointed to the importance not only of accurate train timetables, but of controlled procedures for maintaining and revising them. "[T]he time and manner of running the trains shall be established and published by the Engineer," railroad management concluded, and "no alteration in the times of running or mode of meeting and passing of trains shall take effect, until after positive knowledge shall have been received at the office of the superintendent, that [written] orders for such change have been received and are understood by all concerned."[9]

The use of written records became a central plank in the realization of systematic management. During the late nineteenth and early twentieth centuries, new document technologies and new document genres were invented or adapted to satisfy the growing desire for speed, efficiency, and control. Three technologies were particularly important: the typewriter, carbon paper, and vertical files.

Until the invention of typewriters, office clerks used quills, as had writers for many centuries. A quill is simply a feather, from a goose or turkey, that has been baked to harden it, then cut with a knife to form a writing point. (The term "pen knife" derives from the use of knives to cut quills or pens.) The quill is an extremely fine writing instrument — I recently heard a calligrapher call it "the finest writing implement ever invented" — but it isn't ideally suited for producing large quantities of writing quickly. The point of the quill needs to be regularly trimmed with a quill knife to keep it sharp, and the quill itself will wear out before too long. The manufacturing of steel pen nibs addressed this problem; it made more durable writing implements, but could not significantly accelerate production of documents.

The first commercially viable typewriters were produced in the early 1870s. Initially considered a tool for court reporters, they didn't assume a prominent place in the office until a decade later. In 1887 one writer observed: "Five years ago the type writer [*sic*] was simply a mechanical curiosity. Today its monotonous click can be heard in almost every well regulated business establishment in the country. A great revolution is taking place, and the type writer is at the bottom of it."[10] The great advantage of the typewriter, of course, was that it permitted documents to be composed much more quickly than had been possible through handwriting. A competent typist could produce eighty words a minute, whereas a hand-copyist could produce thirty at best.

Equally important was the development of carbon paper as a means of reproducing documents. Before carbon paper, a document would be hand-copied; alternately, one or two copies of a handwritten letter could be made using a "letter press" while the ink was still wet. Hand-copying was of course slow, and in neither case was it practical to make more than a couple of copies. Carbon paper had actually been invented much earlier, in 1823, but didn't work well with the quills or pens of the time. In a nice example of the synergy between technologies and work practice, it wasn't until fifty years later that the increasing drive for speed brought a much improved carbon paper together with the new mechanical writing device. Even so, it took several decades before this new method of copying displaced the letter press in the office.

Thanks to the typewriter and carbon paper, office documents could be produced more quickly and in greater numbers. This served to highlight the inadequacy of the filing methods of the time. There were two main methods for storing incoming documents: pigeonholes and flat filing. In the first, the document to be saved was folded, a brief description of its contents (e.g., name of sender and date) was written on the outside, and it was stored in a pigeonhole in the recipient's desk. In the second method, a document was stored flat (rather than folded) and horizontal between alphabetic tabs in a letter box or cabinet. (Such letter boxes are still in use today.) Neither method was particularly good at handling large quantities of documents. A typical desk could only hold so many pigeonholes, and finding any one document might require unfolding several, a time-consuming process. Flat filing could accommodate an open-ended number of documents (you could always start a new box), and while the indexing methods employed with them were an improvement over pigeonholes, still it was at best a clumsy and bulky system.

To help bring order, a filing method was borrowed from the library world. Melvil Dewey, the inventor of the Dewey Decimal System, adapted the idea of the library card catalog, a system of small cards filed vertically in drawers, to produce the vertical filing system we still use today. In this system, consisting of hanging file folders stored in file cabinets, it was much easier to add documents to folders, to add new folders, and to move folders around. Vertical files also took up considerably less space than flat files. Along with these technologies came new techniques, new office practices. As one writer observed in a 1913 textbook: "It will already have become evident that it is impossible to sever the problem of finding a good practicable filing system from the whole problem of business organization. This is particularly true of all businesses large enough to be carried on departmentally."[11]

The new vertical filing system was much acclaimed; it won a gold prize in the 1893 Chicago World's Fair. Today, of course, we tend to think of paper files as the problem, not the solution. But at a time when the typewriter, carbon paper, and vertical files are all being challenged if not displaced, it may be useful to realize that they were the radical technologies of *their* time. Even today's radical innovations will turn into tomorrow's legacy systems.

These new document technologies were only part of the solution. What kinds — what genres — of documents would be created, copied, distributed, and filed with them? The philosophy of systematic management stressed the orderly flow of information up and down the organizational hierarchy. Managers needed to be able to send rules and orders downward. They also needed to gather information from the lower levels to keep tabs on how the work was progressing. "Circular letters" — that is, letters that circulated — as well as procedure manuals were developed to accomplish the former, to communicate and document company policies and business procedures. Forms, graphs, tables, and reports were developed to accomplish the latter, to collect statistics on the operation of the company and communicate the results to higher levels of management.

The birth of the form nicely illustrates how documents were streamlined and tailored in the service of ever greater efficiency. Workers at lower levels of the hierarchy — e.g., railroad clerks and shop foremen — were increasingly being asked to document their activities in written reports, sometimes on a daily basis. This could be a time-consuming process. But, it was realized, the process could be standardized and speeded up by printing forms, sheets of paper whose printed material indicated exactly what information needed to be filled in, and where. This meant the worker had less to write; the familiarity of a standard layout also increased his speed. This standardization also facilitated reading and summarizing as the report

traveled up the hierarchy. Except for changes in type styles, these earlier forms from nearly a hundred years ago are essentially indistin-
guishable from those we still use today.

The memo, too, was a product of the search for speed, efficiency,
and standardization. It arose most directly from the letter. Letters as a
form of personal correspondence had of course existed for many
centuries. They were already used in commerce, mainly for external
communication. The conventions of letter writing were well established. These included the date of writing, a formal salutation
("Dear . . .") as well as a formal closing ("Your most . . ."). The opening and closing addresses could be quite flowery, at least to our ears.
But as the letter was increasingly used for internal communication,
within and across departments, the new business experts, masters of
efficiency, argued for a much simplified format. Typing time could be
saved if the company printed up letterheads with fields such as *To,
From,* and *Subject,* and if openings and closings were stripped down
to a bare minimum. JoAnne Yates quotes one expert arguing for just
such a simplification:

> In the first place, all unnecessary courtesy, such as "Fred Brown
> & Co.," "Gentlemen," "yours very truly," and other phrases are
> omitted entirely. In a business where hundreds and sometimes
> thousands of interhouse letters are written daily the saving of
> time is considerable. Next, an expensive letterhead is done away
> with, and this also is a factor in reducing expense. The blank is
> made with simply the words, "From Chicago," "From Atlanta,"
> or whatever may be the name of the town where the letter is
> written, printed in the upper left-hand corner, and underneath
> the word, "Subject." In the upper right-hand corner is the serial
> number of the letter and the words, "In reply refer to No." and
> "Replying to No." It will thus be seen that the only typewriting
> necessary in addressing a letter consists of the location of the
> house to which the letter is to be sent, a short summary of the
> matter contained in the letter for indexing purposes, the number
> of the letter, and date, with the initials of the writer, and the
> number and date of the letter which is under reply (in case there

has been previous correspondence), with the initials of the former correspondent.[12]

The "Subject" field had a double purpose. It of course gave the recipient a quick way to determine what the memo was about. But it was equally important as a resource for a new class of workers, the file clerk. It helped the clerk determine where in the vertical files to store the memo. One authority went so far as to suggest that memos should be limited to a single subject to simplify the task of filing.

Initially, companies thought of their files as a centralized resource, but as memos proliferated (thanks to the typewriter and carbon paper), departments realized they had reason to maintain their own local files as well. Although the memo emerged as a tool of the new management techniques, it also shaped them. (I have perhaps made it sound like the new management methods were invented to solve the control crisis, *then* new document technologies and genres were adapted or invented to satisfy the needs of the new methods. A better way to think of it is that the new management methods and the new document technologies and genres *co-evolved,* with changes in one area affecting the others.)

While these technologies and methods achieved their intended purpose — they made it possible to create and manage large-scale, distributed organizations — they also came at a substantial cost. "Systematic management principles," says Yates, "required depersonalizing the workplace in the interests of control and efficiency."[13] This led to resistance at times on the part of both workers and managers. Decades before these changes swept through the American economy, however, the German sociologist Max Weber had already begun to speculate about the causes of mass bureaucratization and to express concern about its effects. He believed that Western culture was becoming increasingly *disenchanted:* it was prone to value that which was amenable to calculation, to mechanization, and to rational analysis, and to devalue and dismiss "mysterious incalculable forces"[14] — anything that was not amenable to rational control. The West was becoming increasingly depersonalized, he thought. "Bureaucracy develops the more perfectly," he said, "the more it is 'dehumanized,' the more completely it succeeds in eliminating from official business love, hatred, and all purely personal . . . and emotional elements which escape calculation."[15] (Recall Carlyle's complaint that people were becoming "mechanical in head and heart, as well as in hand.")

We can now see, I think, where the horrors of the 27b/6 and the tyranny of correct procedures have come from. They have arisen, in conjunction with industrialization, from a philosophy of impersonal management and rational control. And although neither forms nor standardized work practices can be held responsible for the disenchantment of the world, they are certainly major participants in it. You might think of a form as the attempt to create a highly stylized, scripted, and impersonal piece of conversation. Each labeled field is essentially a question: name? address? marital status? Your job, then, as the form-filler, is to understand what is being asked of you and to respond appropriately. Not only are the questions typically of a highly institutional nature, but the person asking the questions isn't a person at all. He — or it — is the institution itself, which may by law be considered a "person," but shares few of the warm, soft, human features of real people. When you fill out a form, you are essentially engaging in a scripted conversation with a faceless bureaucracy. Is it any wonder that we feel uncomfortable with such documents?

All administrative and bureaucratic documents have something of this impersonal character. The writer or author is essentially an organization, not a person or even an identifiable group. Can you show me, please, Steve's Deli — not the physical place, but the author of my cash register receipt? Even when the document has been written by a real person and signed by him — a letter from your health insurer, for example, in response to a query about denial of service — the writer is still speaking in the name of the corporate entity. The subject matter of administrative documents, too, is typically impersonal and objective: it is about the cost of a tuna sandwich or the time at which a train arrives, not the taste of the tuna or the sound of the whistle as the train roars across the prairie.

Dorothy Smith, a sociologist, has analyzed an example of bureaucratic writing in detail.[16] Her observations are particularly com-
pelling because she juxtaposes a personal account with a bureaucratic
account of the same event, a clash between the police and a crowd of
people in Berkeley in 1968. She examines two documents written in
response to this event. The first is a letter written by a college professor, a witness to the event, protesting what he considered "a
fracas . . . staged and organized by the police in an obvious attempt to
provoke the people there into a confrontation with the heavily armed
cops." He describes how a passing boy, sixteen or seventeen years old,
was grabbed by the police and manhandled; how the police tried to
pry a baby away from a young mother; how another young woman
was beaten with a club while lying on the ground; and how a policeman attacked a man whom the officer thought had thrown a beer
can. "Immediately, the young, cigar-smoking cop sprinted across the
street charging like a vicious bull, the most vicious and horrifying
look of hatred and contempt on his contorted face, his club raised,
shouting. If hate could kill, that savage's look would have killed
everyone in sight. How can a man be entrusted with safeguarding the
law and protecting the citizens, all citizens, if he becomes so easily
the victim of such neurotic behavior that blinds him to all reason?"
The professor's letter was addressed to the Berkeley chief of police,
but was also published in a local paper, the *Berkeley Barb*.

The second document is a response from the mayor of Berkeley. It
was produced as a flyer, and was distributed in banks and stores
throughout the community. It begins with an excerpt from the professor's letter to the chief of police, and is followed by an open letter
from the mayor to the professor. The mayor asserts that he has
checked into the professor's allegations. Subsequent paragraphs present an entirely different picture of what happened: The young man
whom the professor claims was an innocent passerby was in fact "a
juvenile who was arrested and charged with being a minor in possession of alcoholic beverages." As for the woman with the child,
"[i]nvestigation revealed that this young woman was screaming vile

profanity at the police and was agitating the crowd." The other young woman "was attempting to interfere with the arrest of a man who had attacked a police officer." She may have ended up on the ground, but she was, "to the best of my investigation, never struck with a baton or hit with a fist." Finally, it is true that the man the professor identifies did not throw the beer can, but "body-blocked" the officer as he began to pursue the man who had.

Here are two completely different stories about what happened, one accusing the police, the other defending them. But they differ not only in their ascription of innocence and guilt. The professor's is a personal, eyewitness account, a set of observations made from a particular place on the street: "I was walking toward my car parked off Telegraph Avenue." "I was standing just below the corner of Haste and Telegraph opposite Cody's." The mayor's account, by contrast, is institutional. Instead of statements based on direct observation from a particular vantage point on the scene, it offers the results of an "investigation." It is a composite account that has pretensions to objectivity — supposedly offering a God's-eye view of what *really* happened. It gives the impression of simply stating the facts. While the professor offers up vivid details of his experience, including his emotional reactions ("I shall never forget the face of that policeman, his eyes bulging out . . ."), the mayor's report is dispassionate, and seemingly neutral.

But the mayor's account is bureaucratic in another important respect as well. The police actions are justified, he claims, because the police were simply following "proper police procedures." Rather than being the result of "neurotic behavior," as the professor claims, they were the result of reasoned and reasonable institutional action. Each of the people the professor mentions — the boy, the young woman with the child, the second young woman, and the man — can be shown to have acted in ways that warranted the corresponding police action. "Thank you for relating to me your civic concern," the mayor concludes. "I am sure we both share a common desire to cultivate respect for law and law enforcement officers." In the background of the police chief's remarks we can almost hear Lowry's comment to the men from Central Services: "Where would we be if we didn't stick to correct procedures?"

Of course, not all administrative and bureaucratic documents are brutish, demonic creatures. Three chapters back, I was singing a love song to a cash register receipt. And earlier in this chapter I offered train schedules as an example of an innovation that saved lives. There is no doubt that administrative documents make the trains run on time, literally and figuratively, and surely that is a good thing. What I have been after here is the source of our bad feelings about these kinds of documents. We can partly locate these feelings in the sheer quantity of bureaucratic documents, the fact that we are bombarded and overwhelmed by them at every turn. But this explanation doesn't go far enough. There are more books, news stories, and movies than we can possibly attend to, but we don't direct our hostility at them. Something else is going on with administrative documents, something qualitative. They are at once the products, the co-creators, and one of the more visible symbols of our age, an age that bears the mark of the rational, the mechanical, the impersonal, the efficient, and the disenchanted. We may have derived many benefits from a system of efficient administration and production, but we also feel victimized by it.

It is curious to notice how robust our modern bureaucratic systems have so far been. Despite remarkable and rapid change in many arenas, bureaucracy seems to have become only *more* entrenched; it continues to grow and thrive. A hundred years ago, bureaucratic practices and bureaucratic documents were primarily used to regulate the internal working of institutions. JoAnne Yates's story of "control through communication" is about the development of document-centered practices for managing the movements of employees *within* a company. But over the course of the last century, these same techniques have been extended to regulate the interactions between customers and corporate entities. If we resent red tape, it isn't just because we feel enslaved to it in the workplace; it's because we encounter it in almost all our daily practices. If you want your mail stopped while you're on vacation, you don't generally *tell* your mail carrier — you fill out a form. Your dealings with the gas company, the health insurance company, the phone company, the bank, are mediated by forms, boilerplate letters, and bills. In most of these cases we have also been able to speak to someone by phone. But even here, one of the last bastions of direct human contact, the customer service representative, is being replace by automated, menu-driven voice-mail systems.

Rather than freeing us from bureaucracy, computers may actually be locking us only more firmly into what Max Weber called the "iron cage." (It is a term he first used for capitalism, but it applies equally well to bureaucracy.) In a book written twenty-five years ago, *Computer Power and Human Reason,*[17] Joseph Weizenbaum argued that the computer came along just in time to save our massive bureaucratic system. (This is very close to Beniger's thesis, although Beniger puts a more positive spin on it.) The Internet is clearly a powerful vehicle for extending commerce and administration across the globe. Many of the document genres generated in an earlier era to effect control and coordination are already present in digital form. Indeed, the genre that Web developers first produced to facilitate two-way communication was the dialog box — a digital incarnation of the form. The technologies of document construction and distribution may be changing, but at least in the bureaucratic realm, the system looks remarkably like the one created a hundred years ago.

Won't digital technologies at least liberate us from paperwork? In some ways they already have. In the years ahead, more and more of us will prepare our tax returns on the computer and submit them electronically to the IRS. Companies will increasingly offer us the option of receiving bills electronically rather than on paper, and we will have the option of handling our payment electronically too. Companies will offer to handle our bills for us. Business memos and reports, sales catalogs, and advertisements will increasingly appear in digital form, and fewer readers will feel the need to print them out before reading them. In certain areas of our lives, there will certainly be less paper.

But less paperwork — literally less paper to work with — doesn't necessarily mean less bureaucratic tangle. If we think paper is the problem, it is because we are confusing the *medium* with the *mode* of operation. Paper in itself isn't the problem; it is the most visible and tangible manifestation of it. It is true, of course, that stacks of paper are daunting and they require effort to organize and keep organized, but so do digital materials, as we are discovering is the case with e-mail and Web documents. Digital technologies, in their favor, do offer the possibility of increasingly powerful, automated search tools and classification schemes. These, however, are solutions in the spirit of bureaucracy itself: they try to counter the bureaucratic onslaught by giving us more efficient, more mechanized, more impersonal tools. From childhood I remember an episode of the "Little Rascals" TV show. The truant officer has just caught one of the kids playing hookey. He tells the boy that if he's sent to reform school, he'll spend his days breaking rocks with a sledgehammer. Ah, but on Christmas, on Christmas, the truant officer says, all the boys get a special present. What's that? the boy asks. A new sledgehammer, the officer replies.

5

Reach Out and Touch Someone

Remember the old phone company slogan, "Reach out and touch someone"? It suggested you could make intimate contact with a loved one, even though you were physically separated from him or her. Of course, long before the sound of the voice could be transmitted over phone lines, people reached out across vast distances through writing. While letter writing lacked the immediacy of contact we've come to expect from our newest communications technologies, it had — and still has — certain benefits, not least that it leaves a tangible product, something that can be held, kept, reread, and treasured. In my own family, my father has for many years kept and cherished a small note written by my sister. Although outwardly simple, it points to some of the complexity of being in touch, and illustrates, to my continual amazement, how much skill and sophistication is available at a very young age.

The note consists of just one word — "DID" — written in shaky capital letters by my sister Elena when she was perhaps three years old. According to my father, this is what happened: He had come home from the office one evening to find something amiss. He no longer remembers the nature of the problem, but it was the sort of thing a child might well have done. He demanded to know who was responsible. (At the time I would have been five or six, and I may well have been a suspect too, but somehow I never made it into the official story.) My sister denied everything. But a short while later this note appeared on my father's dresser or desk.

It would be easy to see this note as the mere substitution of a written response for an oral one, as if the two were equivalent. But this would miss the important psychological and social work the written version is doing. The note is precious not just because of the vulnerability of its confession, but because of the writing skills displayed by someone so young. Elena switched to writing exactly *because of* the advantages it offered her over direct verbal contact. With the note, she was able to make a confession at a distance. It's as if, in the act of writing, she was separating out a part of herself — impressing the confessing self into the paper — and sending it off to do the work for her. Curiously, the scrap of paper was *her* and *not her* at the same time. Constructing it was both an act of vulnerability (a means of confessing to a misdeed and owning up to a lie) and an act of self-protection (hiding away). She was extending herself to her father — literally creating something that would travel beyond the boundaries of her physical body — and at the same time withdrawing from him. She was both present in the note and at a safe distance from it.

The note was neither psychologically nor socially the equivalent of a spoken confession. It gave Elena the extra distance she felt she needed. It gave my father the same. Had Elena confessed face-to-face, he might have first reacted out of anger. Finding the note, however, gave him extra time to grasp what was being said, to reflect on it, to appreciate it, and to respond constructively. Indeed, the use of a note where spoken words would have been expected (especially with someone so young) effectively communicated Elena's embarrassment and fear. The little note with its delicate writing, too, conveyed her smallness and vulnerability. These qualities might well have been communicated in a face-to-face encounter, but the impact would have been different. It is impressive to see so much skill on display, and to realize at what an early age children immersed in a literate culture can begin to grasp and exploit some of the differences between speech and writing.

Elena's note is in essence a personal letter in embryonic form. It lacks certain conventional trappings, to be sure: the date, the opening salutation, the closing. But it carries a message from one individual to another; it addresses a highly personal subject; and in its hand-produced marks it expresses some of the drama and the pathos of the situation in which it is embedded. While no one would confuse it with one of Mme. de Sévigné's eighteenth-century literary missives or with a modern exemplar of the epistolary art, evaluated on its own terms it must surely count as both persuasive and beautiful.

Lately, a great deal of attention has been paid to the fate of the personal letter in the age of electronic communication. Does e-mail spell the death of the letter? Or does it perhaps signal a revival of the epistolary art, a resurrection in silicon? It depends whom you ask. In 1990, well before e-mail had become a mainstream phenomenon, the journal *World Literature Today* devoted most of one issue to the topic "The Letter: A Dying Art?" John L. Brown, referring to "computerized mail" as the latest in a series of letter-killers, sounded a pessimistic note:

> The letter, it seems, is dying; but its deathbed is surrounded by an unprecedented number of specialists, who find the moribund of great clinical interest, and every one of them seems to have a diagnosis of his own. All agree, however, that the health of the letter has been undermined and finally dealt a fatal blow by the telephone, the telegram, the cassette, the fax, and other technical innovations that have deprived it of its raison d'être. The written word has been vanquished by the audiovisual. The authentic "personal letter" . . . has been further devaluated by the rise of computerized mail. The public now receives masses of "letters," addressed by name and making a pitch for everything imaginable, from political and charitable contributions to "special offers" and "gifts for you alone." The flood of such patently phony missives, couched in terms of instant intimacy, is the "junk mail" which constitutes a major part of the correspondence most of us now receive.[1]

But Leslie B. Mittleman disagreed. In her contribution in the same issue, she claimed that "obsequies on the 'death' of the art of letter writing are premature."[2] She later put it even more emphatically: "the art of the letter is not dying."[3]

Almost a decade (and many billions of e-mail messages) later, the same positions are being argued. Writing in *The New York Times*, Martin Arnold opened his column, "Pen in Hand? Maybe No More,"[4] with an observation and a question. The literary letter "has survived the telephone and the typewriter and the personal computer. Will it survive E-mail?" After quoting various writers, including Joyce Carol Oates and John Updike, none of whom sees much literary potential in e-mail, he concludes with a reference to Samuel Johnson, the great eighteenth-century literary figure: "So the loss of letters on paper can be a serious thing indeed. And can anyone really imagine: sjohnson@therambler.com?"

Apparently someone can. Adam Gopnik, writing in *The New Yorker*, thinks the Internet is "sublimely reactionary." "It doesn't just look back," he says, in a commentary entitled "The Return of the Word," "it looks way back, to around 1730. Swift and Pope and Lord Chesterfield, with a Web page apiece, would have been merrily scribbling short essays, anonymous accusations, flames, and billets-doux. Dr. Johnson would have loved the medium and Boswell would have fancied it so much that he might yet spring back to life for a chance to log on."[5] He concludes on a happy note: "That the triumph of numbers — that is, the digital age — should lead to the return of letters is as happy an irony as will warm this cold millennium."[6]

Writing in an online magazine called *Island Scene*, Bill Harby is equally optimistic. "There's nothing new about global communication at the speed of light," he says. "We've been able to phone Timbuktu for a long time. But email has revitalized and redefined the art and science of letter writing in ways that air mail (mere 'snail mail' by e-standards) and even the fax machine could never do."[7] According to *U.S. News and World Report*, however, James Atlas, critic and biographer, has doubts about the quality of reflection found in e-mail. "When you sit down to write a letter," Atlas believes, "you are making a more serious commitment." In the same article, the novelist Reynolds Price offers a more mixed assessment. At least young people are writing more these days. Besides, it's not as though the art of writing has fallen "from some great recent height."[8]

This last observation seems particularly on point. Our age isn't particularly known for its epistolary triumphs, and it seems unlikely that it ever will be. Why are we even discussing the eighteenth century — surely a very different era from our own — other than as a journalistic hook, or perhaps as a reference point from which to measure our sorry state? The eighteenth century would hardly seem to be a model for our own. It is an era that scholars have called "the great age of the personal letter" and "the golden age of the familiar letter," a period recognized for its great literary correspondences among a social elite. Letter writing, for practitioners of this high art, was "an informed, entertaining exchange carried on between persons belonging to a circle of familiar acquaintances, who shared a common knowledge of literature, history, and . . . social institutions."[9] If they aimed for a certain naturalness associated with speech, this wasn't the naturalness of the speech of the streets, but of "people who take particular care to speak well. Their talk makes incomparably better use of language than does that of the uncultivated."[10]

What's going on, it seems to me, is this: letter writing has come to symbolize the possibility of intimate contact at a distance. For as long as people have written to one another, and with whatever technologies, letters have served a wide range of purposes. Measured quantitatively, personal letters have almost certainly been in the minority. Some of the earliest and most common uses of letters were administrative, commercial, and political, rather than personal. Ancient postal systems, such as those of the Persian and Roman empires, were created to effect control through communication: carrying the messages of the powerful — the military, the administrators, the ruling class — as a means of maintaining political and economic control over a wide area. Yet the letters that have been most carefully preserved, analyzed, and emulated through the centuries are those of a more personal and literary nature, like this one from Seneca to Lucilius:

> I thank you for writing to me so often; for you are revealing your
> real self to me in the only way you can. I never receive a letter

from you without being in your company forthwith. If the pictures of our absent friends are pleasing to us, though they only refresh the memory and lighten our longing by a solace that is unreal and unsubstantial, how much more pleasant is a letter, which brings us real traces, real evidences, of an absent friend! For that which is sweetest when we meet face to face is afforded by the impress of a friend's hand upon his letter — recognition.[11]

Today we are still collecting and publishing exemplary letters. (Recent collections include *Letters of a Nation*[12] and *Letters of the Century*.)[13] We are also still publishing books that offer to teach us how to write letters, and that explain why we should still write them. "The pleasure of sharing ourselves," says Jennifer Williams in *The Pleasures of Staying in Touch,* "is no less important now than it ever was. A letter that takes only ten minutes to write can have tremendous immediacy and give the person who receives it an exhilarating sense of 'being there,' next to you, living in the same moment with you."[14] She concludes her introduction with these inspiring words:

> In the end, writing a letter is an adventure to be embarked upon with a happy, expectant heart. It will give your life more joy and meaning than you can imagine. So, go quickly! Write a letter now, even if it's just a few lines to propose a picnic, relate a dream, or share a sudden thought, joke, inspiration, or memory. Write to say hello, and I'm thinking of you. Write to say I hope you're feeling better. Write to say it's raining and cozy by the lamplight and I miss you. Just write, and wait: An enchanting letter will soon be on its way to you. . . .[15]

But, realistically, who has time to write letters today? (Brief notes and e-mail messages, yes, but long, reflective letters? Hardly any of us, I would venture to say.) If personal letters were as vital a part of our culture today as they once were, we wouldn't need books like Jennifer Williams's exhorting us to write them. If we want to examine the pleasure of staying in touch — as it is actually practiced today, in great volume and to great effect — I suggest we look to a different form. It is one without the literary pretensions or the cultural history of the letter. But it is nonetheless a rich, important, and abundant form, with much to show us about how intimate contact is maintained today through writing. I'm referring to greeting cards.

According to industry sources, more than six billion greeting cards were purchased in 1998.[16] You don't have to travel far to find them on sale: in pharmacies, gift shops, gas stations, bookstores, and shops devoted exclusively to pens, papers, and cards. Walk into any greeting-card store and you will find them neatly displayed row upon row, categorized by the occasion for which they are intended. One large group is concerned with life-cycle events: birth, confirmation, bar mitzvah and bat mitzvah, engagement, marriage, and bereavement. Another set marks events in the cycle of the year: New Year's, Valentine's Day, Easter, Passover, Chanukah, and Christmas, as well as birthdays. Yet another expresses basic sentiments and wishes: I love you, I miss you, Get well soon, Thank you, I'm sorry. Still others are blank: the buyer creates the message for the appropriate occasion.

You might think of greeting cards as prefabricated letters, ready to send. With the exception of the blank cards, they've already been specialized for particular occasions. Of course, letters have long been categorized by function and occasion. Greek and Roman rhetoricians recognized different types of letters: letters of congratulation, letters of thanks, letters of praise and blame, and so on. They wrote the equivalent of how-to manuals, providing models of the different types of letters and offering instruction on how to write them. Following in their footsteps, we still classify letters by function, and books like Jennifer Williams's still coach us in the writing of love letters and valentines, invitations, thank-you notes, letters of sympathy and condolence, and more. What's different today is that you have a choice: you can pen a note from scratch, or you can buy a card that's been prepared in advance. It's the difference between preparing a homemade meal and heating up a prepackaged serving.

If greeting cards are like letters, they also bear a resemblance to business cards and postcards. The connection to business cards is perhaps not so immediately obvious, but there is a strong historical link.

The precursor to today's business card was the visiting card or calling card. (You've probably seen them in the movies when a gentleman hands his card to the servant opening the door of the home he's just entering.) Such cards came into popular use in the eighteenth century. They often contained an engraved scene as well as the name of the caller. The less expensive ones left room for the visitor to sign his or her name; people in positions of higher rank had their names engraved on them. Cards came in two sizes, the smaller ones for gentlemen, the larger for ladies. In the nineteenth century the cards became more elaborate, with fancy borders and hand painting. It also became the custom to include a seasonal message on the card, e.g., Christmas greetings. The first Christmas cards (greeting cards, that is), produced in the mid-nineteenth century, were the same size as women's calling cards. And so it appears that the practice of identifying oneself through calling cards subtly shifted into a practice of sending seasonal greetings. Meanwhile, calling cards — which had in fact been used for business purposes too — eventually dropped the seasonal acknowledgment to become the no-nonsense business cards we have today.

The postcard seems to have developed in parallel with the greeting card. No doubt each influenced the other in multiple ways. Certainly, in order to establish themselves as acceptable vehicles of communication, they had to address — and in a sense do battle with — some of the same social obstacles. Like the memo, the postcard put a premium on conciseness and brevity, only more so. Of course, it had always been possible to write short letters. Yet for much of the recent history of personal letters, the norm seems to have been to write long and substantial ones. British letter writers in the eighteenth century, Howard Anderson and Irvin Ehrenpreis suggest in their essay on "The Familiar Letter," "were perhaps the more likely to take care that their letters should be long and worth reading because throughout the century the recipient had to pay the post, and might be inclined to judge rather critically what he had paid for."[17]

And if the advice offered letter writers can be taken as a clue to habits of the time, letters were still expected to be lengthy well into the next century. The author of Cradock's *Art of Letter Writing Simpli-*

fied, published in 1844, felt the need to explain that proper letters *could* be written in "not more than six or eight lines." Having entertained guests the night before, for example, the hostess could write them the following morning: "Mrs. Thompson's compliments to Mrs. Bennett and the young ladies, hope they got safe home and are perfectly recovered from the fatigues of last night." And the guests' reply could be brief as well: "Mrs. and the Misses Bennett return thanks to Mrs. Thompson for her kind enquiries; they reached home in perfect safety, and are all well, except Julia who has taken a slight cold."[18]

The invention of the postcard, however, created a form where brevity would be the rule rather than the exception. After a short period of experimentation in the private sector, the first postcards used on a mass scale were created by national governments: by Austria in 1869, by Britain in 1870, and by the United States in 1873. At the international postal congress the following year, it was agreed that cards, although varying in size from country to country, could cross national borders without being restamped.

Although the postcard quickly found a public eager to use them — seventy-six million of them were sold in Britain the first year — how exactly, or even whether, they were to be used in polite society was not immediately apparent. The author of *Don't: A Manual of Mistakes and Improprieties,* writing in 1890, warned his readers that "[i]t is questionable whether a note on a postal card is entitled to the courtesy of a response."[19] What was the problem? There was barely enough room to say anything, and certainly no room for the wordy, formal openings and closings that a polite writer would be expected to use. "For the purposes of correspondence," one man observed, "they are practically useless. There is . . . barely room for you to write your name. . . . They are utterly destructive of style, and give absolutely no play to the emotions."[20] Then, too, since a postcard had no envelope, privacy couldn't be guaranteed. "My grudge against the postal card," one writer observed in a letter to *The Atlantic Monthly* in 1877, "is the tendency to read, against your own will, postal cards not addressed to yourself. There is a fascination about the thing which is very like kleptomania."[21]

Postcards also seemed impolite because their use suggested that the writer wasn't prepared to take the time to write a proper letter. Yet this was also their attraction. In 1903 the *Lincolnshire Echo* called the postcard "the spirit of the age — brevity and speed." Three years earlier a Miss Margaret Meadows had observed that the postcard was "a sign of the times" and suited to "a period peopled by a hurried generation that has not many minutes to spare for writing to friends, what with express trains going at the rate of a mile a minute, telegrams and telephones."[22] By the turn of the century, the opinion of polite society was turning. "Postcards are no longer considered vulgar," wrote the *Daily Express* in 1902. The postcard, like the memo a product of the new spirit of bureaucratic efficiency, had achieved respectability.

Today the letter, the postcard, and the greeting card each inhabit their own social niche. Much as my sister's note wasn't the exact social equivalent of face-to-face conversation, neither are these three written genres completely interchangeable. There is overlap, to be sure, in the social territories they cover, and this means we can sometimes choose which to use. You can send someone a letter, a postcard, or a greeting card to acknowledge his birthday. But you will be saying something different with each one — they are not exactly equivalent. Just what significance your choice has, though, will depend on any number of factors. In some circles greeting cards are considered lowbrow — especially the most traditional of them, with their quaint rhyming verse and sweet sentimentality. But in other circles these very same cards are a much-cherished vehicle of intimate contact. Regardless, they are a popular form, standing at quite a distance from the literary letter with all its lofty pretension.

It is perhaps for this reason that I have been unable to find much scholarly work on greeting cards. While there is a rich scholarly literature on the history and function of the letter and similarly of the book, there is remarkably little written about the lowly greeting card. The main source book I have located is Ernest Dudley Chase's *The Romance of Greeting Cards,* a book first issued in 1926 and edited and reissued in 1956. Chase was a greeting-card designer whom the book jacket describes as a "propagandist for the greeting card." Indeed, his tone is more often celebratory and promotional than scholarly. "The story of the Greeting Card," he begins, "is truly a romance. The record of a vital, fast-growing industry, it is a picture of many times and different eras; and it is the story of many men and many women. In carrying messages of love and friendship, the Greeting Card has ever brought people closer together. In these days when continents are but hours apart and soon may be only minutes apart, the importance of one more personal bond between people the world over is self-evident."[23]

Searching for other entry points into the subject matter, I was fortunate to find a source in a rather unexpected place. In the American Anthropological Association's newsletter, I discovered that an anthropologist named Ken Erickson had testified before the Postal Rate Commission on the cultural significance of greeting cards.[24]

The Postal Rate Commission (PRC) was created in 1970 in conjunction with the formation of the United States Postal Service (USPS). In that year the Post Office Department was dissolved and replaced by the USPS, a self-supporting postal corporation wholly owned by the federal government. The mission of this new organization would be "to bind the Nation together through the personal, educational, literary, and business correspondence of the people" by providing "prompt, reliable, and efficient service to patrons in all areas." Authority for the new postal system was transferred from Congress to the postal corporation's management and to a newly created board of governors. And a five-member, independent Postal Rate Commission was established to rule on Postal Service requests for postal rate increases.

In 1997, when the Postal Service requested a $2.4 billion increase, which would include an increase in first-class postage from 32 to 33 cents, the PRC initiated a series of hearings at which the different constituencies affected by the rate hike could air their views.[25] Initial briefs were filed by more than forty special-interest groups, including the American Library Association, the Association of American Publishers, and the Newspaper Association of America. Most of them claimed that the increased cost of mailing personal letters, advertisements, bills and statements, newspapers and magazines, mail-order catalogs, and the like would be harmful to their businesses and, of course, to the consumer. Among those making such an argument was the Greeting Card Association (GCA), a trade association of greeting-card publishers whose members produce ninety percent of the cards in the United States.[26]

The GCA took a novel approach, arguing that the rate increase would do harm to American cultural life. The Postal Service had based its argument for the proposed rate hike on a classical economic analysis of supply and demand, cost and benefit. But the GCA pointed to section 3622(b) of the Postal Reorganization Act, which states that when the Postal Rate Commission is considering a request to change postal rates, it must take into account "the educational, cultural, scientific, and informational value to the recipient of mail matter." An economist, James A. Clifton, testified before the PRC that the rate increase would have negative consequences for American cultural life, regardless of its effect on economic life, if it diminished the number of greeting cards sent and received. The members of the PRC seemed to appreciate this novel angle, one based on cultural rather than economic value, but they questioned whether Clifton had the professional expertise to make it. "Are you a sociocultural anthropologist?" one of the commissioners asked. Clearly the answer was no, but the door was now open to exploring the cultural angle.

Ken Erickson was called to testify before the PRC on the cultural significance of greeting cards. A professor of anthropology at the University of Missouri, he had previously been asked by Hallmark to do a study of Mother's Day cards, which included observing and interviewing people as they shopped for cards in shops. In his testimony, Erickson explained the anthropological notion of gift exchange, and asserted that greeting cards exist simultaneously in a market economy and a gift economy. Greeting-card publishers manufacture them, customers buy them, and for the price of postage the postal service will deliver them. But these money-based transactions, while undeniably a part of the life cycle of greeting cards, don't really get at what they are *about*. For their primary value is cultural, not economic. They "embody as well as mediate social relationships," Erickson said. "They communicate meanings and intentions about relationships and, in so doing, they signal their cultural value. . . . Greeting cards are a way to signal (and sometimes reshape) the cultural value attached to relationships over time."

A greeting card makes the transition from commodity to gift at the point at which you select it. Choosing the right card is serious business. When you enter the card shop, you often already have a person in mind and the occasion you want to acknowledge in sending the card.[27] The hard part is finding a card that properly acknowledges the occasion, the person you're sending the card to, and the relationship you have with that person. The card, says Erickson, has to "match the present state of the relationship with reference to past relationships, relationships that are shaped by the presence (or absence) of other people. A card for a family member with whom you have had a warm and affectionate relationship in the past but do not have such a close relationship now is different from a card for someone with a different interpersonal connection with you."[28] Getting this right means taking all the design elements into account: the printed message, the illustrations (or lack of them), the colors, the card stock. You may not be conscious of all these elements as you choose, but still they will combine to produce an overall feel or mood, and that's what you're after.

Standing there in the card shop, what is foremost isn't the cost of the card (although that may be a factor) but the significance, the value or worth, of the relationship. No wonder that when you watch people selecting a card you'll often see them lingering reflectively — standing there, feeling, remembering, assessing. It's one of those moments, not normally acknowledged in the culture, when we take time to meditate on the meaning, with all their complexities, of our intimate relationships. Erickson suggests that each greeting card stands "between memory and hope." It arises out of an existing relationship with its prior history (memory) and points to an uncertain, but wished-for future (hope). Days, weeks, or months before the card has been received, the relationship is already being invoked by the sender: the giving has already begun.

It's strange, in a way, that the selection of a mass-produced artifact can carry so much meaning. The greeting-card company may have produced thousands or even tens of thousands of copies of this very card and distributed them in every card shop in the country, but the number of outstanding copies has no bearing on the impact this particular card will have on my intended recipient. He or she will receive *this* card, *this* physical object, and will interpret it in terms of its overall message, its gestalt. In this respect, choosing a card is a lot like choosing a book as a present, or an article of mass-produced clothing. In making your choice, how well have you communicated something of significance about your relationship with that person?

The choice of the card (or of the book or the shirt) is therefore a personal act — made by one person for and in acknowledgment of another. But in the case of the card in particular, convention requires that you do more to personalize it. You must address the card ("Dear So-and-so") and sign your name. And in many instances you will add an additional line or two, or more, in your own words. Through these extra touches you personalize a mass-produced item and make it unique. As a sign of its new status, it can't be returned to the shop once you've written on it.

Because personalization is such an important part of the process, receiving a card that shows little attempt to personalize it specifically for the recipient — to reach out and touch him or her — may do little to strengthen the relationship, and may actually undermine it. Or it may serve as a tangible and painful reminder of a broken connection. Some cards just feel hollow, either because they haven't been annotated or because the annotations feel strained or perfunctory.

Annotation is, of course, one of the most basic and important ways we have to tailor a document to particular circumstances of use. Medieval books, with their Bible passages at the center of the page and their surrounding rings of commentary, are perhaps our most magnificent examples of annotational practices. But all around us are

examples of annotation that are no less important for being less beautifully executed. We may write on a memo or a printed copy of an
e-mail message, then fax the annotated copy to someone else. Or we
may write in the margins of a book we're reading, or highlight the
text with a colored marker. Catherine Marshall, a researcher formerly
at Xerox PARC, now at Microsoft, has observed that undergraduates
will search out used copies of textbooks in a college bookstore, looking for those with the most useful annotations.[29]

In inscribing a greeting card, you add a great deal of meaning
through the actual words you choose. Do you say "Dear So-and-so,"
or "My dearest" — or do you write the person's name without further adornment? Do you close with "Love," or "Warmly," or "With
best wishes"? Or do you simply sign your name without any further
closing? What additional message do you add, and how long is it
overall? Is it all contained on the right-hand side of the card? Does it
spill over onto the left-hand side? Or do you need additional sheets of
paper, so that the card becomes a vehicle for a full-scale letter? Personalization, however, comes not just through the words, the new
content you've added, but by the very fact that you have chosen to
handwrite anything at all.

Indeed, handwriting very much carries the mark of the personal.
It means something to us today when we receive a handwritten card
or letter, or even a hand-addressed envelope. The writer is signaling
some sort of personal relationship with us (or an advertiser is trying
to trick us into thinking this). But this "reading" of handwriting as
being personal is a relatively recent cultural development. Until the
printing press was invented, there simply was no alternative to handwriting. Books, letters, and accounting records were written by
hand. Printing, as first conceived, was a mechanical alternative to the
handiwork of the scribe. The products of the hand and of the press
were largely undifferentiated. But over the course of several centuries,
whether or not something was written by hand came to acquire cultural significance. Printed — that is, mechanically produced — works
came to be understood as public and impersonal expressions. The
work of the hand, by contrast, came to be understood as a form of

personal expression. Drawing on the work of Michael Warner (in his book *The Letters of the Republic*),[30] Tamara Plakins Thornton, in *Handwriting in America,* explains this divergence of function:

> [S]ometime in the eighteenth century the cultural trajectories of print and script were set by their respective relations to the hand, and from that time they did diverge. Print lost any association with the hand just as pointedly as script [handwriting] retained it. This association of script with the physical executor of the script endowed handwriting with a unique set of cultural meanings and functions. For if print was defined by its dissociation from the hand, the body, and the corporeal individual that created it, then handwritten matter necessarily referred back to the hand, the body, and the individual in new ways. . . . Words transmitted their authors' ideas; scripts, the authors themselves.[31]

This is very much the point of a greeting card, isn't it: to send something of yourself. Through a combination of prefabricated object and specially tailored annotation, you put into material form not only an abstract message but a portion of yourself. In his classic work on the gift, Marcel Mauss suggested that "to give something is to give a part of oneself. . . . [O]ne gives away what is in reality a part of one's nature and substance, while to receive something is to receive a part of someone's spiritual essence."[32] (He was referring to one specific non-Western culture, the Maori.) This turns out to have been one of the more controversial statements in Mauss's treatment. It was attacked by other anthropologists as a form of mysticism and mystification. "Are we not faced here," said Levi-Strauss, "with one of those instances (not altogether rare) in which the ethnologist allows himself to be mystified by the native?"[33]

Perhaps. But what Mauss claims makes sense to me about our culture. All artifacts, after all, are the materialization of some dimension, some portion, of human life. All documents, then, as the materialized voice or breath of their creators, carry aspects of their creators' "essence." This is as true of an IRS 1040 tax form (which carries a trace of the essence of a massive bureaucratic entity, not a person) as it is of my sister's one-word note. Greeting cards are a highly ritual-ized form of such transfer.

Once the card is ready, the next stage of its existence is its delivery. Ken Erickson naturally focuses on the delivery of the card by mail, since he is testifying before the Postal Rate Commission. Sixty to seventy percent of cards arrive by post in the United States, the rest being delivered by the writer or some other intermediary.[34] The addressing of the envelope, the choice of a stamp and the delivery method (first class, priority, express, etc.) may all have social signifi-cance. How much (or little) do we think about the recipient when addressing the envelope? Does our handwriting in some way reflect our feelings about him or her? Do we make a special trip to the post office, or to a particular branch, in order to see the card off more speedily, or to have it postmarked from one town rather than another?

Finally, the moment arrives when card and recipient meet. It is typically a physical joining as the recipient grasps the envelope and undertakes the delicate work of opening it. (A whole chapter could be written on this alone.) The card is read. The length of time this takes is likely to be small relative to the amount of time it took to choose the card and send it. You might think of this as the whole point of the preceding efforts, but this isn't quite right. For, as we have seen, the time preceding this is equally a part of the ritual, and is equally important. Yet there is no denying that the instant of recep-tion is a crucial moment as the recipient absorbs the printed message, the inscription, the design, and takes in a first impression.

With some greeting cards, first impressions are all we ever get. The Happy Birthday card accompanying the gift is quickly opened in front of the giver as a preliminary part of the ritual, a necessary politeness before tearing into the main event. But with many cards, their work is hardly done at this point. It isn't uncommon for them to be put on display: on the mantel, or the refrigerator, or on a table. In his research, Erickson found that for certain classes of cards — Mother's Day cards in particular — people take future display into account when buying them.

Why is display important? "Changing — or enduring — relationships among family members and friends," says Erickson, "are made visible in the display of cards; the selection and receipt of cards is laden with emotional and cultural baggage." Making the card visible keeps the sender present for the recipient. But equally important, it makes the relationship visible to *others*. Look at the lovely card my son has sent me. See how my daughter is thinking of me. Like the display of another kind of document, the photograph, or like flowers sent to someone's workplace, the card on display is a concrete and public manifestation of connection.

And there may well be yet another stage in a greeting card's life: when it is put away for safekeeping. Many of us hold on to objects having special personal significance, tucking them away in our sock drawer, or in shoeboxes in the closet or the attic. In an informal and possibly unselfconscious way, we maintain a personal archive, a treasure chest of cherished artifacts and the memories they hold for us. This is a very old practice. The word "archive" comes from the Latin *arca,* originally meaning a place to store things, a box or chest. (In English, we still find *ark* used in this way, in phrases like "Noah's Ark" and "the Ark of the Covenant.") In the Middle Ages, Ivan Illich reports, each monastery had an arca, which was "kept in the sacristy to store the treasures: chalices and vestments for the liturgy; relics, mainly the assorted skulls and bones of saints enclosed in precious boxes; and, besides these objects, also books."[35] Kings in twelfth- and thirteenth-century England, according to M. T. Clanchy, also had archives in this sense, but rather than being kept in a fixed place, they would be moved around, as the king moved from place to place.[36] The Latin word for their contents, *thesaurus,* has also come down to us as a document-related term; its original meaning is "treasure."

In the privacy of our own homes we are likely to hold on to any number of treasures: cards, letters, and notes written long ago, photographs, scrapbooks filled with mementoes from an earlier era. We can't throw them out, even if we can't say why. We may look at them rarely or not at all, yet still it is somehow comforting to know they are there. It's as if something of importance is embedded in their very substance. This has less to do with their information content per se than with the emotions they evoke and the personal relationships they signify and embody. Of course, not all these items are documents. And not all those that are documents started out with personal significance. Bureaucratic and mass-produced items — theater tickets and programs, newspaper clippings, even cash register receipts — may acquire a special status if they've come to stand for some significant person or event.

My sister's note became an archival item in my father's care. Initially, it lay in my father's drawer for thirty years or so, passively performing its memory function. During that time he may have come upon it now and then among the pencils and paper clips, the scissors and other artifacts that so commonly inhabit people's desk drawers. In one of these encounters he noticed that the note was fraying, and took steps to preserve it. He mounted it and annotated it, and in this process it was further transformed. For by taking these steps, he was declaring the note to be something worthy of preservation, description, and display. The note suddenly became something akin to a mounted butterfly, a framed photograph, or an artifact in the custody of a museum or archive. In much the same way, greeting cards end up in drawers, or in scrapbooks alongside memorable photographs.

In addition to his fieldwork — observing and talking to shoppers as they bought cards — Erickson conducted a phone survey. These results further confirmed the significance of greeting cards in American cultural life. A strong majority of those questioned, for example, felt that greeting cards helped them to celebrate holidays and special occasions, and to know that they were cared about at times of illness and bereavement. What is perhaps more interesting is that differences in patterns of use exist among different social groups. Generally speaking, African-Americans and those with lower incomes seem to value the exchange of cards more. Just as cards are differentiated by occasion (birthday, Christmas, graduation, etc.) and by mood (humorous, sentimental, uplifting, etc.), so too is their value treated differently within different groups.

The picture that emerges is of a vast web of exchanges taking place around the country, billions of cards being exchanged every year. Each exchange is unique: the pairing of a specific sender with a specific recipient. Each card, ultimately, is unique — purchased, annotated, and sent — and is the material acknowledgment of one specific, ongoing relationship. Yet taken together, Erickson argues, these activities help to "bind the nation together."

In *Imagined Communities,* Benedict Anderson suggests that the idea of a nation as a collection of citizens united through common views and practices was partly achieved by the daily newspaper.[37] As millions of readers received their morning newspaper and read it over breakfast, they could feel that they were part of an extended community: reading the same news stories, and thereby participating in the life of a common culture. Greeting cards would seem to have a similar function — not because everyone is receiving the same cards, but because so many of us are participating in these common rituals of gift exchange.

Today, of course, these very rituals are beginning to shift. E-mail and the Web provide new opportunities for personal communication. Instead of sending your grandmother a handwritten letter, you can send her e-mail. Instead of shopping for a birthday card at the shop down the street, you can send someone a digital card. (There are any number of services on the Web now that will let you choose cards from traditional categories, or even create your own, and will deliver them via e-mail.) You can do the same with digital postcards. What difference does it make whether we choose the traditional forms or the new digital ones?

As far as I can see, it comes down to a few basic differences in how we manage space and time, and to the social significance of these differences. Traditional letters and cards, like my childhood copy of *Leaves of Grass,* are tangible, continuously existing objects. This means that the card I receive in the mail from you is the very one you picked out and handled. There can be great emotional significance in this — not only because I can now hold the tangible evidence of my connection with you, but because I can *hold on to it* in the future as well. Your handwriting makes it all the more personal.

For the moment at least, digital cards and letters (e-mail) don't have these physical properties. But they do offer certain temporal advantages. The most notable, of course, is speed: the selection and transmission of an online card can take place in a matter of minutes, as compared with the effort needed to purchase a card and mail it, and the time needed for the post office to deliver it. The speed of e-mail, in fact, has already produced a novel communicative behavior: some people chat with friends and family throughout the day over e-mail, sending short messages back and forth. Interestingly, there is some precedent for this in a prior era. During the eighteenth century, there were as many as a dozen mail deliveries a day within London, which meant that people could participate in multiple literary round-trips in a single day. Today's e-mail is different, however, not only because it allows so many more round-trips, but because the messages being exchanged are (or can be) more informal — nearly conversational in style.

The difference seems to come down to this: You can have a physical object, possibly handwritten, but it will be slow to arrive. Or you can have a digital transmission, lightning fast, without a unique object. So which is better? It depends, of course. It depends on the particular circumstances under which you are reaching out to someone, what you are wanting to say, what the nature of your relationship is, and what resources are available to you. How important is the creation of a tangible surrogate? How important is the possibility of saving it away? How important is the act of writing with pen on paper, the look and feel of the hand as it glides and hesitates? When is time a hindrance, and when does a slower rhythm of creation and transmission nurture the relationship between sender and receiver? If there are no general answers to this question, it doesn't mean that the choices are without significance. Far from it.

I opened this chapter with a question: What will happen to the letter in the age of e-mail? Many questions are contained here: the future of handwriting, of paper, of the postal service, of literary correspondence, and, of course, of the possibility of real human contact at a distance. It is the last of these that I think is ultimately the most important. All communication is communication at a distance, an attempt to bridge the mysterious gap between sentient beings. Letter writing, now perhaps more in the cultural imagination than in actual practice, symbolizes the possibility of a graced, perhaps even a transcendent, communion between souls. (If the letter is the supreme form of personal, written communication, then surely the love letter is the supreme form of the letter, for just this reason.)

It makes me wonder if the real question being asked isn't about the letter or about e-mail, but about a mode of life. Many of us feel that our lives are speeding up, becoming more fragmented and dislocated. Under such circumstances, what are the possibilities for deep human contact and communion? Will e-mail help us or hurt us? Is it possible that e-mail will enable a true correspondence of souls, or will it prove to be a technology of alienation? This is what I hear us asking, at any rate, even when the words are not spoken as such, even when we seem to be speaking most directly about properties of the new technologies.

6

Reading and Attention

Roughly twenty-five years ago, I witnessed a heated exchange on just this topic. It was the mid-1970s and I was attending a demonstration of an experimental window-based programming environment, called D-Lisp, at the Xerox Palo Alto Research Center. Windows — the framed, rectangular portions of a computer display screen that are now ubiquitous — were still a novelty then. Personal computers hadn't yet been successfully commercialized, and windows were still only a reality within the walls of the research laboratory. The system being demonstrated wasn't the first to make use of windows — that distinction belongs to the Smalltalk system, which had been developed at Xerox PARC several years earlier — but it was the first such environment for the Lisp programming language.

The presenter, Warren Teitelman, demonstrated how multiple windows could be opened and moved around on the screen. At one point, as part of the carefully scripted demo, he received an e-mail message. He shifted his gaze from the window in which he had been programming to the window in which the e-mail message had just appeared. He typed a reply and sent it off, then returned to the programming task that had been interrupted. The point was to show off how a windowing environment could facilitate "multitasking" — performing several tasks at the same time.

In the audience were thirty to fifty computer scientists. One of them, an eminent computer scientist visiting from abroad, was visibly upset by what he had just seen. And in the boisterous, often contentious atmosphere of the early PARC, he made his unhappiness immediately known. This was no way to program, he objected. Why in the world would you want to be interrupted — and distracted — by e-mail while programming? Clearly, more was on display than just a new technology. For here was a conflict between two different ways of working and two different understandings of how technology should be used to support that work. What Warren Teitelman considered a useful feature of the new system, the visitor apparently viewed as a hindrance and a distraction. While Teitelman was eager to juggle multiple threads of work simultaneously, the visiting researcher saw his work as an exercise in solitary, singleminded concentration.

No doubt all of us in the room that day believed that personal computers, networks, and e-mail would become a vital part of future work practices. But I doubt that anyone could have imagined how e-mail traffic would grow, or how its use, along with cell phones and pagers and other communication technologies, would vie for our attention and further complicate our lives. Yet more than twenty years later, many of us are coming to suspect that these technologies are a mixed blessing. Certainly they allow us to stay in touch with friends, partners, children, and colleagues at a distance. They make it possible to do several things at the same time — driving and talking on the phone, for example. But it is becoming clearer that we use these technologies at a cost: they can interrupt us at any time. Although in principle we can choose to ignore the latest batch of e-mail messages or the ringing cell phone, many of us have great difficulty doing so. And thus, although promising to connect us, by contributing to the fragmentation of our lives, they also seem to disconnect us — from our tasks, from our relationships, and even from ourselves.

It is a question of how we use one of our most precious resources: our attention. More than a hundred years ago, the psychologist

William James observed that attention "is the taking possession by the mind, in clear and vivid form, of one out of what seem several simultaneously possible objects or trains of thought. Focalization, concentration, of consciousness are of its essence. It implies withdrawal from some things in order to deal effectively with others, and is a condition which has a real opposite in the confused, dazed, scatter-brained state which in French is called *distraction,* and *Zerstreutheit* in German."[1]

Every moment of our lives, whether consciously or not, we are choosing what to attend to and with what depth of focus. In talking with a friend, we may at one moment be deeply attending to her words. At the next moment our attention may be split between what she is saying and the sight of someone walking by, or we may be momentarily lost in our own thoughts and oblivious of everything else. At any given moment our attention may be highly concentrated or focused on its current object, or we may find ourselves in the "confused, dazed, scatter-brained state" to which James refers, in which we are simply incapable of any real depth of focus. Anecdotally, at least, it does seem that our modern, high-tech world increasingly encourages distraction and fragmentation over extended concentration. Many of us long for a remembered — or perhaps a mythologized — past in which life was simpler, time was more abundant, and we could attend more fully to the dimensions of life that most mattered to us. We also long for those opportunities, perhaps on our next vacation, when we can recover, if only briefly, our composure and concentration.

Like all the objects around us, documents vie for our attention. Whether we are on the Web, sitting in our offices surrounded by stacks of paper, or driving down a freeway lined with endless road signs and billboards, we are faced with constant decisions about which ones to attend to. All of them have the potential to draw and shape our attention, not just because we may focus on them as physical objects but because we have the potential to *see through them.* Indeed, as information-bearing or representational artifacts, they direct us beyond themselves and speak to us of other aspects of the world. Much like a window — or, perhaps even better, a crystal ball — they direct our gaze and our imagination elsewhere. Reading, the name we give to this form of directed gaze, thus has a double attentional quality: by attending to certain properties of the artifact literally at hand, our attention is drawn to other places and other worlds. (In an essay famous in typographic circles, Beatrice Ward suggested that fine typography, like fine crystal, should be invisible, all the better to reveal its contents.)[2]

As literate members in a literate society, we read all day long, mostly unconsciously. We glance at the headlines of a neighbor's newspaper as we ride on the bus. We read road signs as we drive to work. We scan the menu in a restaurant, our latest credit-card bill, the ingredients on a can of soup, the headers of newly arrived e-mail messages. These forms of reading tend to be shallow and of brief duration. Yet there are times when we read with greater intensity and duration, when we become absorbed in what we are reading for longer stretches of time. Some of us, indeed, don't just *read* in this way but think of ourselves *as readers*. And although we have the potential to read any form of material in this manner — newspapers, magazines, journals, even the backs of cereal boxes when necessary — it is books that are the primary target of our attention.

I have long loved Wallace Stevens's poem "The House Was Quiet and the World Was Calm" for its reverential (and, to my mind, accurate) portrait of just such a reader. In a mere sixteen lines, Stevens describes a man sitting alone, reading late into a summer night. There is no mistaking the focused, contemplative quality of this practice. In the stillness of the evening, the calm of the night, the reader seems to merge with his object of study:

> The words were spoken as if there was no book,
> Except that the reader leaned above the page,
>
> Wanted to lean, wanted much most to be
> The scholar to whom his book is true, . . .

For this reader at this moment, there is a graced unity of experience. The quiet and calm, far from being the background for this experience, are inseparable from it. Book and reader, quiet and calm are one.

> The quiet was part of the meaning, part of the mind:
> The access of perfection to the page.
>
> And the world was calm. The truth in a calm world,
> In which there is no other meaning, itself
>
> Is calm, itself is summer and night, itself
> Is the reader leaning late and reading there.

There is even, I would venture to say, a sacred quality to this act of reading. I don't mean to suggest that the reader is reading "religious" scripture. Nor do I mean to suggest that he is engaged in an overt act of worship, prayer, or meditation. But there is a reverential quality to this act, an aliveness and attentiveness, which I think of as sacred, even when the material being read or studied is of the kind we would normally call secular. It has more to do with the quality of attention and care being brought to bear than with the nature of the object of study.

The book of course has its roots in distinctly religious territory. The codex — the form of the book made by binding folded sheets of paper or animal skins together into a single volume — is about two thousand years old. It was first adopted for use within early Christian communities as a vehicle for their version of the Bible. Jewish communities wrote their sacred scripture on rolls or scrolls, and by moving to the relatively new codex form, Christians may well have been visibly demonstrating the rupture with their Jewish roots. At any rate, Christian communities seem to have embraced the codex by about 100 C.E. Its adoption took much longer in other communities and for other forms of content. Two hundred years later, Roger Chartier reports, a full fifty percent of Greek literary and scientific works were still being produced as rolls.[3]

If reading can be a sacred act, it can be many other things as well, and recent scholarship has been exploring its multiplicity of forms and functions. An interdisciplinary field of study known variously as the history of the book, print culture history, or just book history has taken reading as one of its central preoccupations. In earlier eras, literature was thought of as a succession of books — or, more exactly, *texts*. Much scholarly attention was devoted to studying the transmission of texts as they were copied and recopied, printed and reprinted. Textual critics and scholars collated and evaluated variant manuscripts and editions, attempting to reconcile them and to ferret out errors. Using highly sophisticated sleuthing techniques, some even managed to determine the exact order in which pages were printed, locating individual pieces of type (say, a letter *n* with a broken serif) and watching where they were reused.

Practitioners of the new book history — historians, literary scholars, sociologists, anthropologists, and librarians — have been less concerned with books or texts per se than with the human activities within which these are embedded. As Robert Darnton, one of its preeminent practitioners, explains, this new field "might even be called the social and cultural history of communication by print, if that were not such a mouthful, because its purpose is to understand how ideas were transmitted through print and how exposure to the printed word affected the thought and behavior of mankind during the last five hundred years."[4] From this perspective, to study books is to attempt to reconstruct how they have been made, used, and viewed at particular times and in particular communities — and how they have been *read*. "Literature itself," says Darnton, "no longer looks like a succession of great books by great men, or '*l'homme et l'oeuvre*,' according to the old French formula for imposing order on it. It is not even a corpus of texts. Instead, it is an activity: readers making sense of symbols printed on pages, or, in a word, reading."[5]

What this new focus has brought to light is how little we actually know about past reading practices, and, for that matter, how little is known about the range of reading practices people engage in today. As the literary theorist Tzvetan Todorov has observed: "Nothing is more commonplace than the reading experience, and yet nothing is more unknown. Reading is such a matter of course that, at first glance, it seems there is nothing to say about it."[6] Yet it is exactly such practices, invisible in their ordinariness, that have the potential to be rich sources of insight. Recent books with titles like *Reading the Romance, Reading in America, Reading Books, Listening for the Text,* and *The Ethnography of Reading* point to an expanding set of investigations into the range of reading practices in different eras, among different classes, and within different communities.

Reading, it turns out, is far more than the simple transformation of visible letterforms into meanings; it is a complex set of physical, cognitive, and social practices that have varied with time and place. Wallace Stevens's silent, solitary, intensely concentrated reader, far from illustrating the one true form of reading, represents instead a particularly modern archetype of what it means to read. Until the twelfth century, for example, most reading was done aloud. A text was akin to a script — something to be spoken. (In this respect, a book really *was* a talking thing, made to speak through the reader's mouth.) Even when someone read alone, to himself or herself, it was still generally by vocalizing. To read was therefore to hear: to hear one's own voice and thus to hear "the voices of the pages."[7] Monasteries were hardly the silent places we now imagine, but were instead "communities of mumblers," in Ivan Illich's words, since the practice of devotional reading, an essential ingredient in monastic life, produced a constant murmur.[8]

To be sure, silent reading was known and practiced as far back as Greek and Roman times. But it seems to have been a relative rarity. Although silent reading was known in ancient Israel, Daniel Boyarin notes, the principal meaning of the Hebrew verb that we now translate as "to read," was to call out — that is, to read out loud, to proclaim in public.[9] And in his *Confessions,* Saint Augustine reports his surprise at discovering that Ambrose, the bishop of Milan, could read without making a sound: "When he read, his eyes followed the pages and his heart pondered the meaning, though his voice and tongue were still."[10] The adoption of silent reading as a normal and unremarkable practice from the twelfth century on seems to have been occasioned by a number of factors, including the introduction of word separation.

In our modern cultural idealization, as illustrated in Stevens's poem, reading is a solitary activity. We may be surrounded by others — in a library reading room, on a train, in bed beside our partner — but we are "alone with others." For many centuries, however, reading was not only a vocalized process, it was an explicitly social activity, accomplished with and for others. If you read aloud, you were likely to be reading to others. And those *listening* were themselves considered to be reading — not because they were looking at the text, but because they were *hearing* it. "All those who, with the reader, are immersed in this hearing milieu are equals before the sound," says Ivan Illich, speaking of monastic reading. "It makes no difference who reads, as it makes no difference who rings the bell."[11] (Of course, reading is still at times a group activity: parents read to children at home, librarians read to children in public settings, authors read to adults at public events called "readings." It is also worth noting that solitary reading always was, and still is, inherently social: how we read is ultimately determined by social conventions and community membership.)

We also take for granted easy access to large numbers of books. To be a reader today — and certainly to be a *serious* reader — is to read many books, to compare them, to browse, peruse, skim, and scan them. But for many centuries, reading was generally a kind of re-reading. Few books were available, and those that were — most notably the Bible — were read deeply and repeatedly. Today's reading habits — which scholars call "extensive reading" to distinguish them from earlier "intensive" practices — are the product of a number of changes over a number of centuries: the shift from vocalized to silent reading and from a meditative to a more scholarly approach, the greater availability of books thanks to the invention of the printing press and the adoption of paper, and dramatic increases in literacy.[12]

But changes in the technologies and the character of modern life may be putting an end to reading in depth. That's the fear, at any rate, in some quarters. In a short essay called "The End of Bookishness?"[13]

the literary theorist George Steiner suggests that the five-hundred-year history of modern book culture may be coming to an end, and, with it, certain habits of deep reading. It isn't that the book has gone away, but rather that the cultural conditions for this kind of reading — "the economics of space and of leisure on which a certain kind of 'classical reading' hinges" — are fast disappearing. ("Already the silences, the arts of concentration and memorization, the luxuries of time on which 'high reading' depended are largely disposed," he puts it nearly a decade later, in a review of Alberto Manguel's *A History of Reading*.)[14] And yet, even as Steiner sees the writing on the wall, he looks to the survival of that thread of deep reading which has stretched over centuries, if not millennia. "I would not be surprised," he says in the penultimate paragraph, "if that which lies ahead for classical modes of reading resembles the monasticism from which those modes sprung. I sometimes dream of *houses of reading* — a Hebrew phrase — in which those passionate to learn how to read well would find the necessary guidance, silence, and complicity of disciplined companionship." Ivan Illich echoes Steiner in hoping that people "who discover their passion for a life centered on reading" can be initiated "into one or the other of several 'spiritualities' or styles of celebrating the book."[15]

Steiner and Illich seem to suggest that the reading of books can only survive as a marginal, almost cloistered, practice. Theirs turns out to be a surprisingly moderate position, at least as compared with the hyperbolic extremes in the ongoing debate about the future of the book. On one side of this debate are the technological visionaries, for whom the book is a technology, like the gramophone or the typewriter, whose time has gone. Book lovers, according to these technophiles, are simply "addicted to the look and feel of tree flakes encased in dead cow" (as one commentator, William J. Mitchell, so provocatively put it in his 1995 book *City of Bits*).[16] They just need to get over it.

The bibliophiles are equally fervent, however, and equally intransigent. They see themselves as defenders of one of humankind's greatest sources of wisdom and light. For them, the technophiles are uneducated and misguided *engineers* (for God's sake!) — hardly a group to be trusted with the divine gifts of truth and beauty. Simon Jenkins, a columnist in the *The Times* of London, sees digital technologies — specifically the Internet and the Web — as just the latest in a series of grand, overblown visions that are doomed to failure. "The history of technology is littered with such crassness," he says.[17] All the current talk about hypertext as a medium that will liberate the reader from the tyranny of the author is pure hype. He cites *The Future of the Book,* a collection of essays edited by Geoffrey Nunberg,[18] as one of the sources of such "rubbish." Yes, the Internet has its place, alongside the microfiche, the Filofax, and the telephone. But take a good hard look at the way it is *really* shaping up — as "a sex-and-shopping medium, plus intranets for specialists."

Besides, and most important, the book's future is secure simply because of what it is. The book is "an artifice of undying appeal." It is eternal, "a shelter for the human spirit." It "stands as the supreme artifact of human creativity." "The book needs no helping hand," he concludes. "It stands majestic on its own two covers, a thing of beauty and a joy forever."

And so it goes, back and forth. The technophiles are for progress, for human evolution, for the solution of humankind's social and economic problems. The bibliophiles are secretly (or not so secretly) Luddites, hoping to return to an idealized past. Or is it the bibliophiles who are the true social prophets, the caretakers of the human soul? Perhaps *they* are the true visionaries, seers of the civilizing function of the book. In which case it is the technophiles who are the Luddites, afraid to embrace the true sources of human evolution. As Deborah Tannen has pointed out in a recent book, we live in an "argument culture," in which the complexities of life are conveniently reduced to the play of polar opposites.[19] Both sides represent extremes, and in this dispute, as Nunberg notes, each camp is guilty of fetishizing the book.

This has the feel of a religious argument, and not just because each camp sees itself as true believers struggling against the infidels. The book does indeed have religious roots, as I've already noted. If in our bodies, in our genetic material, we carry traces of our ancestors, then there may be a sense in which the form of the book also carries resonances of its sacred content and uses. (Form may not be so easily divorced from content.) Certainly Steiner and Illich see modern bookish practices drawing on earlier, explicitly religious forms of reading. And Carla Hesse, a professor of history at the University of California, Berkeley, sees in the makeup of the modern system of book production and consumption a bias toward a slower, more reflective approach to life. The book, she argues, is a form of deferral — "a slower and longer form of expression than a pamphlet or a broadside." Libraries, "the places of many books," carry these values too, for they "are modes of configuring reading that are slower and longer still. Libraries . . . are not simply points of access for documents, they are places of deep investigation, concentration, reflection, and contemplation. . . . Libraries are the cathedrals of the modern secular world. They are our most cherished spaces of contemplation and reflection upon human experience."[20]

If the bibliophiles are operating from, and defending, religious values, so too are the technophiles. For technophiles, the materiality of the book is an encumbrance ("tree flakes encased in dead cow"). Its pages, its binding, its general weightiness confine and limit what is ultimately most important about the book: its information content. If we could only liberate this information from its physical circumstances, like liberating the soul from the body, then it — and we — could breathe and operate with greater ease and freedom. Indeed, digital technologies now seem to hold out just this possibility. Paul Duguid has labeled this hope *liberation technology*. "Technology," he says, "is . . . called upon to do for information what theology sought to do for the soul. But this liberation technology is quite distinct from liberation theology, for where the latter turned from tending the soul to tending the body, liberation technology turns in the opposite direction, away from the text's embodiment toward information's pure essence."[21] He cites various technologists and hypertext aficionados who give voice to this view — among them Jay Bolter, who talks of "freeing the writing from the frozen structure of the page" and "liberating the text."[22]

Indeed, information seems to have become a kind of god for many of us today. Our assumption is that if we can just get the right information at the right time, good things will happen. (We will be liberated?) This is such a central plank in our information society that it is hard to see it as an article of faith, no less so than the belief that books will set us free. But what exactly is this stuff, information, that has such remarkable properties? In some ways it is like the ether, the hypothesized, invisible substance once thought to fill the universe. Information is all around us, morsels of fact and data. In itself it is pure (hence "pure information"): it has no shape, size, color, or weight. But it can be embedded in, or poured into, physical containers or carriers: documents, databases, and human heads. And it can be transferred from one container or vehicle to another, as when I read a document, thereby gleaning the information in it.[23]

Unfortunately for us, though, there seems to be too much of it. Daily, we face information in such abundance that it threatens to overwhelm us. Twenty years ago, long before the Internet had become a household utility, Herbert Simon, the Nobel laureate in economics, was suggesting that it might just be possible to have too much of a good thing. "In a world where information is relatively scarce," he said, "and where problems for decision are few and simple, information is always a positive good. In a world where attention is a major scarce resource, information may be an expensive luxury, for it may turn our attention from what is important to what is unimportant. We cannot afford to attend to information simply because it is there."[24]

More recently, Richard Lanham, a professor of English at UCLA, has pointed to a certain irony in the phrase "information economy." Economics, as he understands it, is concerned with the management of scarce resources. But "[i]n a society based on information, the chief scarce commodity would presumably be information, not goods." Sounding a good deal like Simon, he goes on to say, "we are drowning in information, not suffering a dearth of it. Dealing with this superabundant flow is sometimes compared to drinking from a firehose. In such a society, the scarcest commodity turns out to be not information but the human attention needed to cope with it."[25] His point is that what we lack are tools and strategies for managing this scarce resource.

Observations of this kind have in recent years led to calls to formulate an "economics of attention." Warren Thorngate, a psychologist, has proposed six principles of attentional economics.[26] The first of these, the principle of *Fixed Attentional Assets,* states that "attention is a finite and non-renewable resource." The second, the principle of *Singular Attentional Investments,* states that "attention can, in general, be invested in only one activity at a time." Whether we think of these as noble "principles" or simply commonsensical observations, together they serve to remind us that we are finite creatures with a tiny attentional capacity. The implication is clear: that we should spend our attention well, that we must make careful decisions about what we will pay attention to if we are to live well and fully. But Thorngate's fifth principle adds an important cautionary note. The principle of *Exploratory Attentional Expenses* states that "whenever we search for and choose attentional investments, the acts of searching and choosing themselves require attentional investments." To spend our limited attentional budget well, we must make wise choices, but the act of choosing will cost us too, sometimes dearly.

And so we come back to the sad truth that there is too much to read and too little time, so that we are continually being faced with decisions about what to read, when, and to what depth. On airplanes and trains you see people with book bags and attaché cases filled with books, papers, and newspaper and magazine articles, which are being carried about in the hope that they will finally be read. Ours is certainly not the first age to be overwhelmed by masses of materials. (Geoffrey Nunberg notes that this very complaint has been raised in a number of eras, stretching back three centuries at least.)[27] But we live in an age where the reading we practice seems more and more to involve short bursts of shallow attendings.

Michael Joyce, a professor of English at Vassar and a hypertext author and enthusiast, has suggested that this will be our primary mode of reading in the future. "[I]n an age like ours," he proposes, "a sustained attention span may be less useful than successive attendings."[28] It is not so much the books that threaten us (who has time to read books?) but the information fragments — sound bites, factoids, data — flying at us from all directions and all media. The Web seems to be the latest manifestation of this: a technology that can link and lead us to endless information fragments. "Reading what people have had to say about the future of knowledge in an electronic world," Nunberg observes, "you sometimes have the picture of somebody holding all the books in the library by their spines and shaking them until the sentences fall out loose in space."[29]

Under such circumstances, reading becomes a kind of a mining operation. We dig into and work with the materials before us to extract their essence, their information content. (Or someone else does this for us: the editors of *Reader's Digest* or *Cliff's Notes*.) Always in a rush, we want to liberate just the information we need, as quickly as possible: to find that client's phone number or e-mail address, to get the latest stock quotes for the companies we've invested in, or the weather report for the city we're about to fly to. The more efficiently and effectively we can do this, and the less we are distracted by, or beholden to, the physical embodiment of the materials before us, the better off we will be. No wonder that the technophile sees the physical properties of the book as an encumbrance, a restraint.

But it should be clear enough that Wallace Stevens's reader is doing something else. In his reading practice, it is perhaps not so easy to distinguish the essential from the inessential, the wheat from the chaff. For this reader is more concerned with the *experience of reading* than with the (mere) extraction of information. As I find when I read *Leaves of Grass,* it is the whole that matters: the weight of the book as held in the lap, the texture of the paper, the sound the pages make when they are turned, the look of the typeface, the nature of the illustrations, will all inevitably contribute to the reading experience.

That the book is a physical object and that the reader is a sensing, material being are integral, and unavoidable, dimensions of the experience. The qualities of the surrounding environment matter too: the light, the air, the furniture (how it supports the book and the reader's body).

All these features come together — the material being read in its form and content, the reader's state of mind and body, the physical environment — to produce a unique reading experience. And as any serious reader knows, the states of attunement and awareness that sometimes arise can have a transcendent character. Indeed, transcendence isn't a bad word to characterize both kinds of reading. Reading for information aims to transcend the physical properties of the document, the reader, and the reading process to glean the essence of what is being read. Reading as experience aims to enter into the reading itself — the reading process, the material being read — and thereby to achieve, in its own quite different way, a measure of higher, or transcendent, understanding.

But in a world in which the acquisition and manipulation of information is primary, deep reading *as an experience* appears to be a luxury. It has no justification in the language of information; it is something we simply can't afford to do. The reader "leaning late and reading there" (in Wallace Stevens's words) is doing something else, which can't be explained as information-seeking or foraging, or even as knowledge management. And when George Steiner and Ivan Illich express the hope that houses of reading might be created, it is because they see the need for, and the possibility of protecting, this mode of life.

If the contrast between bibliophiles and technophiles is extreme — and, to a large extent, artificial — then so too is the distinction between reading for information and reading as experience. Surely when we read for information we needn't ignore all properties of the reading experience. In fact, we can't. Whether or not we're conscious of it, the visual — and, more generally, the physical — properties of the document provide us with clues, with information, which help us interpret what we're reading. And when we read for experience —

for pleasure, for insight, or perhaps even as prayer — we needn't ignore the information content of what we're reading. Just as our attention is continually shifting when we're in conversation with a friend — between her words, her person, our thoughts, the environment — so too will attention continually shift in any act of reading.

Still, this stark and somewhat overdrawn distinction between two kinds of reading has its uses. In the endless discussions about books, computers, information, and the Internet we all seem to be having these days, someone inevitably leaps to defend the book. "You can't take a laptop to bed," that person will say. Or he will make reference to the feel of paper, or even the scent of a book. Remarks like these tend to be the kiss of death. The speaker is immediately labeled as suspect — as soft, romantic, retrograde. The problem is that we don't have the language for talking about these dimensions, and so, when people begin to wax poetic about, say, the smell or feel of books, they are immediately marginalized (a curious expression). To be sure, in such statements there can be a clinging to the old simply for the sake of familiarity. But that needn't — indeed, isn't — all that is being said. Unfortunately we are now so oriented toward information-seeking and use that we have increasingly become blind to other, equally important dimensions of reading — and, I would even say, of living.

What's more, to voice any concerns about the direction in which technology is taking us is taken to mean that you are necessarily an extremist; it suggests you are a Luddite, wanting to pull the plug on the whole enterprise. But this needn't be the case, and it certainly isn't the case for me. By pointing to other forms of reading and other bookish practices, my aim is to contribute to a healthier mix and a healthier balance. There is no denying that information-seeking and reading for information are important skills. But when taken to an extreme, they lead to the atomization of our written forms and to the corresponding fragmentation of attention. We need a more varied diet, I am convinced, and it is helpful to be reminded that our bookish roots still carry the resonance of other ways of reading and other ways to spend our limited attentional budget.

In arguing about the future of the book, we have a tendency to talk *past* one another. When we are attacking or defending the book, *which book* are we talking about? What exactly is it that we care so fervently about, whether for or against? Is it the form of the book, the codex? Or certain kinds of traditional bookish content, i.e., literature? Or are we perhaps arguing about certain modes of approaching the world, more-contemplative ways of reading and thinking? (This hardly exhausts the possibilities.)

Certainly the book functions as an important symbol in our culture, and it can symbolize many things, among them the weight of history, cultural authority, and modes of knowing. Unless we are clear about what we are after, and which values we wish to preserve, we risk losing by winning. It is possible, for example, that the codex will survive the onslaught of digital technologies having been stripped of the bookish practices that, to my mind at least, make up its heart and soul. It is also possible that the codex will disappear but we will find other vehicles around which more-contemplative forms of reading can arise. (Who is to say that e-books won't serve this purpose? Surely it is too early to tell.) And it is even possible, although I doubt it, that reading itself in all its various forms will disappear, but our culture will find other arenas in which to exercise its need for reflection. (Reading is hardly the only guise in which reflection and contemplation appear today.) What is it we want to hold on to, and what is it we want to move toward?

7

Libraries and the Anxiety of Order

SOME YEARS BACK, I was shocked when I walked into the Saks Fifth Avenue in the Stanford Shopping Center. Instead of finding the brightly lit store with aisles full of expensive merchandise beautifully displayed — the shop I'd visited many times before — I found a dingy, rundown excuse for a store. Paint was peeling off the walls, display counters were nicked and tattered, and the merchandise was in disarray; it had a slightly used air about it. This could well have been a dream, the anxious sort where you return home to find that everything has changed. But it wasn't. I walked outside, just to make sure I had found the right building, but also to clear my head from the shock and confusion. As I entered the building the second time, I noticed a sign I hadn't seen the first time. The sign explained that Saks was closing and that the building was being used as a "seconds" store for Saks merchandise.

Evidently what I had encountered was a store in decline. Through their elaborate and highly tuned order (lighting, displays, music, and so on), fancy department stores like Saks try to suggest a timeless and perfect order, an effortless happiness, which can be ours if we will only buy the right things. We are never meant to see the huge amount of work that is required to maintain the illusion. I had come upon the inevitable decline that occurs when the invisible, ever-ongoing work of maintaining order is withheld. And what I experienced was not just the shock of the unexpected but a confrontation with the chaos that lies just behind the carefully maintained façade.

Of course it isn't just stores or shopping malls that need to be constantly maintained. Everything does. Gardens go to seed, bridges fall down, clothes become frayed and stained, and human relationships wither without regular attention. The same is true for documents. Without proper care they decay, lose their intelligibility and intellectual currency, and become inaccessible. And this isn't just true of paper documents. We are quickly discovering that digital materials, too, need to be properly tended. Web pages disappear and links break. Digital media — floppy disks, CD-ROMs, and so on — degrade after a matter of years, and the files stored on them have to be copied to new media if they are to be preserved.

These problems are only magnified and compounded when we have more than a couple of documents. For now we have to organize or arrange them in some more or less systematic fashion. There are so many places in our lives where documents tend to pool or congregate. And in each of these places we have to do something with them, if only to sift through them as needed. People's bookcases are an obvious enough collection point. (Henry Petroski has recently written a book-length meditation on just this subject.)[1] I am an inveterate browser of people's bookshelves, always curious to see what other people have been reading, and which books they choose to display. But I am equally curious about the manner in which they array them. Are their books neatly aligned, like the leatherbound books in the Levenger catalog, or do they teeter on the shelf at odd angles? Do they use bookends, or the sides of the bookcase, for support? Does there seem to be an intellectual ordering to the books (cookbooks here, travel books there)? Are they arranged by size, or is there no discernible organizing principle? ("To arrange a library," says Borges, "is to practice, in a quiet and modest way, the art of criticism.")

Less obvious, but equally intriguing, are people's refrigerators. There you will find collections — unselfconscious collages — of photographs, newspaper articles, theater tickets, kids' drawings, calendars, and all manner of flyers and announcements of future events.

It may be hard to discern an ordering principle at work, but generally there is one, however partial. When you've run out of space on the refrigerator door, which sheets do you decide to take down first? Or if you are going to double up more than one page using the same clips or magnets, which one goes on top? Do you stack them or overlap them? Even if you don't have a single organizing principle (such as putting the most current announcement on top), this doesn't mean that you aren't organizing the refrigerator's display.

Our wallets and purses provide a different kind of collection point. Refrigerators and home bookcases tend to reside in the more-public spaces of our private dwellings. You don't generally display items there that you don't want others to see. Wallets and purses, by contrast, are most definitely private territory: you don't poke around in someone else's wallet or purse without permission unless you've found it in a public place and you're trying to identify the owner, or unless you're up to no good. Many of the materials there have a certain bureaucratic or commercial power — paper currency, credit and debit cards, and driver's licenses. But here too you may find newspaper clippings, photos, fortunes from fortune cookies — some of the same materials you find more publicly displayed on refrigerators. Compartments of different sizes encourage at least a minimal sorting and separating by genre and function: IDs versus paper money versus photos versus tickets.

We are possessed of a remarkable range of technologies for organizing our document collections, especially those realized on paper. This should hardly be surprising, since paper has been such a crucial medium for so long. Just walk down the aisles of an Office Depot or your local stationer, and you will find a seemingly endless array of tools and devices: file folders and filing cabinets; bookcases; stacking trays for the desk; pushpins and cork bulletin boards. In some cases we have a number of alternatives to accomplish (at least superficially) the same aims. This is particularly true when it comes to keeping sheets of paper together. Do you staple them, or perhaps clip them with a paper clip (large or small, silver or colored), or with a binder clip? Do you place them in a manila file folder, in an envelope, or in a clear plastic cover? Do you punch holes in them and insert them into a ring binder? The decision may partly be an aesthetic and a personal one, but there can also be a functional component: How likely are you to want to separate the sheets, or insert new ones?

Grouping — or sorting, or categorizing, or classifying (call it what you will) — is one of the most powerful intellectual tools we have for managing our lives. It is something we do all the time. "To classify is human," Geoffrey C. Bowker and Susan Leigh Star say in their book *Sorting Things Out: Classification and Its Consequences.*

> We all spend large parts of our days doing classification work, often tacitly, and we make up and use a range of ad hoc classifications to do so. We sort dirty dishes from clean, white laundry from colorfast, important e-mail to be answered from e-junk. We match the size and type of our car tires to the amount of pressure they should accept. Our desktops are a mute testimony to a kind of muddled folk classification: papers that must be read by yesterday, *but that have been there since last year;* old professional journals that really should be read and even in fact may someday be, *but that have been there since last year;* assorted grant applications, tax forms, various work-related surveys and forms waiting to be filled out for everything from parking spaces to immunizations. These surfaces may be piled with sentimental cards that are already read, *but which cannot yet be thrown out,* alongside reminder notes to send similar cards to parents, sweethearts, or friends for their birthdays, all piled on top of last year's calendar (which — who knows? — may be useful at tax time).[2]

Of all the places where documents pool and accrete, people's desks are undoubtedly my favorite. They offer such a rich snapshot of modern life, of modern practices and pressures. Looking at one is a bit like examining a tidepool. At first it seems static and uninteresting. But once you start to pay attention, you begin to see what a complex ecosystem is present, and how much richly structured and diverse activity is going on right before your eyes. On someone's desktop, you're likely to see a heterogeneous mix of documents: some bureaucratic and administrative; some personal and private; some published. On my own desk right now I have three small images propped up against the wall, two photographs and a postcard. In addition, I have drafts of various chapters of this book, some in colored file folders, some loose, some stapled, some clipped. They are loosely organized into two piles, with drafts and notes for the current chapter spread out over the piles and drifting onto the bare desktop. I also have a handwritten to-do list, my Filofax (calendar), and a vertically arranged stack of bills and other correspondence still to be dealt with.

Each of these documents has its own trajectory and its own rhythm. They only appear to be static, like Zeno's tortoise, if you look at them in the moment. Some, like the to-do list and certain chapter drafts, are just passing through, and are destined for the trash in short order. Others, like the postcard and the photos, are meant to stay for a while. Some of the book drafts will eventually make their way to my files. Other documents have an even more complex future ahead of them. The utilities bill, for example, is a composite document, and its various parts will eventually be sent off in different directions: when the bill-paying urge finally strikes, I will tear the lower portion of the bill at the perforation and send it back to the utilities company with a check in the envelope provided, while I file the upper portion "for my records" (which probably just means tossing it in a box in the closet). At the same time I will throw out the envelope in which the bill first arrived, as well as the newsletter advising me on water conservation.

But I am not interested only in the range of documents on the desktop, the strategies for organizing them, or their life stories; I am equally interested in the psychological stresses our desktops evoke in us. It is the rare person who isn't somewhat traumatized by the state of his or her desk. People don't seem to worry too much about the state of their refrigerators — what's on the outside, at any rate. We don't tend to apologize if there are lots of announcements, photographs, and shopping lists posted on the door. It's a very different matter, though, when it comes to our desks, either at home or in the office. We are embarrassed by our own documentary clutter and mess and invoke standard jokes to express and manage our embarrassment ("a clean desk is the sign of a disorganized mind"). We judge our desks by standards that are not our own: the one obsessively neat person we know whose desktop is always tidy; the executive whose files are managed by an assistant; the professional organizations, libraries, and archives, that work, day in and day out, to keep their collections in order. But in all these cases — and in libraries especially, I believe — if you scratch the surface you will find the same anxieties of order and disorder being played out.

Libraries have been in the business of collecting, organizing, preserving, and providing access to documents for thousands of years. If we think our individual efforts are daunting, imagine the pressures on institutions responsible for overseeing thousands, even millions, of culturally significant documents. (The mission of the fabled Library of Alexandria, created more than two thousand years ago, was nothing less than to amass "the books of all the people of the world."[3] It is thought to have held as many as 500,000 scrolls.)[4] Because of the scope of their enterprise, libraries have been forced to develop highly systematic methods of organization — methods that could work relatively satisfactorily for huge numbers of works, and that could transcend the skills and knowledge of particular individuals.

Central to these systems has been one simple but extremely powerful documentary form: the list. Lists were one of the earliest forms of writing, no doubt because of their usefulness in accounting and administrative practices. The anthropologist Jack Goody notes that of the clay tablets dating to the fourteenth century B.C.E. excavated in one Syrian town in 1929, the vast majority are lists: tax lists and lists of rations, occupational lists, census records, and so on.[5] Much as lists could be used to keep track of people, taxes, crops, and livestock, they could also be used to keep track of documents. This seems obvious enough to us now. But I can only guess that a leap of imagination was required to realize that written forms could be used to manage other written forms.

Lists of library holdings — or catalogs (from the Greek *katalogos*, meaning "list") — are therefore quite ancient. When the French

Egyptologist Auguste Mariette excavated the "House of Papyrus" at Edfu in the 1860s, he found none of its contents, but still discernible on its walls were inscriptions listing the library's holdings. This early catalog was divided in two: one list covered works on magic; the subject matter of the second — with titles like "The Book of what is to be found in the temple," "The Book which governs the return of the stars," and "The Book of places and of what is in them" — is harder to discern.[6] For the Library of Alexandria, the poet Callimachus is said to have compiled a catalog filling 120 volumes.[7] This long history notwithstanding, it is only in the last 150 years that cataloging as a systematic, professional enterprise has emerged. Indeed, the catalog produced through these professional practices, the modern catalog, is inseparable from the birth of the modern library. Both are products of industrialization and bureaucratization.

In the United States, much of the initial energy for the development of modern libraries came from the desire to supplement public education. The first public library opened its doors in Boston in 1854. The argument for it, as articulated by its chief sponsor, George Ticknor, was a lofty one. It would complement and extend Boston's system of public education: "Why should not," Tiknor asked, "this prosperous and liberal city extend some reasonable amount of aid to the foundation and support of a noble public library, to which the young people of both sexes, when they leave the schools, can resort for those works which pertain to general culture, or which are needful for research into any branch of useful knowledge?"[8] The idea spread rapidly. By 1875 nearly two hundred publicly funded libraries had been created around the country.

The following year, a hundred librarians met in Philadelphia and formed the American Library Association. One of the central figures was Melvil Dewey. Dewey was only twenty-five years old at the time, but through his energy, ambition, and inventiveness he was already making a name for himself. While still an undergraduate at Amherst College he worked as an assistant in its library. During this time he invented the scheme that still bears his name, the Dewey Decimal Classification (DDC). The DDC was an attempt to sort or group books into useful categories. Naturally there are endless ways to group books — by size, by number of pages, by author's last name — some of which will prove to be more useful than others. The DDC aimed to classify them by their content or subject matter. What makes this such a daunting task is that books can be written about virtually any subject in the world. So if you're going to create a classification scheme for the subject matter of books, you've got to create a set of categories that span all of creation — at least insofar as human beings conceive of, speak, and write about it.

Dewey was hardly the first person to undertake to classify all of human knowledge. Nor was he the first to seize on such a scheme to organize books. In the early seventeenth century, Francis Bacon had created a highly influential classification of knowledge that was used as the basis for innumerable library catalogs from the seventeenth to the nineteenth century.[9] What seems to have been most original about Dewey's work was the way he used a classification of books to "mark and park" them — to place them on shelves. Up to that time, books were kept in fixed locations. Dewey was struck by "the waste of time and money in the constant recataloging and reclassifying made necessary by the almost universally used system where a book was numbered according to the particular room, tier and shelf where it chanced to stand on that day, instead of by the class to which it belonged."[10] In his rethinking of this system, books were given a unique (decimal) classification number once and for all, which could be used to shelve them relative to one another. This reduced the effort required of the library staff, and made searching and browsing easier for patrons at a time when public library stacks were being opened up to the general public.

Time management was a central obsession of Dewey's, beginning in adolescence. As the historian Dee Garrison tells it, Dewey's relationship to time was part of a larger pattern, an obsessive-compulsive need to control the world around him.

> The attempt to control all eventualities presented time as a special problem to Dewey. Time, an enemy to be overcome, was a threat

to all his plans and projects. Since a guarantee of the future was his prime concern, he experienced time in the present as being wasted unless it were filled to the brim. The present did not have significance in itself because his interest was solely in the future. . . . Day after day was consumed in a futile and desperate struggle to control the passage of time itself. Unable to tolerate ambiguities and unpredictabilities, Dewey sought to dismiss time as a realistic limitation on his life. He craved certitude — desired to foretell, foresee, and exert control before the fact. Thus Dewey's lifelong concentration on detail is best understood as a measure of self-protection.[11]

In the service of this vision of time-saving as a path to greater life, Dewey became an "irrepressible reformer," in the words of another biographer, Wayne Wiegand.[12] By the time he was eighteen he had already identified four time-saving crusades he would pursue throughout his life: simplified spelling, the adoption of the metric system, shorthand, and written abbreviations. (The simplified spelling of words like *catalog* and the naming of the New York State Thruway are directly attributable to Dewey's influence. Dewey also changed his own given name, from Melville to Melvil.) But it is his library work that in the end was the most successful of his reformist enterprises and for which he is most remembered.

In trying to locate the magnitude and significance of Dewey's work for his time, Francis Miksa, a professor of library and information science at the University of Texas, resorts to the language of *our* times. He casts Dewey as a savvy businessman, an entrepreneur: "But the fact is the DDC was an entrepreneur's dream, a brilliant invention which would have thrilled anyone who had a business sense and appreciated the value of innovation. It was like an 1870s DOS or Netscape in that it did something that no one else had ever successfully done before — it organized books in a reasonably efficient way in libraries."[13] This was clearly a major achievement in itself. But Dewey also played a central role in establishing librarianship as a profession. He had a strong hand in the formation of the American Library Association and its journal, the *Library Journal*. He founded the first library school in the country, at Columbia University in 1887, which was groundbreaking not just because of its subject matter but because he insisted on admitting women to the program.

Dewey also founded the Library Bureau, a commercial venture, in 1882, to develop and sell equipment to libraries and businesses. A few years ago I was lucky enough to stumble upon a copy of the 1909 Library Bureau catalog in a secondhand bookstore. (By coincidence, it was discarded from the library of the college I attended as an undergraduate.) It contains highly detailed illustrations of the equipment they sold. Nearly all this equipment is instantly recognizable as the equipment we've seen and used in public libraries: cabinets with long drawers to hold catalog cards; library tables, benches, and chairs; inkstands, paperweights, and stamps; and a whole range of paper forms, including the "borrowers' cards" stuck in the backs of library books to record when books were borrowed and returned.

The Library Bureau sold practices as well as products. Imbued with Dewey's missionary zeal, it aimed to teach libraries how to create vast efficiencies through the use of its equipment. In the opening paragraphs of its 1909 catalog, it makes clear that it views order or organization in the service of users as the central function of the library:

> The development of library science during the last quarter century has made it evident that a library in the true sense is not merely a certain number of books, but rather a collection of books so arranged that they may be conveniently used for reading or reference. Five thousand well-chosen volumes classified and administered according to modern methods may better deserve the name of library than four times the number carelessly or erratically arranged, even though the larger collection might contain every volume to be found in the smaller group.[14]

If Dewey isn't better known outside the library profession, it is perhaps because of a number of personal flaws that offset his genius for organization. He was intense, arrogant, driven, and possessed of an exaggerated moralism. He was racist and anti-Semitic. He could be duplicitous. And "he crafted into the normal practices of institutions he created the striking character flaws and social prejudices he himself embodied." "That there is so much to dislike about Melvil Dewey's character," says Wayne Wiegand, "may explain why his legacy has been under-studied in recent decades."[15]

Yet despite all this — or perhaps because of it — there is something mesmerizing about Dewey. He made a deep impression on people. A schoolgirl who met him in 1892 described her impression on being ushered into this office. Observing him, "[i]t was like watching a fine machine, an electric machine — the air about him was vibrant with energy. . . . His decisiveness, the sparkling darkness of his face (dominated by his vivid eyes), his intense energy impressed me deeply. Indeed, I was a little awed . . . I had come into contact with an immense force."[16] And more than a hundred years after this observation, the force of his crazy brilliance still attracts notice. For Dee Garrison, he is to be studied for what he can teach us about a certain type of personality, a "reforming 'savior' mentality."[17]

My own fascination with Dewey comes from a somewhat different angle. On the one hand, I see him as a product and symbol of his age. He lived through a period that worshiped the god of efficiency and created bureaucratic systems of control on a scale and to a degree that were previously unimaginable. With his exaggerated fears and anxieties, and his enormous energy and intelligence, he represents that spirit well. But at the same time that he speaks from and for this particular era, he also embodies a response to life that is found in all of us to varying degrees. For there is, it seems to me, a degree of anxiety embedded in all our attempts to order and organize, to control the world around us. The discomfort we feel when faced with our disorganized desks, our cluttered offices, our messy homes, is emblematic of a more general aversion to mess. Here is how I understand this.

Clutter or disorganization, first of all, alerts us to real, often immediate problems in our lives. The cluttered desk speaks of the amount of work awaiting us, the sheer volume of it. And the fact that the desk's contents aren't better organized speaks of a lack of time and attention. (With more time and attention, we would get better organized, wouldn't we?) Who wouldn't be anxious when faced with too many tasks to do, in too little time? What's more, because we aren't better organized, we are likely to work less effectively. Who wouldn't feel terrible when being strangled by paperwork?

There is ample reason, then, to see mess — or clutter, or disorder — as a signpost pragmatically alerting us to trouble ahead, like a road sign warning about icy road conditions. But I think there is more to it than that. My sense is that the anxiety provoked by disorder is intimately connected with some of our most basic fears about survival and well-being. As human beings, we seem to crave order as much as we crave anything in life. With our minds — through the pursuit of science and religion, for example — we seek to discover a larger, meaningful order in the universe. And through our actions, we are continually working to create orderly patterns of behavior. Human culture, human society, is the collective enterprise by which we establish and maintain shared understandings and ways of behaving. Laws are a big part of this, as are ethical systems of conduct, codes of politeness, and group norms. To live with others is to participate in making, living out, and policing individual and collective conduct.

There is clearly survival value in such practices. Without guidelines for behavior that aim to minimize conflict and to manage it when it arises, great harm can come to individuals and to entire groups. We have only to look to the former Yugoslavia, or to Africa, to see what happens when dark destructive human tendencies take precedence over orderly conduct. Or we have only to look to the scenes of natural disasters to see how illness can achieve epidemic proportions when human-created systems of water purification, food storage, and burial are disrupted.

At times, it seems that human cultural order is no more than a thin veneer overlaid on a much wilder, uncontrollable, unknowable, and dangerous world. To the extent that this is so — to the extent that we live with this sense, however unconsciously — then order-making will be tinged with anxiety. And what makes the process of order-making all the more charged is the knowledge that it must continually be kept up. Rundown barns in the countryside, roadways with potholes, the state of our homes when we've neglected our cleaning duties, all testify to the decay that befalls any human enterprise that isn't continually maintained. Is it so farfetched to see our messy desks as silent reminders of the chaos that lies just beyond the trim lawns and cultured sensibilities of civilized life?

And so I see Dewey as a kind of anti-Whitman. The man portrayed in Whitman's poetry — "Walt Whitman, a kosmos" — is the great embracer of life. Far from needing to regularize or standardize or control it, he takes things as they come. The world is enough just as it is; there is an order, a logic to it, just as it is. Even death is to be accepted, celebrated. But for Dewey, the world must be shaped, bent, controlled. Far from accepting death, Dewey was terrified of it. "[T]he central key to an understanding of Dewey's personality is his over-riding preoccupation with death and the passage of time," Garrison says. This she sees as a characteristic of the obsessive personality. "The obsessive feels besieged, at every moment. The forced drivenness of his existence is to him a real life-and-death matter and if he does not do as he is driven to do, he is filled with panic. Dewey behaved as if his existence were continually threatened; he seemed to live in an imaginary jungle where the threat of death necessitated a constant guard."[18]

It is a curious fact that both Whitman and Dewey are known for their catalogs. Whitman's are free-flowing celebrations; their logic is that of the ecstatic witness proclaiming what he sees. In "Song of Myself" (my childhood copy), he takes note that:

> The pure contralto sings in the organ loft,
> The carpenter dresses his plank, the tongue of his foreplane
>   whistles its wild ascending lisp,
> The married and unmarried children ride home to their
>   Thanksgiving dinner,
> The pilot seizes the king-pin, he heaves down with a strong arm,

The mate stands braced in the whale-boat, lance and harpoon are
   ready, . . .

(He continues like this for nearly two pages.)

Dewey's catalogs, by contrast, are carefully constrained works of
bureaucratic order. Dewey, says Garrison, "had realized the obsessive's dream — to place all of human knowledge into *ten* tight
holes."[19] He created a *system* for manufacturing carefully constrained
catalogs. Here is what a small section of his classification scheme
looks like (a hierarchy of subject matters and the decimal numbers
associated with them):

600	Technology (Applied sciences)
610	Medical sciences Medicine
612	Human physiology
612.1	Blood and circulation
612.11	Blood
612.112	White corpuscles[20]

I am not so concerned with whether Whitman the man actually
lived his idealization or simply performed it. Nor with whether
Dewey was as obsessively compulsive as Garrison makes out. What
interests me most is the tendencies these men exemplify: one toward
observation and acceptance, the other toward control and reform.
Surely all of us possess both tendencies, in different combinations and
to different degrees.

Thanks to Whitman's gift and inspired efforts, we have access to a
particular mystical vision of the fullness of life. Thanks to Dewey's
gifts and inspired efforts (and the efforts of many others along with as
well as after him), we can identify all the editions of Whitman's work
and locate copies of them. Whitman begat Allen Ginsberg, Woody
Guthrie, Bob Dylan, and many others. Dewey begat a huge network
of libraries and librarians. In the United States alone there are 9,000
public libraries, 3,500 academic libraries, and 10,000 so-called special

libraries. In most of those institutions there are reference librarians devoted to helping patrons find just what they're looking for: a particular book, books on a particular topic, information needed to solve some problem or other. And hidden from normal view, from patrons' eyes, are catalogers and other "technical service" professionals, doing the ongoing work of collection development, cataloging, and so on.

Lately, however, the continued existence of this whole institution has come into question. The buildings the philanthropist Andrew Carnegie built, the systems Dewey invented, the ongoing efforts of many thousands of librarians, are now threatened by the latest technical innovations and by new types of materials, digital materials. But why *threatened,* you might ask. In one sense the latest digital technologies are a boon to libraries. Online catalogs and collection management tools hold out the possibility of improving library service: helping libraries keep track of their collections and make them available to patrons. Using scanners to read the bar codes in books, just to choose one specific example, greatly simplifies the process of checking out books, to the advantage of both library personnel and library users.

What's more, libraries have successfully accommodated to new materials in the past. Systems and practices first set up to handle books have been expanded to accommodate maps, serials (newspapers, magazines, and journals), microfiche, film, audiotapes, videotapes, and computer software. Not only have libraries been able to incorporate new materials, they have also met the challenge of incorporating new *technologies* — electric lights and ventilation systems in their early days, as well as typewriters, microfilm viewers, film projectors, computer workstations, and so on.

So, in one sense, the new digital documents are just another in the series of materials needing to be cataloged and made accessible. But in another sense, they seem to threaten the entire edifice, literally and figuratively. It is just possible that something bigger is afoot this time. The talk now is of *digital libraries,* perhaps as a replacement for the traditional, bricks-and-mortar kind. Many questions are now being asked: Will we really need more library buildings, essentially huge warehouses for books, at a time when digital materials can be stored so very compactly? Do we really need separate library institutions, for that matter, when the Web is, or gives evidence of becoming, a global library without walls? How necessary are cataloging and the library's other traditional order-making functions in this new environment? And what exactly are *digital libraries,* anyway? No one is quite sure.

Francis Miksa divides library history into eras. He calls the current era, which began in the mid-nineteenth century, the "modern library era," and he cautions against thinking of "the library" as a unitary phenomenon across time. "[L]ibrary historians," he points out, "typically assume a continuity in the history of libraries that goes back much further than a century or so (some going back to Mesopotamian civilization)."[21] Certainly all libraries have features in common, including collections of documents and catalogs of some sort or other. But,

> were we able to jump back in time to any but the most recent manifestations of the library — for example, to libraries before 1850 or so — the further back we traveled, the more uncomfortable we would find ourselves in calling what we found at any one point a library. Our discomfort would arise from using the modern library as a standard for measuring libraries of the past. I do not simply mean discomfort with the infrastructure of the library, although that would be a factor. Rather, I mean discomfort in terms of "subjective" differences — for example, that such agencies would not have the "feel" of the modern library, that they would not go about their business in the same way, that they would not have the same sense of goals.

The modern library, Miksa suggests, is the product and the expression of particular, time-bound social conditions. The modern library — and here he means the academic and the research library as well as what we have come to call the "public library" — came into being as a public institution, publicly funded and committed to making information broadly available for the sake of society. In the service of this mission, it drew on the philosophy and methods of modern bureaucracy.

Miksa believes we are now entering a new library era. The public space within which the modern library operated, and which it helped to sustain, is closing down. In its place will come private libraries. Thanks to computers, the Web, and who knows what else, we will all be able to create our own private "libraries in a box," with collections tuned and organized to our own specific needs. "Only a little reflection will show," he says, "that this new kind of library is not only a denial of the modern library's public space and general target population orientation, but it actually represents something of a return to the library era that preceded the modern library, when a library generally represented the private space of an individual or of a small group. Frankly, this reversion makes eminent sense to me for, ultimately, is not an excellent library one which is as personal in its selections and access mechanisms as the personal nature of the information seeking that prompted it?" Of course, we are likely to need help in creating such libraries and organizing them. Enter the librarian, who in the future, Miksa suggests, "will function primarily as an enabler, as a person who can help others create their own personal-space libraries, who can help families make their own family-space library systems with individual modes for family members, or who can help businesses create any one or more necessary personalized information systems."

These are certainly provocative words, and there is much here to question and debate: Must new kinds of libraries necessarily replace older kinds? (Surely private libraries continued to exist during the modern library era. Could we perhaps agree that private libraries will increase in number without assuming that libraries as public institutions will disappear?) Is the loss of public space and public funding inevitable, as Miksa makes it sound, or would it be a consequence of choices made explicitly or implicitly in the political realm — choices that *we* might have a say in?

What I find most useful about Miksa's analysis is the attention he directs to the word *library* and to the multiple societal conceptions that it can name. In the modern library era, the term has come to evoke a particular kind of social institution (one committed to providing communal access to information) that is realized by a particular organizational structure (the modern bureaucratic organization). As Miksa makes clear, this is a highly time-bound notion. Yet alongside this is a notion of libraries that is common across all eras: the notion of a collection. When Miksa talks about personal or private libraries, this is essentially what he means: personal or private *collections*.

This ambiguity between institution and collection is carried through in the phrase "digital library." For some groups, most notably librarians, the phrase refers most directly to *institutions that oversee digital collections,* while for other professions, primarily computer and information scientists, it refers to *digital collections,* without regard to the institutional settings (if any) in which they might be managed. (Notice that the phrase "software library" means a collection of computer programs or routines, and makes no reference to an institution.) *Digital library,* it seems to me, draws much of its power from this ambiguity: it provides a name for collections of digital materials that invokes the aura of the modern library and its social mission (library as social institution). But it does so without actually making any commitments to the public good (library as collection).

Library, however, carries yet another common meaning, which doesn't resonate in the phrase "digital library." A library is also a building — one that houses collections and the staff who tend them. In the modern library era, this sense of library is also rich with cultural commitments, for the library building is a public space in which citizens are guaranteed not only access to information but a space in which to read, write, and reflect. It is a shared sacred space held open through secular civic funding and participation.

It is by no means clear what will happen to libraries, in any of these senses. What *is* clear, however, is that digital materials will need to be ordered and organized. There is no getting away from this kind of invisible work, whether in department stores, in our offices, or in our homes. Someone has to do it. What also seems clear is that new methods of organization will be needed, methods that are unlikely to be simple extensions of those Dewey and his contemporaries concocted more than a century ago. Whether traditional libraries (or traditional librarians) develop and implement these methods seems less important than that this all-important work be done.

Roger Chartier has observed that after the invention of the printing press it took an "immense effort motivated by anxiety" to "set the world of the written word in order."[22] It seems likely that we are at the beginning of a new immense effort, one surely motivated as much by anxiety as by excitement and fascination with new possibilities. This anxiety is broadly felt: by individuals concerned about the future of their livelihoods and by the loss of familiar, stable practices and artifacts; by institutions no longer certain of their missions or the means of fulfilling them. It is the messy-desk syndrome, an anxiety of order, but on a national, perhaps even a global, scale. The messy-desk analogy, however, breaks down in one important respect. Even when our desks have become desperately disorganized, the materials on them still have a stable and recognizable nature. But in the current transition, the new materials are still being formed — the clay is still wet. What sense can we make of this new cyber-substance?

8

A Bit of Digital History

S O MANY GRAND CLAIMS are now being made about digital technologies: how they are all radical, new, groundbreaking, earth-
shattering. It is hard to separate hype from hope, and both of these
from current reality. It is hard to see how, and in what ways, the
"new" technologies *are* truly new and different, and *do* represent a
radical break with the past; and how, and in what ways, they are continuous with the past, and in a sense just more of the same. Sorting
this out is complicated by the fact that so much of the current discussion — in books and magazines; on television, radio, and the Internet — is highly technical and jargon-filled. If you don't know what
XML or ASCII is, or what T1 lines or ISPs are, you are immediately
lost. But even if you do understand the ins and outs of standards and
protocols and such, you risk getting so caught up in the intricate
technicalities that you lose sight of what is most simple and straightforward.

So, in a spirit of inquiry, I want to look closely at the nature of
digital documents, at their basic architecture. What are they made of?
How are they structured and constructed? What dimension of reality
do they inhabit? My hope is that by addressing these questions conceptually (with little recourse to technical jargon), we can begin to
sort out what's new and what is not.

As a starting point, I will make a broad claim of my own: Much of what is powerful, but also confusing and uncertain, about digital documents comes from their schizophrenic nature. Digital materials have undergone a kind of schizophrenic split, at least as compared with their counterparts on paper. A paper document is complete in itself, with the communicative marks inscribed directly on the writing surface — one or more sheets of paper. The ensemble is a self-contained, bounded object. It weighs a certain amount, feels a certain way, and is always located somewhere: on your desk, in a briefcase, on your refrigerator, or folded and stuffed in a pocket.

Its digital counterpart, however, has a divided existence; it lives a double life. On the one hand, you have a digital representation. This is the collection of bits stored on a floppy disk, on the hard drive embedded in your workstation, or on a fileserver. This is your Microsoft Word or WordPerfect file (for a mainly textual document), or your JPEG or TIFF file (for a scanned photograph), or your JavaScript (for a piece of animated graphics), or your MP3 file (for recorded sound). While the digital representation is necessary, it is hardly sufficient. For the simple, and possibly profound, truth is that you can't see the bits. You can't see them, you can't hear them, you can't touch or smell them. They are completely inaccessible to the human senses. Which means that they can't communicate with us, they can't talk to us or for us. Not directly, anyway. This makes the digital representation, in and of itself, an extremely poor choice as a medium of communication.

But the digital representation is only half the story. It serves as a generator for other things that *are* directly accessible to the senses, that can speak to us and for us. From the Microsoft Word file a sequence of letterforms can be displayed on the screen or on paper. From a JPEG or TIFF file, an image can be similarly realized. From the JavaScript, an animated sequence can be produced on a workstation screen, and from the MP3 file, voice or music can be made to ring forth. Digital materials are made up of both the *digital representation* and the *perceptible forms* produced from it.

The digital representation is a kind of "master," a generator that allows you to make an indefinite number of copies. There are two different senses in which you might be said to make copies from a digital master, and I want to be careful not to confuse them. On the one hand, you can make copies *of* the representation itself, the bits. (You do this when you make a copy of a Microsoft Word file, for example.) But you could also be said to make copies *from* the digital representation: when you create perceptible forms, say, by printing your Microsoft Word file or displaying it on your computer screen. It is this second sense of copying I am particularly interested in here, because this is how you go from the bits to something you can read or hear.

This method of making copies is actually quite ancient. For several thousand years at least, people have known how to create stamps, templates, or patterns from which a set of identical artifacts could be manufactured. Coins are one of the first instances of this. As long ago as the fifth century B.C.E., gold and silver coins bearing inscriptions were minted from bronze dies.[1] The use of seals and signet rings to impress a "signature" (or some other identifying mark) is even older.[2] The Louvre, for example, has in its collection the cylindrical seal of an Akkadian scribe that dates to the twenty-third century B.C.E.[3] Block printing, which involved carving text and images on a wood block, then inking the block and transferring its images onto smooth surfaces (skins, fabric, or paper), was known in the East as early as the eighth century C.E.[4] The same technique was widely available in the West by the fourteenth century.[5]

In all these cases, the stamp or pattern is a unitary thing. Letterforms or other images are carved into a single block of wood, for example. This makes it hard to correct a mistake. If you've misspelled a word, you may just have to start over again. It also means you're unlikely to be able to reuse a portion of the text or image (as opposed to the whole thing) for some other purpose. The invention of movable type changed all of this. With movable type, each time you want to create a new pattern — for a page of text, say — you select the individual, previously cast stamps you need and arrange them to suit your current purposes. Mistakes are correctable — small ones easily, others less so — by replacing or interchanging the individual stamps. And when you're done, all the individual stamps can be recovered and reused for new projects.

The Chinese are credited with first coming up with the idea. In the eleventh century C.E., a technique was developed whereby individual characters could be fashioned from earthenware, fired in a kiln to harden them, and assembled in an iron form.[6] It never took off, however, apparently because of the huge number of Chinese characters that would have been needed. The idea reappeared in fifteenth-century Europe, independently invented by Gutenberg and his contemporaries. This time, the stamps (or *type,* as they are normally called) were cast in metal. And the smaller number of symbols needed to write Western languages made it a much more practical scheme.

In Gutenberg's technique there are actually three separate manufacturing steps in which a template or pattern is produced and used. In the last of these, individual pieces of type are selected, arranged, and "locked up" in a metal frame called a *chase* to produce a *forme* from which multiple pages can be printed. For this scheme to work, however, you need to be able to produce lots of type, both to spell out all the words on the page — a typical page of text may have a hundred or more lowercase *e*'s — and to replace type that has become worn. Gutenberg's solution, like the one found by the Chinese inventors before him, was to cast each individual piece of type from a pattern — or a *matrix,* as it is usually known. But how do you impress the shape of the character into the matrix so it can be used to cast the type? The answer — as Gutenberg, a jeweler by trade, developed it — is to cut a metal stamp, or *punch.* (Think of a rubber stamp for a letter, except smaller and made of metal.) This, when pounded into the soft metal of the matrix, leaves the concave impression of the character.

At first blush, there is something distinctly odd about this process. Why would you cut a punch to create a matrix to cast a piece of type? Why not just carve or cut the individual pieces of type directly, thereby eliminating two time-consuming steps in the process? The answer is simple: cutting either a punch or a piece of type is itself time-consuming. It would take an extremely long time to carve by hand all the pieces of type you'd need for printing — thousands of pieces.[7] But whereas cutting a piece of *type* gives you, in the end, a single piece of type, cutting a single *punch* makes it possible to manufacture a great many pieces of type. From a single punch for the letter *e,* you can make many matrices, and from each matrix you can cast many pieces of type. The whole point is to make *lots* of copies.

This method of printing is called *letterpress* — a technique in which the raised, inked surfaces of the type are *impressed* directly onto the paper. In Gutenberg's day, this was the only method available, and it was all done by hand: the punches cut, the matrices made, the type cast and composed (arranged), and the pages printed. From the nineteenth century on, however, in the attempt to meet the growing market for print publications, these steps were automated, and new techniques were developed, such as phototypesetting, that eliminated the need to cast pieces of metal type. If we can now compose and edit documents on computers with relative ease, it is because this stream of developments met up with another stream of innovation: the invention of the digital computer.

The idea of linking the printing press and computers actually precedes the modern era of computation. In the 1820s, Charles Babbage designed and partly implemented his "difference engine," a computer intended to calculate tables of mathematical functions to the twentieth place. This machine, like its modern descendants, needed to do more than make correct calculations: it needed to present the results in a form a person could understand. Babbage took this into account and designed the difference engine so that its results could be printed from plates without a human intervening to typeset the results.

The first modern, digital computers date to the 1940s. (ENIAC, completed in 1945, was designed to help the war effort by computing artillery firing tables.) Over the course of the next two decades, punched cards, punched and magnetic tape, and paper were adopted as the output media on which both programs and data could be printed. For the computer to cause a letter *a,* say, to be printed on a piece of paper, it needed to send a signal or code to the output device that amounted to the command "print a letter *a.*" Character codes — numerical codes standing for the letters of the alphabet, the numerals, and punctuation marks — had first been developed in conjunction with the telegraph.

The telegraph, invented in the early nineteenth century, is a device for sending electrical signals representing characters across a wire to a receiving device. The sender would translate a message (made up of letters, numerals, and punctuation) into a sequence of long and short taps on a telegraph key. In Samuel Morse's first version of the 1830s, the electrical signals corresponding to these taps caused a device on the other end to emboss dots and dashes on a paper roll. Twenty years later the more familiar device was invented, which translated the received signals into audible sounds: *dits* and *dats.* In either case, a human operator was needed to translate these codes back into a more comprehensible form: spoken or written language.

Later still, teleprinters were invented; these were essentially electric typewriters that could send an electrical signal when a key was depressed, and could print the corresponding character when its code was received. The best known of these devices is AT&T's *teletype,* which was developed in the 1920s. The use of teleprinters effectively eliminated the need for human translation and interpretation of the character codes. Now, rather than translating the letter *a* into a sequence of dots and dashes, the operator simply pressed the *a* key on the teletype.

For those most directly involved in the invention of modern computing, the printing of a result was generally of secondary importance. The main act was the computation the computer was performing. Clearly, you needed to supply certain inputs to the computer (the data) and get back the results of the computation. But for the mathematicians and engineers designing the computers and the programs that ran on them, what went on under the hood held their greatest fascination: the design of the hardware and software, the working out of elegant algorithms to compute results. The mind of these early computer scientists was firmly fixed *inside* the box.

But sometime in the 1960s — when exactly, I'm not sure — a subtle shift began to take place, a partial reorientation of focus. Greater attention began to be paid to the inputs and outputs. The first step in this movement was the development of tools (software) that could help programmers write and modify computer programs. Sitting at a teletype, for example, a programmer could type in computer instructions line by line. The program would be saved in the computer's memory, and the programmer could display lines of it and modify them. The purpose of the program, of course, was to get the computer to do something, to perform some kind of calculation. The written program, displayed on the teletype, was an instrument for something else, a computation.

By the mid-1960s, however, it had begun to dawn on programmers that tools for displaying and modifying computer programs could be used to modify and display other kinds of textual material — documents — intended solely for human consumption. Conceptually, this was a huge step. Now, instead of seeing text just as an *input* to the computer, as necessary but of secondary importance to the computation inside the machine, text in these new cases became the *primary object* of the user's attention, with the computations inside the computer (the operations needed to edit and display the text, for example) taking a back seat. I don't mean to suggest that this awareness was necessarily present in people's minds as such, but with hindsight we can see that the effect of these developments was to give text a new, privileged status.[8]

In 1967, Peter Deutsch and Butler Lampson, two computer scientists who would play prominent roles at Xerox PARC in the next decade, wrote a journal article called simply "An Online Editor." In it they argued for the value of a new kind of software, called an "editor," which could be used to edit not only programs but "reports, messages, or visual representations," and which, they claimed, was superior to a keypunch. Listen to them trying to explain distinctions that are now second nature to us:

> One of the fundamental requirements for many computer users is some means of creating and altering *text,* i.e., strings of characters. Such texts are usually programs written in some symbolic language, but they may be reports, messages, or visual representations. The most common means of text handling in the last few years has been the punched card deck. Paper tape and magnetic tape have also been used as input, but the fact that individual cards can be inserted and deleted manually in the middle of a deck has made the keypunch the most convenient and popular device for editing text.
>
> With the appearance of online systems, however, in which text is stored permanently within the system and never appears on external storage media, serious competition to the punched card has arisen. Since the online user has no access to his text except through his console and the computer, a program is needed, however minimal, to allow him to create and modify the text. Such a program is called an editor and presupposes a reasonably large and powerful machine equipped with disk or drum storage. The user therefore gains more convenience than even the most elaborate keypunch can provide.[9]

These early editors were quite primitive by today's standards. Users were stuck with whatever typeface was available on the printer connected to their mainframe computer — typically a fairly primitive, fixed-width typeface, akin to a typewriter font. (In some cases, printers printed only in capital letters.) And if users wanted to do even the simplest arranging or formatting of their text, such as centering a title or creating a tabular format, they needed to do the work by hand — e.g., by inserting spaces or tabs themselves. The early text editors were a lot like typewriters, with one major exception: the computer maintained a memory of your text, and you could modify it.

At roughly the same time, programmers began to develop another kind of document preparation tool, called a formatter. This was a program that could take an unformatted text (produced by a text editor) as input, and could produce a formatted text as output; centering, underlining, and the setting and justification of margins were some of the early features. To make this work, the user had to supply formatting codes, embedded in the text, indicating, say, that a particular phrase should be centered or underlined.

So, by the late 1960s, the basic architecture of digital documents was in place. What you had was the ability to create and store the digital representation of a text. The elements of this representation were character codes, each code standing for a letter, a numeral, a punctuation mark, or a control command. You could also display the text so represented: the character codes could be translated into commands to a printer to display the corresponding visible symbols on paper. The digitally encoded text could be stored on external media: tapes, disks, and cards. And the text could be modified by the user and again printed or stored.

One other innovation extended these capabilities in important ways: the use of display terminals as input and output devices. The first displays were made from cathode ray tubes (CRTs), still one of the main computer display technologies in use today. (Invented in the late nineteenth century, the CRT found use in early television in the 1930s and in radar during World War II.) The advantage of such a technology was obvious enough: marks on a screen, as opposed to those on paper, could be quickly — indeed instantly — changed.

Once CRTs were coupled to computers, programmers began experimenting with techniques to display and edit text on them, and some of the basic capabilities that are now second nature to computer users all over the world were invented. You could, for example, type on a keyboard, and as you typed, the characters would appear on the screen, much as with a typewriter. But unlike a typewriter, you could press the backspace (or rub-out) key, and the characters would be erased; they would simply disappear. You could also insert characters into a line of text and have the characters following the insertion point move to the right; or you could delete characters and the characters to the right would move left to fill in the gap.

By the early 1970s the following setup was common in well-equipped academic and industrial computer laboratories: If you wanted to write a paper, say, you could sit down at a display terminal connected to a time-shared computer. There you would type in your text, edit it, and save it in a file. You could print out the text directly on a line printer. Or, if you wanted a better-looking result, you could insert formatting codes into the file (codes to indent and right-justify paragraphs and to insert page numbers) and run the formatting program. The result could then be printed on the printer.

But in the mid-1970s, a new type of document preparation tool was developed that integrated editing and formatting capabilities, and that tried to eliminate (or at least minimize) the differences between marks on the screen and marks on paper. This type of editor was given the name WYSIWYG, an acronym standing for "what you see is what you get." Using such an editor, you could create rich textual displays on the screen and when you printed out this material on paper (using a laser printer), the result would look "the same" as it had appeared on the screen. You could type in text and see it immediately displayed on the screen. This much wasn't new, but in addition you could change the "look" of selected portions of text on the screen by issuing commands with the keyboard and mouse. You could select a portion of text and italicize it, make it bold, or change the typeface. You could change the margins, the interline spacing, the paragraph indentation, and so on. And (this was the WYSIWYG part), no sooner had you issued these commands than the changes appeared on the screen. You could *see* the word italicized, the paragraph now indented, the space between lines increased. Not only that, but when you printed out the document, it looked exactly the same on paper as it appeared on the screen — typefaces, spacing, and all. This is what WYSIWYG meant: what you see *on the screen* is what you get *on paper*. If these abilities are obvious enough now, it is because the tools we use today are direct descendants of these early prototypes. Microsoft Word, for example, is a direct successor of the first WYSIWYG text editor, called Bravo, which was developed at Xerox PARC.

The way WYSIWYG works is conceptually quite simple. As you type, adding text to your document, each keypress causes an electronic code to be generated. This code, the character code for the key you've just pressed, is inserted by the editor into the template, the file, it is maintaining for your document. As each character code is received, the editor also issues a command causing the letterform corresponding to that character code to be displayed on your computer screen. In the days of the typewriter, the relationship between keypress and visible mark was of course much simpler, a single causal step. By pressing the key, you caused a hammer with a piece of type at the end of it to strike an inked ribbon lying against a piece of paper. Now the relationship between keypress and image is indirect: pressing the key first causes a character code to be recognized and saved; this character code is then used to generate a visible image.

What happens, say, when you italicize a portion of your text? You typically do this by sweeping your mouse across a portion of text on the screen and issuing a command to italicize the selected portion. What actually happens takes multiple steps. Each character on the screen corresponds to a character code in the file. But the editor also keeps track of *where* the characters are on the screen and exactly which character code in the file each character corresponds to. So when you sweep the mouse across the screen (this is actually indirect too, since your rolling the mouse on the table causes a cursor on the screen to move), the editor figures out which character codes in the file are being selected. When you then issue the command to italicize, the editor in effect appends a note to the character codes in the file, indicating that they are now italic. It also issues commands to the screen to display the italicized versions of the characters. Here too, then, the operation proceeds indirectly: from characters on the screen to character codes in the file and back to characters on the screen.

What WYSIWYG does, however, is to hide all this indirection and backstage manipulation. It maintains the illusion that there is no separation or distinction between the digital representation and the marks on the screen. You're meant to believe that there is just one thing, one unified thing: your document. And when you print "it" out, the result on paper is meant to look just like what appeared on the screen — as if there were no distinction here either, between marks on screen and marks on paper. But the truth is, no matter how masterful the illusion, there really *are* three different kinds of materials in use: the invisible digital representation, the visible marks on the screen, and the visible marks on paper.

Up to this point I have been focusing on the ability to create and manipulate text by digital means. But the brilliance of the digital architecture I have been describing is that it accommodates other communicative forms just as well. So long as you can develop the right codes (digital representations) and input/output devices capable of trafficking in these codes, you can display and edit these nontextual forms as well. And so, over the course of the last thirty years or so, tools and techniques have been developed to create and manipulate diagrams and other still images, moving images (both synthesized animation and recorded movement), and sound.

The groundbreaking work in manipulation of static graphics was Ivan Sutherland's Sketchpad, a computer program developed at MIT in the early 1960s. Sketchpad allowed the user to construct complex line drawings. These could be displayed on the screen, and they could be modified on the screen as well. Using a lightpen as an input device, the user could edit drawings much as the user of a text editor edited text. With the lightpen, for example, the user could select a line segment by pointing to it on the screen, then issue a command to delete, move, or stretch it. Thirty-five years after Sutherland first demonstrated such capabilities, they have been absorbed into our regular cultural practices and it is hard to remember how remarkable they were. So it may be helpful to hear what Ted Nelson had to say, writing in his 1974 manifesto, *Dream Machines:*

> If you have not seen interactive computer display, you have not lived.

Except for a few people who can imagine it . . . most people just don't get it till they see it. They can't imagine what it's like to manipulate a picture. To have a diagram respond to you. To change one part of a picture, and watch the rest adapt. These are some of the things that can happen in interactive computer display. . . .

For some reason there are a lot of people who pooh-pooh computer display: they say it's "not necessary," or "not worth it," or that "you can get just as good results other ways."[10] [Emphasis in original.]

It was Ted Nelson who first coined the word "hypertext." Nelson and Douglas Englebart are considered to be the fathers of *computer-based* hypertext, the ability to link fragments of text together via computer, allowing the reader to follow a link from one piece of text to another. (The more recent term "hypermedia" is a further generalization of hypertext, in which not only text but other media types, such as static graphics, animation, and sound, are linked together.) Vannevar Bush is generally credited with coming up with the idea of hypertext (but not the name); his Memex system — envisioned in a paper published in 1945 but never implemented — stored text fragments on microfiche. Yet the notion of non-linear Webs of text is an ancient one — surely as old as annotation — and other hypertext-like designs precede Bush's in the twentieth century.[11]

What makes computer-based hypertext and hypermedia possible is the basic architectural premise of digital documents: the separation of digital representation and perceptible form. One of the basic building blocks of modern computing since its early days has been the notion of a link or a reference: the ability to embed within a sequence of computer instructions a pointer to some other location in the computer's memory and to the instructions or data there. At its heart, a computer program is a sequence of instructions, like a cookbook recipe: do this, then this, then this. Early on, however, programmers realized the importance of breaking the linear sequence of steps. At times you might want to "jump" to a different set of instructions, stored elsewhere in the computer's memory.

Nelson and Englebart (and no doubt others too) noticed an interesting parallel between a computer executing instructions and a person reading a text. In both cases, following a linear sequence was the norm; and in both cases there were times when you might want to break the sequence and jump somewhere else. And so, by embedding within a sequence of character codes a link or pointer to another sequence of character codes, you could let the reader decide whether to keep reading on linearly or jump to the second piece of text.

It would be remarkable enough if development had stopped with the creation of stand–alone computers operating, in effect, as digital presses, and with the expansion of linear sequences of text to webs of hyperlinked materials. But in parallel with many of the inventions I've been describing, computer networking capabilities were also being developed. The creation of the Arpanet (a precursor to the Internet) in the 1960s made it possible for people to exchange data rapidly among computers distributed around the country, and even around the world. E-mail predates the invention of the Arpanet — it had been developed as a communication technique among users of time-sharing systems — but the development of standards for the exchange of e-mail on the Arpanet allowed users to transcend the boundaries of their particular computer systems.

What e-mail did for point-to-point communication, the World Wide Web and Web browsers did for formatted documents and for hypertext. From the early days of the Arpanet, users could exchange data and text files using an application called ftp (file transfer protocol). You could "ftp" a formatted text file from some other computer to your own, and provided you had the right software, you could display, print, and edit this file. In the late 1980s and early 1990s, inspired by Nelson and Englebart, Tim Berners-Lee developed a scheme for linking texts that were stored on different computers. And with the development of the Mosaic browser and its commercial successors (from Netscape and Microsoft), it became possible to display these texts (to translate the digital representations into perceptible forms) on your computer screen, no matter where in the world they had originated (were stored).

As a result of all these threads of invention and adaptation, a global infrastructure for the production, distribution, and consumption of digital documents is now emerging. Although outwardly quite complex, at its heart it is remarkably simple. And it is based on an ancient technique for manufacturing objects from templates or patterns. Putting it this way stresses the radical continuity of current developments with the past. There is nothing new under the sun, the author of Ecclesiastes observed several thousand years ago.

But this isn't quite right, either. For although we have borrowed the architecture of the printing press (and its antecedent forms of manufacturing), we have improved upon it, creating a "just-in-time" manufacturing technique for written forms. When you ask to view a digital document — by opening a file on your local disk or downloading a document from the Web — you are essentially asking that it be manufactured for you on the spot. (The "it" here, of course, is the perceptible form.) If you've asked for the document to be printed, the whole thing will be manufactured for you on paper. If, on the other hand, you want to see it on the screen, then only that portion of it that will fit inside the current viewing window will be manufactured (displayed). And when you scroll forward or backward, just the new portion is manufactured for you.

It's worth pointing out that a just-in-time scheme isn't entirely new in the realm of documents. Audio, film, and video are based on the same premise. From a recording tape, sound and images are manufactured in real time — just in time for our eyes to see motion and for our ears to hear intelligible sound. These techniques have been around for about a hundred years. But in going digital we are accomplishing several extremely powerful and impressive things: we now have a single medium (ones and zeros) in which to represent all our documentary forms: text, graphics, photographs, sound, and moving images. And we have the beginning of a global infrastructure in which these forms can be represented and realized. This new state of affairs can be summed up in a phrase: "more, faster, farther, easier, cheaper." It is quicker, easier, and cheaper than ever before to produce more copies and more variants of documents, and to send them farther at less expense.

These advances come from the way we've managed to split apart documents. Paper is heavy, but bits are light. Digital representations can be modified without leaving a trace; it's much harder to do this with marks on paper. The more we can work with the bits, only transforming them into perceptible forms when we need them (just-in-time), the greater the speed and flexibility and the lower the cost. But there are significant costs to this scheme as well. The financial implications of making this global infrastructure work are staggering: the cost of networks, of computers, of upgrades and maintenance, of training, of the reorientation and rethinking of work. In addition, however, we now live with certain deep confusions and uncertainties about the nature of these new documents, what they are and how they are to be preserved. To a large extent, these questions arise from an aspect of the new digital architecture that I have thus far made little of: the dependence of digital documents on a complex technical environment.

Here is the problem in a nutshell: In the world of paper, documents are realized as stable, bounded physical objects. Once a paper document comes into being, it loses its dependence on the technologies that were used to manufacture it. The photocopied memo takes leave of the photocopier, and never looks back; the printed book takes leave of the printer and bindery, and never looks back. But a digital document, because its perceptible form is *always being manufactured just-in-time, on the spot,* can't ever sever its relationship to a set of manufacturing technologies. It requires an elaborate set of technological conditions — hardware and software — in order to maintain a visible and useful presence.

Of course, this isn't an entirely new problem: it exists in the case of analog recorded audio and video. (Analog recordings are continuous in nature; digital recordings, by contrast, are made up of discrete values, ones and zeros.) Without a tape player in working condition, without the right kind of tape (VHS, say, rather than Beta), without the right encoding standard (NTSC or PAL, for example), no performance can be realized. Provided such conditions are met, however, you can take your tape of *Groundhog Day* to any number of videocassette players around the world and you will see the same show, more or less, as you would see on any other video projection setup. I say "more or less" because, inevitably, there will be visual differences between performances on different machines. The monitors may be of different sizes (so the image sizes will differ), the color balance is likely to be different, as well as the quality and volume of the sound. But by and large, for a non-specialist audience, these differences will be insignificant, and no one is likely to claim that he isn't seeing an authentic performance. (Within specialist audiences, however, it may be quite different: seeing the film on a small screen, rather than on the big screen the producers assumed, could be considered a serious liability.)

This scheme works well to the extent that we've been able to standardize the various components. There are standards for the production of the physical cassettes, there are standards for the analog encoding of images and sound on them, and there are standards for the players that turn the encodings into perceptible forms (or performances). If you stay within the bounds of these standards, you are pretty much guaranteed that you can continue to view *Groundhog Day* again and again. Up to a point, that is. For at some point, after some years or decades, the physical tape will begin to deteriorate. Its record of sound and images will begin to fail. (For just this reason, the National Film Preservation Board reports, fully half the film stock for movies made before 1950 is no longer available.)[12] But even if the tape remains in good shape, it can still become unusable if the proper players are no longer available. This has already happened to a large extent with eight-track tape, and, who knows, in not too many years, VHS may go the way of Beta.

To a first approximation, digital production is the same as analog audio and video. Instead of a recording (audio or video) tape, you have a digital file, whether stored on a floppy, on a local hard drive, on a CD-ROM, or on a server somewhere on the Internet. And instead of a tape player, you have a computer equipped with the appropriate viewing/editing software. You can then insert the floppy into the computer's floppy drive and (if the material is textual, say) scroll forward and backward in the text, much as you would rewind and fast-forward a video. The same modes of failure exist in the digital case: the storage medium can degrade, and, in effect, lose its charge. (None of our current digital modes of storage are thought to be good for more than about fifty years, which is quite striking when you realize that paper can preserve its content for hundreds of years, and animal skins for thousands.) The proper technical environment needed to view the file may also cease to exist. (What will happen to the digital manuscript of this book when, someday, Microsoft Word, Macintosh computers, and PCs are gone?)

To this extent, the cases are parallel. Both are deeply dependent on the health of their storage media and the technologies for using them to produce human-sensible products. The primary difference, however, is the extreme — indeed, radical — sensitivity of digital products to their technical environments. To begin with, digital hardware and software has been changing much more rapidly than have the technologies of analog audio and video. Just think of the rate at which new releases of software have been emerging and the limits of compatibility among versions. When you want to move a text file from one computer to another, you need to be concerned not only about whether it has Microsoft Word, but whether it has a compatible version of it. (There is really no equivalent for this in the world of analog video.)

What's more, there are further and finer dimensions of sensitivity in the digital case. Fonts, for example. Having moved a file to another computer, I may discover that it doesn't have the font in which the document was originally composed. (Whether or not this matters will depend entirely on the particular circumstances of use. At the very least, it can be crucial in the legible display of diagrams.) Or the problem of ongoing editability: How do I guarantee not only that the document will look the same, but that I will have the same capacity to modify it as I did in the previous environment?

What seems clear is that we are just beginning to figure out how to stabilize digital documents — how to guarantee fixity and permanence. In an environment in which every viewing is a newly manufactured form, and every form is highly sensitive to the technical conditions under which it is manufactured, how do we ensure that a document will remain the same in whatever ways matter?

These problems aren't only particular to digital documents. Every time we make a photocopy of something, we are asking, perhaps only subconsciously: Does this reproduction satisfy my needs? Do I need to copy both sides (perhaps because there are pencil annotations on the back of some of the pages)? Is making a black-and-white copy of this color document sufficient? Does it matter whether I reduce the double-size foldout map to a single eight-and-a-half-by-eleven-inch format? Archivists and librarians face these questions when attempting to preserve a deteriorating document for future use. Some techniques involve making a copy of the original (e.g., making a "preservation photocopy"), which raise the same challenges I've just been discussing. Others involve preserving the physical artifact: repairing torn pages and binding or deacidifying the paper, for example. But even these latter techniques require trading off certain features for others.

What is new in the digital case is not that we have to make decisions of this kind, about what to preserve and how to preserve it. What is new is that the technological means of production and preservation are new and poorly understood. What is new is that production and preservation are not separable. What is new is that instead of a continuously existing, physical artifact, we have just-in-time creations, cooked up on the spot.

We aren't yet able to grasp, literally or figuratively, what these new creations are made of. And so the word *virtual* is bandied about as a way of talking about the distinction between physical and digital "matter." Paper documents, we often hear said, are *real:* physical, material, weighty, tangible. Whereas digital documents, by contrast, are *virtual:* immaterial, weightless, and intangible. With such pronoucements, I think we are trying to get at something important about the new technology, but we haven't yet gotten it right. Digital documents are *not* immaterial. The marks produced on screens and on paper, the sounds generated in the airwaves, are as material as anything in our world. And the ones and zeros of our digital representations are equally material: they are embedded in a material substrate no less than are calligraphic letterforms on a piece of vellum. It may be true that digital representations can move around extremely quickly, that they can be copied from one storage device to another, even when they are separated by thousands of miles. But at any one moment, the bits for a particular document are somewhere real and physical. And if the bits have symbolic value, so too do letterforms. Both digital representations and written forms have both a material *and* a symbolic existence.

What *is* true, however, is that in the digital case the digital representations have come to assume a priority, an ongoing importance, at least equal to that of the perceptible forms they are used to generate. In the case of the printing press, the formes (the locked-up type) used to print a text were quickly dismantled (that was the whole point of movable type, that it could be recycled) and the reader never even had to know of their existence. In the case of video or audio, we are more aware and more knowledgeable about the generators, the tape cassettes, but perhaps because these have a conventional physical form and are themselves tangible artifacts (you *can* hold a cassette in your hand), they haven't challenged our sense of reality. But in the digital case, the intangibility of the bits, the ease with which they can be moved around, the ability to store them invisibly beyond our sight and physical grasp, and to move them around so that place no longer seems to matter has us searching for ways to understand what is going on.

People tend to refer to the file on their computer as "the document," I have noticed. This makes a great deal of sense, since the file is the locus of both editability and relative permanence. Because I have the file for this chapter on my laptop, I can continue to edit it as I see fit. I can save it, view it on the screen, and print it. And eventually a copy of a later version of it will be sent off to my publisher. As far as I'm concerned, this file simply *is* the chapter. But it is the chapter in a meaningful and useful sense only because I assume, and can rely upon, a technical environment that includes my laptop,

Microsoft Word, and a printer thanks to which I can see intelligible marks on a screen and on paper. Under such circumstances, is the file really "the document"? Or should I say that the document consists of the file plus the requisite technical environment? Or must I also include the perceptible forms as well? There are no answers to these questions at the moment. While they are philosophically interesting, they will also have profound practical consequences.

Here is a whole new class of talking things, and we are busy fashioning them to do all manner of work: to tell public stories, to facilitate intimate correspondence with one another, to keep the wheels of industry rolling. But we don't yet know what we can count on them for. This is partly a function of the technologies, in the ways I've just been describing, but it is a function of the technologies in the service of human — that is, social — aims. We can't make sense of these things as bits generating words and images without taking account of the ways they work with us and for us to make and maintain the world.

9

An Immense Effort

Look at any document: a cash register receipt, a book of poetry, a child's handwritten note, a greeting card. Each one is tailored to operate within a particular sphere of life: to regulate a sale, to sing the praises of the world, to offer a confession, to say happy birthday to a loved one. Examine it, and you will see the materials from which it is formed, the symbols through which it speaks, and the circuit in which it travels. And if your eyesight is good enough, you will also see the behind-the-scenes work, the invisible infrastructure, that mends and tends it: the cash register manufacturers, the book catalogers, the writing teachers, the postal system.

Now broaden your gaze. Imagine seeing the whole planet, all the documents on it, all the activities in which these documents are embedded, and all the people participating in these activities. Here someone is jotting down a phone number, having just run into an old friend on the street. There someone is leafing through mail-order catalogs looking for Christmas presents for the remaining people on his list. Elsewhere someone is dozing on the subway, a novel resting on her lap, a recently received postcard serving as a bookmark. Someone else is making a plane reservation on the Web for a conference she is about to attend, at the same time writing the conference paper she will deliver there.

What are all these documents doing for us? While each has its unique place and role, all of them together are helping us make and maintain the world. What else could they be doing, for world-making is what we humans do. We create the material, social, symbolic, and spiritual environment we inhabit: we build cities; we tell stories; we manufacture goods; we develop knowledge of the world and ourselves; we fashion individual and group identities and ideologies. In short, we create culture.

This world-making, or culture-making, business is an immense effort, ever ongoing. Without it we would be lost: nowhere, nothing. And documents are our partners in this enterprise. We fashion them to take on some of the work: to help us exert power and control, maintain relationships, acquire and preserve knowledge. There is hardly a dimension of life in which these sorcerer's apprentices don't figure: in business, in science and the arts, in religion, in the administrative practices that support nearly all our organizations, in the management of our private lives. Virtually all the cultural institutions and practices that help us make order, that help us bring meaning and intelligibility to our lives, draw heavily on documents for support.

We have relied on these beings for many centuries, but never so fully as we do now. Never before have we lived in a world so thoroughly saturated with, and dependent on, these creatures. And never before has a technology (or set of technologies) threatened the material underpinnings of our documents and document practices so thoroughly or so quickly. Certainly, over the last hundred years, we have seen the adoption of microfilm alter the practices of scholarship and librarianship, and film and video technologies change the nature of entertainment, but these interventions were confined to particular cultural sectors, whereas digital technologies are now insinuating themselves into nearly every corner of the world in which documents operate — which means virtually everywhere. Such broad-scale changes are therefore destabilizing the institutions and practices that depend on the stability documents help engender, as well as the institutions and practices that help stabilize documents. Is it any wonder that our institutions and practices, our modes of living and working, are shaking?

To see the nature of this disruption in a bit more detail, I suggest we look at what is happening to our genres online. For genres are the social identity of our talking things. They are the forms we give materials to participate in human life. Their current instability is one of the more visible indicators of our cultural distress. Looking in greater detail at them can therefore show us something of the immense effort that's been required to make stable documents and a stable world; it can help us see the immense effort we're undertaking now; and perhaps also help us to appreciate why it's currently all so confusing.

Sometime back I happened upon an odd little Web page. "Expecting to find THE PARANOIA FAMILY TREE?" it announced in large, orange, sans-serif type set on a navy background. "Nice try." And then, in much smaller, light blue type it went on:

> Did you really think it would be so simple? You thought you could just log right on, didn't you? "Hey, I'm a spy," you thought. "Maybe I'll check out the Paranoia Family Tree right now and use the wealth of information contained within to slander and defame the staff of Word!" "Maybe," you thought, "I'll use my little microchip to erase their brains, then escape into a pyramid with my spaceship!" Well you're very, very clever. But so are we.

Its final paragraph read: "We're not 'ready' yet for you to view the Paranoia Family Tree. Why don't you try again in 2000? Get it? 2000??"

But I didn't get it, although I made several stabs at it. Perhaps the Web page was a teaser, a kind of advertisement for a commercial Web site or a new publication. I thought of ad campaigns, like the one Apple conducted for the iMac ("I think therefore iMac"), whose initial obscurity was meant to pique your interest. Or the series of ads ABC Television created to advertise its new programming in the fall of 1997, whose basic message was "Television rots your brain, and that's just fine."[1] Perhaps this was simply the product of someone's quirky sense of humor. God knows, there is plenty of that on the Web. Like the site claiming that Bert — of Bert and Ernie fame — is evil. (It displays a mug shot of a very treacherous-looking Bert.) Or the one that claims to originate from the Bureau of Missing Socks, which is "the first organization solely devoted to solving the question of what happens to missing single socks. It explores all aspects of the phenomena including the occult, conspiracy theories, and extraterrestrial." It also occurred to me that this Web page might be the product of a disturbed mind — or of someone on another wavelength, to put it more kindly. None of these possibilities was provable, however — or for that matter, disprovable — since the Web page simply failed to provide consistent clues about just what it was.

Still, there was a fair amount that I *did* understand about it. I had a pretty good sense of its technological underpinnings: how the various technologies worked to produce an image on my screen. And I had no trouble parsing its sentences and making local sense of their meaning. What I couldn't grasp was its social character. What *was* it? Who was speaking through it? How did they imagine that I, or anyone, would come upon this page? What place or role did they intend it to fill in people's lives?

And this, the Web page's incomprehensibility, is ultimately what interested me about it. For it managed to demonstrate, in just a few lines of text and a couple of colors, what it's like for a document to fail to register in social space, to fail to have a social identity, and thereby to fail *to be* a document. To say that it was uncategorizable, that it was unrecognizable as any particular genre, is simply to summarize this state of confusion. Had I been able to identify it *as* an advertisement or *as* a parody or *as* a work of art, I would have understood its mode of communication and the sphere of life within which it was meant to operate.

It has always been possible to come across unintelligible or uncategorizable documents. But huge amounts of work have been done in the past, and continue to be done now, to minimize this likelihood. Over the centuries a complex network of institutions and practices has grown up to create and maintain meaningful and reliable paper documents. In the world of book publishing, for example, think of the work of agents, editors, publishers, and printers who select and shape authors' manuscripts; the book distributors, librarians, and booksellers who make them available to readers; the system of copyright and the courts that creates and oversees the right to produce and use these products; and the book reviewers working within another sector of publishing — newspapers, magazines, and journals — to summarize and evaluate books for potential readers.

Thanks to this ongoing work, books today are firmly situated within a network of visible signs, institutions, and practices that collectively and consistently attest to what they are. Just wander into a bookstore and pick up a book from the "new and noteworthy fiction" counter, or from the travel section. By virtue of the book's physical presence in a reputable shop, you have a great deal of information about it. That it has made its way there tells you that it has made its way through established publishing channels and is therefore vouched for by the system. Where it appears in the shop — on which counter or in which section — also tells you something about its content and mode of presentation: that it has been classified as fiction or travel or whatever. For a recently published, well-received book, a copy of the review from a reputable periodical may also be on display as further evidence of its social respectability.

In addition to these external cues, the internal makeup of the book helps establish what it is. Its physical format — bound pages between covers — declares that it is a book (a codex), while the printed pages, including a detailed and standardized title page, identify it as a mass-produced, published work and specify who wrote it, who published it, where and when. Further information is likely to be available from the volume too. The size and shape of the book, as well as the cover design, may help in classifying it: compare the cover of a detective novel with that of a work of literary criticism, for example. There may well be a blurb offering a summary of the book and a brief biography of the author.

Most of this system is less than five hundred years old, having arisen in the wake of the printing press, as Chartier has observed, "to put the world of the written word in order." Although title pages existed prior to printing, they were neither standardized nor heavily used until print was well established. The various book genres we now take for granted didn't emerge until well into print history. (The modern novel, for example, emerged in the eighteenth century.) And well into the seventeenth century, books still hadn't achieved the stability and reliability we now take for granted. Pirated and variant editions were common, and authorship was contested. Unlike today, there was no guarantee that the book you put your hands on was a reliable edition, or that the author named was indeed its creator.[2] The system of authoritative publication, which is now largely invisible to us, had not yet emerged.

So it should hardly be surprising if the digital world isn't all neat and tidy. We are just at the beginning of figuring it all out. We have a new technology base, a new kind of material, which itself is still evolving. And we are just beginning to figure out what kinds of creatures to make from this material: what they'll look like, how they'll behave, what kinds of tasks we'll ask them to perform for us. Truly it is an immense effort. And it is made all the more complex and confusing by the fact that the technologies, the genres, and the work we're asking them to do are co-evolving, continually influencing one another. As a result, there's no place to stand that isn't itself unstable, or at least uncertain.

Fortunately, we don't have to start from scratch. We have an existing base of genres and practices from which we can borrow: publications like books, magazines, and newspapers; bureaucratic documents like forms and receipts; personal documents like letters, postcards, and greeting cards. In fact, we have no choice but to borrow from existing genres. It isn't an accident that film first adopted the conventions of the theater, that television adopted the conventions of film, or that the Web has adopted the conventions of print and TV culture. Without some prior basis for making sense of the communicative conventions in a new medium, we would simply be adrift, like tourists in a land whose language and script we didn't know. The alternative — a Web largely populated with Paranoia Family Trees — would simply be unworkable.

But moving existing genres online doesn't guarantee that they'll be stable. Indeed, it pretty much guarantees that they won't be. Having been dislodged from the complex practices in which they had previously operated and through which they were maintained, they are subject to — both affecting and being affected by — the shifting sands of their new, uncertain habitats. It is therefore inevitable that the initial copying of genres, arising from the need to maintain intelligibility in a new environment, will lead to a cascading set of incremental changes whose endpoint can't be foreseen.

E-mail is a good case in point. As one of the first digital genres, arguably the very first, it has been around long enough for us to see some of the many changes it has undergone. The first e-mail systems, created on time-sharing systems in the late 1960s, allowed users to send textual messages to one another. Although the technology itself was new to many users (the details of how you logged on, how you wrote and sent messages), the form itself wasn't hard to comprehend. The idea of composing a letter or a note to someone was hardly new to anyone. Neither was the business of specifying the address of one's addressee (even if the form, a user ID, was new). And the arrangement of fields at the top — To, From, Subject — mirrored the conventions of the memo.

Right off the bat, then, e-mail was a blend of old and new. It made immediate sense to users because it drew on established conventions of postal correspondence (letters, postcards, and even greeting cards), handwritten notes, and business memos. It didn't require a major shift in thinking to understand that you could now exchange messages with a fellow student who used the same university computer, or with a colleague who used the same corporate mainframe.

Yet while e-mail drew from earlier forms, it was identical with none of them. It was unlike a letter in that you didn't need to supply a return address (street number and name, city, state, and Zip code) in the upper right-hand corner; nor could you append a handwritten signature at the end. Unlike most letters and postcards, the message had to be *typed* rather than handwritten, and you could expect instantaneous delivery. (Indeed, the whole idea of delivery was at once familiar and odd.) Your writing style was more likely to be casual than in a memo, at times even chatty. In keeping with the tradition of the memo, you could "Cc" others — that is, carbon-copy them (clearly an anachronism) — but unlike the memo, this required no additional human effort; it essentially came for free. And if, in its ability to facilitate broad distribution, it was like publishing or broadcasting, it was also unlike these media because anyone could send a message.

In those first years, e-mail could be exchanged only among those who had shared access to the same computer system, thus limiting contact to academic and research communities. But beginning in the early 1970s, e-mail appeared on the Arpanet, which meant that people using computers connected via the network could correspond with one another. In addition, in the early 1980s, large-scale proprietary systems — some within corporate environments, others providing commercial services for a fee to individuals (precursors of America Online and Compuserve) — gave a great many more people, distributed throughout the world, access to e-mail, if not the Arpanet. It therefore became easier, and much more common, for people who had never met one another face-to-face to correspond in the informal manner that e-mail users had come to adopt. The development of bulletin boards and distribution lists organized around common interests (parents of dyslexic children, hobbyists, vegetarians, etc.) made "posting" a message to a large number of people, mostly strangers, an everyday occurrence.

Early on in the use of e-mail, a form of behavior emerged which came to be called flaming (sending angry, vitriolic messages to others). Hacker culture was from the beginning confrontational; when online, people seemed more likely than usual to talk in blunt, even hostile terms. "Flame wars" might then ensue, the rough equivalent of a shouting match, among a number of correspondents. The social conventions of polite speech didn't seem to operate, at least not to the usual extent. E-mail correspondence, especially that on bulletin boards and in chat rooms, was different from informal letter exchange among friends (where the participants knew each other). It was also different from business or bureaucratic communications in which the norm was a certain disinterested formality. It wasn't surprising, then, if combining informal and personal correspondence with broad distribution led to bumpy times. It is understandable that attempts at humor and irony might be misunderstood when broadcast within a community of strangers.

And so the novel social and technical circumstances of e-mail began to produce new communicative conventions. These days it isn't unusual for e-mail communities to establish rules of proper conduct (netiquette) governing how one communicates with others (interpersonal style) and what topics are fair game to address. And the new written symbols, called smileys or emoticons (smiling and winking faces made from parentheses, semicolons, and other punctuation marks, such as ;)), are concrete evidence of the ongoing transformation and evolution of the genre. Indeed, the rise of these little symbols nicely illustrates a central feature of the way documents, document technologies, and human activities continually co-evolve. You can see how, in this case, textual communication of a new sort (e-mail) based on new technologies (digital) produced new social circumstances (informal textual communication among strangers), and how this in turn led to the development of new communicative conventions (rules of politeness tailored to the online environment), including the minting of new textual symbols (smileys). It is exactly because genres are so tightly bound to particular technologies and social contexts that change in the genre is likely to take place when either the technologies or the social contexts change.

Another example of this ongoing co-evolution is the use of Bcc, or blind carbon copy. In the days when office memos or circular letters (as they were earlier called) were typed on paper, a single copy might be circulated to the relevant parties with the aid of a routing sheet. The routing sheet listed the intended readers in the order in which they were to receive the memo. Once you'd received the memo and read it (or were simply done with it), you checked off your name on the routing sheet, or placed your initials there, and forwarded the memo (the very copy you'd just read) to the next person on the list. Unlike the recipients named in the To field or on the routing sheet, those named in the Cc field were to receive a separate physical copy, literally a carbon copy. Often a carbon copy went to the files for informational and legal purposes, as well as being sent to specific individuals.

With the advent of inexpensive photocopying, however, the practice shifted. Now it became more common for everyone — those on the To list and those on the Cc list — to receive a separate physical copy. This meant that each recipient could keep his or her own local copy. But it also had an effect on the political and rhetorical significance of annotation. When a single copy circulated among a number of people, anything written on that copy would be seen by those next on the list. You would therefore be sure not to write anything you didn't want others to see; conversely, you could mark annotations specifically to make them visible to others. This practice changed, of course, once you had your own personal copy. Now your annotations could be for your own personal use; they could be as private as you wanted. But you were then also free to circulate *your* copy to others not originally on the list, and by first annotating it and then copying and sending it to *your* list, you could put your own spin on its content.

Clearly it was of crucial significance what was visible and what was not, who was privy to what, and who was excluded. Not only did these concerns apply to possible annotations but to the identity of the memo's recipients. With a To list or a routing sheet, anyone who glanced at the circulating memo could see all of its intended recipients, with all the political implications of such knowledge. Of course, it was always possible to distribute copies to people who were listed on neither the To list nor the Cc list. (Before photocopying, this would most likely be done at the point where the memo originated.) This practice was invisible from the point of view of the recipients.

Once e-mail was developed, however, a Bcc (blind carbon copy) field could be added to the memo that reified the earlier practice. And so in e-mail now, if you want a copy of your message to be distributed to someone, you've got to specify that person's address in some manner. Adding a new field very neatly solved the problem of distribution and invisibility. Your copy of the message (if you were the originator) would show the list of those Bcc'd, but no one else's copy would. From this point of view, their copy would be different from yours.

The creation of Bcc therefore changed the intellectual and physical form of e-mail (by adding a new field), and changed practice (by giving writers a choice among three categories of recipients). But as a recent article in *The New York Times* indicates, the uses of Bcc are continuing to evolve.[3] Specifically, people are making increasing use of the option as they see the potential perils of disclosing the addresses of their intended recipients. The article recounts several cautionary tales of abuse. In one case, a man named Spencer Grey sent out a change-of-address notice to a large number of recipients. Subsequently, a friend who'd received the message sent a party invitation to everyone on Grey's list that included a joking reference to drug use. But Grey's change-of-address message had been sent to business clients as well as friends. "If I have learned anything," Grey is quoted as saying, "it's the value of the Bcc option." In another case, a list of recipients was used by one recipient for marketing purposes, again crossing the line between friendship and business. The article offers its moral in the concluding sentence: "Cc at your own risk."

No doubt this is good advice. But the real question is *when* to Cc and *when* to Bcc, which the article calls the "to Cc or to Bcc dilemma." Clearly, there is a need to balance privacy and disclosure, invisibility and visibility.

> On one hand, privacy concerns have increasingly made Internet users skittish about sharing their e-mail addresses — a view that in some cases extends to friends' addresses. On the other hand, it can be a bit disturbing to receive a party invitation via e-mail

> where the To field says "undisclosed recipients" or "recipient list
> suppressed" — phrases some e-mail programs insert when all of
> the recipients have been blind Cc'd on a message.

One woman reports resolving the "to Cc or to Bcc dilemma" according to the type of message she's sending combined with the size of the recipients list. So she will use Bcc for change-of-address and other similar professional announcements. For party invitations, if the list is small, she'll generally use the Cc option, while for larger parties she makes use of Bcc. Clearly the conventions governing the appropriate use of Cc and Bcc are still being written. And they will no doubt continue to shift with changes in the legal, social, and technical environment on the Internet.

The "Cc or Bcc dilemma" serves as a cautionary tale about trust in the online environment. It is a small example, to be sure, but it is emblematic of the problems we encounter when previously established pathways of communication and social interaction become unstable. Monkeying with trust is serious business. For trust, as social philosophers have pointed out over the centuries, is the glue that binds a society together. "How could coordinated activity of any kind be possible if people could not rely upon others' undertakings?" asks Steven Shapin in *A Social History of Truth*. "No goods would be handed over without prior payment, and no payment without goods in hand. There would be no point in keeping engagements, nor any reason to make engagements with people who could not be expected to honor their commitments. The relationship between teacher and pupil, parent and child, would be impossible if the reliability of the former as sources of knowledge were not to be granted."[4]

How can we trust our documents, though, when the very systems and practices that have worked to ensure their trustworthiness are currently unstable? This came home to me in a very personal way not long ago. I had gone to the emergency room on the advice of my doctor's office (my doctor was out of town) to be examined for the (unlikely) possibility of a serious ailment. The doctor examining me needed to know something about the trigeminal nerve, one of the cranial nerves in the head. It was a detail, he frankly admitted to me, he didn't remember from medical school. He found a medical reference book in the emergency room, but it didn't have the information he sought. Half in jest, I suggested he look on the Web.

To my surprise, he liked the idea and we walked a few feet to a workstation, where he proceeded to do a search of the Web. A huge number of hits came back (in the thousands), and he began looking through some of the top-rated results. A number of these Web pages looked quite official — they had the look and feel of pages from a medical textbook. The information he found confirmed his vague recollection of what he'd learned in medical school. "But I'll check three sources, just to be sure," he said.

Clearly he knew that the medical information he found on random Web sites couldn't be trusted in the same way he would trust a textbook or a reference work published by a reputable medical publisher and used by reputable practitioners. So he took a comparative approach, deciding to check for agreement across sources. This is, of course, a risky and unreliable strategy, as I once discovered for myself. Unsure how to spell "Caribbean" (how many *r*'s? how many *b*'s?), I had done a search on the Web for the spelling I thought was correct, "Carribean." When I got thousands of hits for this spelling, I assumed I was right. But I wasn't: many other people don't know how to spell Caribbean either. (This was a stupid thing to do, of course, and I should have known better. Authoritative knowledge, unlike elective office, isn't simply established by a show of hands.)

Even with this recent experience in mind, I chose to hold my tongue. Much as my doctor was evaluating his sources, I was evaluating him, including his evaluation strategy. We both knew his strategy was faulty, but in the particular circumstances in which we found ourselves — the limited likelihood that I was ill and the relative reliability of his partial memory — it was probably good enough. Had the circumstances been otherwise, he would have insisted on more reliable sources, or I would have.

Had my doctor been able to consult an established, printed medical reference book, the trustworthiness of its information content would have been immediately apparent. But the truthfulness and transparency of its medical knowledge would come not from the marks on the page alone — these are merely the tip of an enormous iceberg — but from the trustworthiness of the publisher and its placement within a vast network of Western medical practices. Even if one of the sources he consulted had been an online version of an authoritative text, it *still* wouldn't have had the same authority as its print-and-paper counterpart. How could he know that the same strict quality controls had been applied to the online version, or that the online text hadn't been tampered with?

Issues of trust and quality are always central considerations in the publication process. As it has taken shape in recent centuries, publishing is more than just "making public" — it is the circulation of socially sanctioned, authoritative knowledge. Indeed, you might think of the modern publishing industry as a cultural mechanism for ensuring the reliability of certain genres. Nowhere has this vetting process been more prominent or of greater significance than in academia, which relies on elaborate processes of peer review and where reputations are made and broken based on scholars' publication records. Academia is also the corner of publishing in which digital technologies have so far made the deepest inroads.

So let's have a look at academic publishing in transition as it struggles to come to terms with the digital medium. While the details are certainly interesting and important in themselves, I offer them here primarily as an extended example of the immense effort required to stabilize published documents in a destabilized environment.

Today the movement online of genres of scholarly communication is taking place within a climate of great ferment and anxiety. Fundamental questions are being raised about the future of scholarship, the pursuit of knowledge, and the process of education. Some of this soul-searching, however, predates the current digital transformation. Since 1970, while books have risen in price at roughly the rate of inflation, journals have increased by well over ten percent per year.[5] This has led academic libraries (the main purchasers of academic journals) to cut back on their subscriptions, while publishers, seeing their market shrink, have raised prices further. And despite these cost-cutting measures, the proportion of library budgets devoted to journals has increased, causing them to cut back on the purchase of scholarly monographs (books) as well. The net result is that academic libraries have been purchasing an ever-smaller number of the publications faculty and students want.

In recent years a great deal of scholarly attention has been directed at the problem: entire conferences, issues of journals, and books have been devoted to the subject. The result has been a fairly clear understanding of the problem, if not consensus on how to fix it. What is clear to everyone is that "journals are the lifeblood of scholarship — libraries and researchers cannot function without them," as a recent *New York Times* article put it.[6] Or as Charles Bazerman says in *Shaping Written Knowledge:* "Knowledge produced by the academy is cast primarily in written language. . . . The written text, published in journal or book, serves as the definitive form of a claim or argument, following on earlier printed claims and leading to future claims."[7] It is therefore fairly inevitable that disruptions to journals will be felt throughout the entire system of scholarship.

The journal article, like the postcard and the memo, is an outgrowth of the letter. The first scientific journals, originating in the mid-seventeenth century, were essentially collections of correspondence. But it was only in the nineteenth century, the same period that saw the rise of modern bureaucracy and the modern library, that the journal in its contemporary format emerged. For this was the period in which the modern university emerged as a secular institution and became "the great factory of knowledge and education."[8] And it was in this redefined institution that the world of knowledge was partitioned into innumerable disciplines, each with its own publication channels for the production and circulation of its specialized knowledge.

For a century, more or less, the academic system of knowledge production and consumption has worked like this: Professors perform research and write scholarly articles and books to disseminate their results. University presses and scholarly societies take responsibility for the publication process: they oversee peer review (the process by which members of the author's scholarly community vouch for the integrity and quality of his or her results), as well as for the editing, printing, and distribution of research results. Academic libraries then buy these publications, making them available to faculty and students. The result is a closed circuit in which written knowledge circulates from scholars to publishers to libraries, then back to scholars. Quality control through peer review has a double role in this system, shaping the quantity and quality of the knowledge that circulates and also helping to determine academic promotion and tenure, because academics must "publish or perish."

For most of the twentieth century this was a highly effective system. It can be credited with enabling the tremendous growth in scientific and technical knowledge. But it seems to have fallen victim to its own success. In the aftermath of World War II, as large sums of government money were poured into academic research, the number of journals and monographs mushroomed. And although publication to this point had largely been in the hands of nonprofit academic presses and learned societies, commercial publishers saw the possibility of making a profit. The profusion of publications, along with commercial publishers' increasing control of publication channels, has made it impossible for libraries to collect — that is, to pay for — all the materials scholars and students may want, thus creating the current crisis.

So what can be done about it? Many people now look to the Internet for the solution. Perhaps the most radical proposal has been advanced by Stevan Harnad, a cognitive psychologist at the University of Southampton in England, who suggests that scholars should take back control of their own publication processes by self-publishing their works on the Web (he calls this "self-archiving"). Academics, Harnad believes, unlike the authors of trade publications, aren't fundamentally concerned with making a profit. They are already paid by their academic institutions, and the kind of reward they look for from their writings has more to do with the circulation of their ideas, and with the attendant prestige and promotion. But they have been forced "to make the 'Faustian bargain' of trading the copyright for their words [to commercial publishers] in exchange for having them published."[9] Scholars, in other words, not unlike Lewis Hyde's artists, would prefer to operate in a gift economy, but have been forced into a market economy out of the need to cooperate with commercial publishers.

Fortunately, Harnad claims, a solution is now at hand: scholars need only publish online. It is a much less expensive alternative — electronic journals, he insists, can be produced for twenty-five percent of the cost of their paper counterparts — and this will allow authors to regain control of their works. What's more, the shift to a pure gift economy could happen instantaneously. "So what is the strategy for ushering in this brave new era? It is a simple subversive proposal that I make to all scholars and scientists right now: If from this day forward, each and every one of you were to make available on the Net, in publicly accessible archives on the World Wide Web, the texts of all your current papers (and whichever past ones are still sitting on your word processors' disks), then the transition to the PostGutenberg galaxy would happen virtually overnight."[10]

But this isn't a proposal to open the floodgates of publishing to one and all. Harnad thinks the Web in its current unregulated state is a "global vanity press."[11] This simply won't work for scholarship. He acknowledges the importance of quality control, and an essential condition of his subversive proposal is that peer review be maintained for online publications. But this would be straightforward, he asserts: scholars already perform this service for free (when asked to do so by current journal and monograph publishers), and since peer review is "medium independent,"[12] it could easily be transferred from paper to digital publication.

Needless to say, Harnad's proposal is controversial. While it doesn't cut publishers and libraries completely out of the picture, it doesn't necessarily leave a whole lot of room for them, either. Commercial publishers currently making a healthy profit on journal subscriptions aren't likely to show much enthusiasm for his proposal. Within the scholarly world itself, a range of questions and criticisms have been raised: Is electronic publishing really as inexpensive as Harnad claims? Is instituting peer review of online publications as simple a matter as he suggests? Are there perhaps better ways to achieve quality control than peer review in an online environment? Do we really want to move the current system of scholarly communication onto the Internet (is it realistic to attempt it), or is it time to rethink the whole system in more fundamental ways?

Meanwhile, as this admittedly extreme proposal is being debated, many changes are already taking place. More and more journals are appearing online. Some of these are established paper-based journals that have decided to create a parallel, digital presence. Others are new journals, created just for the Web, and some of these have made the bold decision to appear in digital format only. The initial movement has been fairly conservative, with online versions maintaining the look and feel of their paper precursors. But changes, both in format and in the rhythm of publishing, have already begun to appear.

In paper journals, the cost of paper and printing has been a major determinant of the length of articles and the total number of pages in an issue. In online journals, however, the cost of printing isn't a factor and articles can be, and in some cases have been, as lengthy as author and publisher wish. The concept of an issue or edition — the binding together of a set of articles all produced at the same time — is also an artifact of the print world, and online journals are now beginning to "unbundle" their articles: rather than putting up a collection of articles (an issue) at one time, individual articles are being "issued" to the Web site whenever they are ready. Journal publishers are also now providing hyperlinked citations between articles, something that was impossible on paper. And new kinds of content — video, simulations, interactive displays — are being incorporated as well.

Perhaps a more fundamental shift is already happening in the publication process. In 1991, Paul Ginsparg, a physicist at the Los Alamos National Laboratories, first put together a database of physics "preprints" (research papers not yet published). Prior to this, physicists already had a tradition of sharing research results before publication. Ginsparg's system provided new technology to support these existing practices and was quickly embraced; over the last decade it has become a stable element in the practice of physics. Similar services, now called "e-print servers," have been developed in other disciplines, including computer science, psychology, and medicine. While these systems don't require any form of review for submission, there is nothing to prevent individuals or groups from setting up systems of peer review or other kinds of quality control on top of the base layer of unrefereed articles. But rather than the simple yes/no (published or not published) decision made by traditional journals, the potential exists to establish a whole range of quality measures (how many people have read a given article, who has commented on it, etc.) and for users to search the archive for papers that satisfy the criteria they are most interested in.

Journals aren't the only scholarly form in transition. There are equally important questions about whether the scholarly monograph or book will survive, and if so, in what form. Clifford Lynch, director of the Coalition for Networked Information (a consortium of major academic institutions), believes that even bigger changes are in store for the monograph than for the journal article. "The digital monograph," he suggests, "is likely to become a larger scale, collaborative effort."

> In print we might think of a series of interrelated but distinct and independent works, such as a critical edition of the writings of an author and a number of works of criticism and analysis that make reference to this authoritative edition. In the digital environment, all of these resources may be woven together into an encyclopedic work of multiple authorship. It will also be possible to link sites in a more extensive and intimate way than can be accomplished through traditional bibliographic citation. In the print world, reviews are separate from monographs; on the web, the comments of one scholar can be directly integrated into the living work of another. And websites, particularly if they involve digitized source materials and multimedia, are often the products of teams rather than individual authors.[13]

Nor is it just scholarly communication that is in transition. There is much talk these days — excitement but also concern — about the way the Internet may contribute to a profound rethinking of the entire educational process. The Web, e-mail, and Internet-enabled video conferencing are now being used to create online courses for students who are located at a distance from the instructor and from a physical campus. It isn't yet clear whether this kind of "distance learning" simply offers students more educational opportunities — the choice to be located remotely or on campus — or whether it signals the beginning of a more significant reworking of educational practices. Certainly, the University of Phoenix, a for-profit university whose teaching is centered around distance learning, has sent a wake-up call to traditional bricks-and-mortar institutions.

At the moment, then, there is no real clarity about how academic scholarship, publication, or indeed the entire educational system will be transformed. No one doubts that publication will remain central to scholarship. But at the same time no one is certain how far new, online genres will diverge from their print-and-paper predecessors. Nor is it clear how the competition among today's stakeholders — scholars and scholarly societies, academic libraries and presses — for a piece of the future pie will shake out. Even more disconcerting is the uncertainty about the future forms and purposes of education and scholarship.

It is interesting to compare this creative ferment in the academy with what is happening in mainstream publishing. In the area of serials (newspapers and magazines), the pattern is quite similar to that of scholarly journals: the creation of online counterparts to print-and-paper publications; the creation of brand-new publications online without any prior counterpart; the loosening up of the notion of editions and the unbundling of articles.

Although there has been much talk of digital books, so far there has been relatively little action. Most of the books now available in digital form — through sources like Project Gutenberg and the Bartleby Library — are works whose copyright protection has expired. Holders of current copyright have been understandably reticent to put their books online for fear of widespread, unauthorized copying. E-books — portable computers meant to display digital works loaded into them — are still in a fairly primitive state, although this could change quickly. And, thus far, no new book-like genres have emerged, despite significant experimentation in hypertext fiction over the last decade or so.

Perhaps the greatest challenge to the current system of book publication at the moment comes not from the evolution of genres or the availability of new hardware but from the potential transformation of the publication process itself: who does it and in what manner. Although Stephen King's experiment in self-publication was a failure by the most obvious standard of success (money), it does suggest how other stakeholders may choose to enter the arena. Perhaps even more suggestive, and immediately challenging, are the companies now offering "print on demand" services. For a small fee they will take any author's manuscript and "publish" it: put it in digital form so it can be printed, bound, and sold to a reader on demand. To traditional publishers this is upsetting, not just because it has the potential to break their monopoly, but because it threatens the quality-control process by which, from their point of view, only the best works enter the public realm. In a short piece in *Harper's,* two editors at commercial publishing houses reprimand one of these companies, Xlibris, for opening the floodgates when in fact "[t]he book industry has many problems; publishing too few books is not one of them."[14]

And so we are back to issues of trust, reliability, and quality, surely some of the most central concerns not just for published works but for personal correspondence and administrative and commercial documents as well. It takes a great deal of parenting, and perhaps even a village, to raise a responsible child. It takes a complex, largely invisible infrastructure to create stable talking things that will reliably do our bidding, and that will help us in our ongoing efforts to make a meaningful and orderly world. It should hardly be surprising if a disruption to these efforts of the scale we are now experiencing would be unsettling. Whose job, whose career path, whose sense of self and of an orderly life, isn't perturbed by such developments? And given the complexity of the forces now at work, the subtle interplay among genres, technologies, and work practices and institutions, it should hardly be surprising if we can't see how it will all turn out. While this might seem like an adequate explanation of our current dis-ease, I suggest we go one step further and examine the existential roots of our striving after, and our anxiety of, order.

10

The Search for Stable Ground

THE LOMA PRIETA EARTHQUAKE struck Northern California at 5:04 P.M. on October 17, 1989. The earth shook for only twenty seconds, but in that brief time, its immense power was felt as far away as San Diego and western Nevada. Buildings collapsed in the Marina district of San Francisco, some sinking several stories into the liquefied ground. One section of the Bay Bridge, which links San Francisco with Oakland, fell. Many deaths occurred when the Cypress Street section of Interstate 880 collapsed like a pancake, killing those on the lower level.

At the time of the earthquake, I was at work in Palo Alto. I remember huddling in the vestibule of the men's room, wondering if this was the big one. I remember watching as a jagged crack formed, as if in slow motion, in the wall in front of me. As soon as it seemed safe, I rushed outside to the open-air parking lot. Others had already turned on their car radios to determine the extent of the damage.

In the first hours following the earthquake and into the next day, there was a palpable giddiness. We were alive; everything was okay. But then a collective stupor seemed to descend. In San Francisco, it became oddly still as people walked and drove around in shock, unable quite to grasp the reality of the event. We needed time to come to terms not just with what had happened, but with what it *meant:* that we lived our lives on shaky foundations.

Some people found this reality more than they could handle and moved away, presumably to safer ground. Most of us stayed. But in the weeks and months following the quake, we lived with strong memories of the event and with its emotional aftermath. Because PARC's main building, where my office was located, had suffered significant damage, we weren't allowed back in for several weeks. I discovered that whenever I was in a stairwell, the walls seemed to shake. This reaction, presumably a form of post-traumatic stress, lasted for weeks. But for several months more, whenever I drove under an overpass on the freeway, I was briefly gripped with fear that it might collapse. And if I happened to be stopped in traffic under an overpass, my anxiety increased with the passing seconds. In time, of course, these reactions subsided. The memories of the quake faded, as did the awareness of my vulnerability.

The existential significance of this whole experience was summed up by one odd little coincidence that happened in the first day following the quake. For several weeks I had been house-sitting for acquaintances in San Francisco, and had been commuting between San Francisco and Palo Alto, a distance of about thirty-five miles. Because the condition of the roads was uncertain immediately after the earthquake, I decided not to venture up to the city that night. The next day, as I headed back to the house, I was understandably concerned about what I might find. So I was relieved to discover that the house was still standing, and seemed not to have suffered any noticeable damage. As I conducted a tour, room by room, however, I discovered something — an accident? a meaningful co-occurrence? — that gave me pause for thought.

For a month or so prior to this, I had been taking a class in Biblical Hebrew at Stanford. Our assignment for the week had been to translate Psalm 104 from Hebrew to English. There on the kitchen table was my class notebook, exactly where I'd left it the morning before. It was open to the last line I had translated on the morning of the earthquake. My translation of line 5 read:

God has set the earth on a firm foundation so it won't shake.

But there was more. This was a home filled with books. Bookshelves lined the walls, yet hardly a book had fallen throughout the house. But when I went downstairs to the study, where my computer was installed, one of the owner's books had fallen onto the desk from a bookshelf above it: Immanuel Velikovsky's *Earth in Upheaval*.

This immediately struck me as funny. Upstairs, one source declared that the earth doesn't shake; downstairs another proclaimed the opposite. Here was a divine riddle, or perhaps a Zen koan: How is it that the earth shakes and doesn't shake? Whether by chance or design, this juxtaposition of messages seemed to pose a series of related questions: Where does our stability come from? Where can we find solid ground? In the end, what can we really rely on?

It is curious that the Book of Psalms played a role in posing these questions. Over several millennia, many millions of people have looked to this book — and the Bible more generally — as a source of answers to life's great questions. Living through trying and uncertain times occasioned by earthquakes, wars, illness, divorce, and the nearly endless forms of human suffering, countless people have found comfort in the words of sacred scripture. Not just the words, though, but the physical volume — solid, substantial, lovingly tended, and perhaps handed down from generation to generation — has itself served as a symbol and a reminder of cosmic safety and security. And the fact that the book was mobile, that it could be carried from place to place, meant that it could serve as a traveling reminder — that it could, in effect, provide a sense of home away from home.

George Steiner makes this very point in an essay called "Our Homeland, the Text." He suggests that for Jews living in exile over many centuries, the Bible, or Torah, as it is called in Hebrew, has been their homeland, "the literal-spiritual locus of self-recognition and of communal identification."[1] Jews have figuratively carried the Torah on their backs, and it has provided them with "an unhoused at-homeness in the text."[2] Of course, it isn't only Jews but Christians for whom the Bible (admittedly a somewhat different collection of texts) has provided a sense of identity and stability. Nor is the Bible the only "book" that has anchored faith communities. Muslims, Buddhists, and Hindus (to name three prominent traditions) have all drawn strength and direction from a small set of canonical texts. In each case, a community's sacred literature has helped its members address some of the most basic, existential questions of human life: Who am I? Where do I come from and where am I going? What is death — and, for that matter, what is life? What is to be valued, and in what can I place my trust? What is the nature of the universe, and how should I act in it?

Of course, it isn't only sacred literature that has provided this kind of practical, moral, and at times spiritual orientation. Just look at the role the U.S. Constitution has played in establishing and maintaining American culture and identity. The Constitution is more than the founding document of the American nation and the basis for its legal system; it is the locus of many of the nation's values, and, through a process of ongoing interpretation, the formal mechanism by which the society has set its moral and practical compass. In a related manner, the Western canon — the collection of culturally authoritative literary and philosophical works stretching from Plato to Shakespeare and beyond — has also served as a source of identity and stability akin to the Bible or the Constitution. Indeed, the "culture wars" of the last decade or two can be seen as a religious struggle over whose literature (and whose values and worldview) should predominate.

So it isn't hard to see great documents like the Bible, the Constitution, or the works of Plato and Shakespeare as sources of stability, providing meaning, direction, and reassurance in the face of life's uncertainties. But I would venture to say that this is true of all our documents, from cash register receipts to children's notes, from greeting cards to Web pages — for all of them aim to provide some measure of stable ground in an unstable world. You probably wouldn't want to say that a cash register receipt offers answers to the great questions of life the way the Bible aims to, or that it is the basis for practical guidance on the scale of the Constitution. Yet in a curious and profound way I do believe that documents — *all of them* —

address the great existential questions of human life. I'm also convinced that we can't see documents most fully for what they are without framing them in existential terms.

Before I can elaborate on these statements, though, I need to say something about the existential dimension of cultural order. On this subject, I have been strongly influenced by the work of the cultural anthropologist Ernest Becker and his writings on the relationship between death, anxiety, and culture. In his Pulitzer Prize–winning book *The Denial of Death,* Becker argues that death — our inability to come to terms with our mortality, our fear and denial of it — is the primary fuel for all of human culture. Death, he claims, quoting William James, is "the worm at the center of the apple," the inescapable condition of human life, which eats away at our projects, our sense of ourselves, our hopes and dreams. How can there be lasting meaning and value in the face of our fragile and temporary existence?

Building on other existentialist thinkers, most notably the Danish philosopher Kierkegaard, Becker sees human anxiety as the result of our inability to come to terms with our finitude. Although it may manifest itself in particular issues in our lives — in concern for our health, for our family's well-being, or for our own career advancement — this anxiety actually springs from a deeper source, the core of our being, and has less to do with specific conditions than with our relationship to life itself.

But death, in and of itself, can't be the cause of our anxiety, Becker observes. Death is only a problem because we *know* that we will die. Most other creatures on the planet presumably live in blissful ignorance of their ultimate end. This makes human consciousness a mixed blessing at best, for it is at once the source of humankind's unique achievements and also of its greatest terror. Following Kierkegaard, Becker reads the story of Adam and Eve's expulsion from the Garden of Eden as a parable on the emergence of human consciousness. Adam, upon eating from the Tree of Knowledge, discovers his dual nature: that he is a mixture of earth and divine breath.

We therefore live with a nearly unbearable burden — not just the knowledge of our mortality, but the anxiety that accompanies this knowledge. Because we cannot live with the awareness of our small-ness, our incompleteness, our mortality, we find ways to suppress or deny the reality of our plight. We try to build ourselves up, to make a "success" of ourselves; or we give ourselves over to something larger: a leader, a cause, an ideal.

Becker sees human culture as the playing field on which this drama is continually enacted. There are endless ways in which we attempt to make something of ourselves and thereby "outlive or outshine death and decay."[3] Some of us pursue wealth and power. Others attempt to create lasting works or monuments, or to excel in sports, or to raise children who will accomplish what their parents failed to do. But these attempts at heroism are only possible because human culture creates the conditions for them. (You can't be rich without a com-munal notion of wealth, or powerful without social structures of hierarchy and dominance. What are works or monuments or sports or families, apart from the human lifeworld through which they are defined?) Apart from what it allows us as individuals to do, human culture — the whole continuous run of it from thousands of years ago into the indefinite future — is our collective immortality project.

A second, more recent work adds an interesting twist to Becker's analysis of the human condition. In a book called *Lack and Transcen-dence,* David Loy, a philosopher, builds on the groundwork that Kierkegaard, Becker, and others have laid. He too sees in human life a retreat from chaos and an attempt to escape anxiety. But he disagrees with Becker that the root cause of our dilemma is the fear of death. Loy observes that for each of us death is *in the future*. While death may certainly be terrifying to contemplate and fearful to anticipate, there is something even more terrifying *right now*, and it is this that is the true source of our anxiety.

Loy calls this something *lack*. This is the sense that we are incom-plete, that we are flawed, inadequate, not enough. Much as Becker suggests that we will do anything to avoid facing our mortality, Loy suggests we will do anything in the attempt to escape from or to nullify our sense of lack. Driven by lack, we are constantly searching for more: more material possessions, more status, more love. But, alas, we discover again and again that the latest attainments provide only temporary satisfaction. There is still more we lack, and we go chasing after it.

But such efforts to acquire enough, or to become enough, as a way of escaping our lack are doomed to failure. Drawing on Buddhist philosophy, Loy suggests that the sense of lack is a necessary concomitant of the self. Each one of us, by virtue of having a self, is continually struggling to discover "ourself" and to know that we are real. What drives us is the suspicion that "I" am not real. Descartes's famous dictum, "I think therefore I am," was one attempt to resolve this dilemma. (The very fact that I doubt I am real is proof that I am.) Buddhism, however, doesn't accept this way out. "Rather than being autonomous in some Cartesian fashion," Loy says, "our sense of self is mentally and socially conditioned, therefore ungrounded and . . . fragile."[4]

We want to know that we are real, that we stand on firm existential ground, that we are whole. But this longing is doomed from the start, because our true nature can only be found in our relatedness; in our very being we are inseparable from one another, nature, the universe. It is an unfortunate property of the self — an inherent property — that it sees "itself" as independent, can't find the grounds for proving this (because no such grounds exist), yet persists in searching obsessively for them. This hole at the center of the self leads us to acquire and to accumulate, to plan, to try to build ourselves up. "To the extent I come to feel autonomous, my consciousness is also infected with a gnawing sense of unreality, usually experienced as the vague feeling that 'there is something wrong with me.' Since we do not know how to cope with such an intimate sense of lack, it is repressed, only to return in projected form as the compulsive ways we attempt to make ourselves real in the world. . . ."[5] Even the fear of death, Loy suggests, is a result of this lack. Rather than face our incompleteness *right now,* we project it onto a future time, the time of our death. This future event becomes the source of our anxiety, rather than the more immediate, and therefore more terrifying, realization that we are inadequate right now, and can never be made whole.

Ultimately we long, both Becker and Loy agree, to transcend our finiteness and incompleteness. Both agree that it is through our cultural projects and products that we try to transcend death or to fill our lack. Where Becker talks about the attempt to carve out "a place in nature, by building an edifice that reflects human value," Loy suggests we need "to organize the chaos of life by finding a unifying meaning-system that gives us knowledge about the world and a life-program for living in it, informing us both what is and what we should do."[6]

Here is a story that makes sense of order and anxiety — and the anxiety of order — in existential terms. The human search for and construction of order, it says, is our response to the profound mystery, and the accompanying anxiety, of existence. Emerging into an unfathomable universe and fearing that we are nothing within it, we strive to create a meaningful and ultimately immortal place for ourselves. Like Marlon Brando's character in *On the Waterfront,* we long to be somebody, "instead of a bum, which is what I am." Culture creates the conditions for a meaningful existence, for us to play out our games of physical and symbolic survival. But it is an ongoing performance, a play we can never stop performing, lest we see the backstage gears and levers and be reminded of the mysterious and terrifying backdrop against which we are performing it. Of course we are always coming upon gaps in the play: when a loved one dies, when war makes a mockery of our pretensions to civility, when we wander into a deteriorating department store, or are awakened in the middle of the night with physical or psychic pain, or even when a messy desk threatens our ability to cope with our ordinary, everyday chores. But these failures of performance are quickly fixed or covered up or, when this isn't possible, denied and forgotten.

Here too is where documents reenter the story. For they are death-transcending, lack-filling artifacts of major proportions. Perhaps they can't literally prevent our physical demise or fill our deepest sense of lack. But they are central participants in our attempts to do so. Every one of them — each cash register receipt, each greeting card, each Post-it note — makes a contribution to the collaborative edifice we call human culture. Although few carry the cultural weight of the Bible or the Constitution, all of them inform us of "what is and what we should do." And in concert they help us create and sustain an orderly and meaningful human lifeworld. But all our cultural products do this, so what, if anything, makes documents special?

What makes them special, what makes them unique, is that we have created them in our own image. We are, in the language of the ancient rabbis, *ha-medabrim,* talking beings, and we have created *ha-medabrim.* We are body and breath, in the language of Genesis, and so are our documents. This perceived parallel has given rise over the centuries to a unique possibility: that we might preserve ourselves in and through our documents. Indeed, since ancient times writing has been seen as a vehicle of immortality. Writers have attempted to preserve their words and ideas, to fix them in a permanent medium, to have them resurrected in the bodies of future readers. By embedding some portion of their essence (their voice, their soul) in stone, in parchment, or in some other durable medium, the hope has been that they might live on — that they might "outlive or outshine death and decay."

At times this strategy has been more than a metaphor. In ancient Greece, where reading was typically vocalized, to read an author's words aloud meant to be controlled by the author. To have one's words read meant "to take control of somebody else's vocal apparatus, to exercise power over the body of the reader, even from a distance, possibly a great distance both in space and in time. The writer who [was] successful in getting himself read [made] use of the internal organs of someone else, even from beyond the grave."[7] From this perspective, through one's writings, one might hope to live on through others.

Today, however, it isn't so easy to see documents as part of a literal immortality project. We know too much. The attempt to preserve ourselves on paper or even in stone seems no more realistic than Egyptian attempts to achieve immortality through mummification.

We know how fragile and short-lived is paper. We know that Web pages, for the moment at least, are likely to survive a matter of days, less than an instant in cosmic time. We know that even when words and phrases *are* preserved for long periods, meaning and interpretation continue to shift. Documents cannot save us — at least not in this way.

Still, in their very essence, documents carry a protest against the passage of time, against change, and against human mortality. The very fact that we have *tried* to hold our voices and our messages fixed in stone or in some other medium is surely a testament to a powerful longing within us. The fact that we have invested so much cultural energy in the enterprise — mastering materials, creating systems of communication, teaching literacy — over so many centuries is surely evidence of the strength of this drive. And even if documents ultimately fail to solve our crisis of mortality, that they manage to achieve *any measure of fixity at all* in a world of continual flux is surely a remarkable achievement. Their moments of stolen fixity are like temporary steppingstones in the river of time. It is remarkable how a cash register receipt or a one-word note provides just enough stable ground to carry us the needed distance in a desired direction, then dissolves or loses its potency.

What's more, since documents are reflections and materializations of ourselves, their stability, however brief, is an assurance of our own. By making graven images of ourselves, we keep trying to see and know ourselves, and to make ourselves real. Some of these reflections we explicitly acknowledge and accept. Many of us keep personal journals as a way of knowing ourselves by putting ourselves on paper. Other reflections we explicitly disown. Who among us wants to see the massive tangle of bureaucratic documents as reflections of ourselves, as external manifestations of our tendencies toward depersonalized control?

No arena better shows off our sense of lack — how we are, or can be, driven by it, or how documents can be used to address it — than advertising. Most straightforwardly, of course, advertisements simply promote awareness in the hope that we will be moved to act. They tell us "what is" (a product or service) and "what we should do" (buy it!). If this were all ads did, their existential roots would be clear enough. But they actually go one step further, not only telling us *what* we should buy, but *why*. And it is in this second step that they most directly play on our sense of lack. For they hint, sometimes more explicitly, sometimes less, that through our purchase we can be made more real, more whole.

Let me illustrate with an example, an ad that appeared in magazines in the late 1990s. It shows the new Mercury Villager, a sport utility vehicle, parked on a beautiful tropical beach. As it sits there on the sand, close to the water's edge, a woman in a bathing suit, presumably its owner, is lounging nearby in a beach chair. The ad's message seems clear enough: Just look at the beautiful places this van will take you. (Never mind that you can't drive from New York, or even from California, to Hawaii.)

But on closer inspection, there is something curious about the rendering. One detail seems out of place. The van is actually parked *between* the woman and the water's edge. Why would you drive to the beach only to position yourself in a way that obscured your view of the water? I can think of two reasons: to shield yourself from the sun or from the wind. Yet neither of these explanations seems to work. There is no evidence of wind, and besides, the van's sliding doors are open: a wind coming off the water would likely pass directly through them. And as for the sun, well, this woman is hardly shielding herself from it. She is basking in it, in evident delight. The ray of sunlight illuminating her is passing *through* the van to get to her. It enters through the right rear passenger door and exits through the left passenger door, and as it is refracted through the vehicle, its gray hue is transmuted into a golden glow.

On a literal level, this image is showing off one of the new Mercury Villager's distinguishing features, that it has sliding passenger doors on *both* sides. But you're unlikely to understand this — it's almost impossible to read from the image — unless you already know it to be so. Something else is going on here, and it is this anomaly that points to the deeper message being conveyed. While on the surface

the ad speaks of travel to beautiful places, and extra doors for easy entry and exit, its deeper message is of transformation and illumination. This vehicle won't just take you to the *beach,* it will take you to *heaven.* It is a remarkable double offer being made here: a means of practical mobility and a route out of our fallenness.

Light is a common symbol of higher states of knowledge and well-being across cultures. While it often has overtly religious overtones, its symbolic value is equally invoked in secular contexts (as in "the Enlightenment," the name for the period of political emancipation and scientific progress in the eighteenth century). The designers of this advertisement have clearly borrowed traditional religious iconography, whether consciously or not, and have adapted it to suit their purposes in late-twentieth-century consumer culture. In Christian art, a ray of light commonly signifies the Annunciation, the announcement to Mary that she will bear a child. In Carlo Crivelli's late-fifteenth-century painting, for example, a heavenly ray falls on Mary, piercing the wall of the room where she kneels in prayer. In the ad, where Mary has been replaced by a woman in a bathing suit, there is something almost sacrilegious about the sunbather's suggestive pose. And yet there is something right about this too, for in her open state, she is receptive — ready to accept the light, to be transformed by what it has to offer.

Once you start looking at ads in this way, you find that many of them address our most basic human concerns. Some are even more explicit about their higher message, using text and image to reinforce one another. An ad for another large passenger vehicle shows an ocean liner with lifeboats mounted above the deck. In place of one of the boats is a Chevy Blazer. The caption reads, "A little security in an insecure world." Surely it is a great comfort to know that we will be safe when the ship (which ship? the stock market? the planet? our life?) goes down. (Unfortunately, this powerful message of protection in difficult times is undercut, hilariously, by one small detail. In the lower right-hand corner is the Blazer logo and motto that reads: "Blazer/Like a rock.")

As the Blazer example illustrates, not all advertisements make their appeal in explicitly religious terms. Yet in an odd sort of way, they are

like prayers. Perhaps they *are* prayers. Certainly they are expressions of our deepest hopes and longings: to be happy, loved, safe, powerful, wise, knowledgeable; to live full and meaningful lives; to have and to be *enough*. Perhaps some future civilization will come upon our TV and radio broadcasts, our magazines and newspapers, our Web pages ("click here for . . ."), and will recognize the sacred quality in these fervent appeals, more so perhaps than we can now.

But I would go a step further and suggest that all our documents have a sacred quality about them, that all of them are religious in nature. For all of them, insofar as they attempt to extend our reach, to cultivate relationships, and to augment our knowledge and understanding, are responses to the mystery of existence. They are concrete manifestations of our longing to be more powerful, more connected, more in-the-know. And in this sense they are religious — not because they necessarily give voice to particular religious ideologies (although some of them certainly do), but because they arise from the same deep, existential source as do our religious traditions. Why do we want more power, more love, and more knowledge, if not because we feel we don't have enough?

It should hardly be surprising if these same longings — existential longings, religious longings — are present in the claims for our newest technologies and our newest documents. *The Web and the Internet will give us so much more of what we really want.* This is the structure of nearly every claim now being made, whether in business, in education, in government, or in social and communal relations. Much of the power of these claims comes, I believe, not from the utility of the goods or services being offered, but from the deeper longing or lack being touched, and the hint that it will be satisfied. Therein lies the danger. It is one thing to buy a new Mercury Villager because you want to get your kids to the beach. But it is something else again if you spend the money in the hope of being liberated from the suffering of the world. How can we begin to separate hype from hope, without acknowledging and examining the depths of our humanity, including our fears and anxiety, and our desperate search for stable ground?

11

Scrolling Forward

IT IS MORE THAN TWENTY YEARS since I left the world of computers behind in search of greener pastures, expecting never to return. Without quite realizing it at the time, in moving to London to study calligraphy and bookbinding, I was making a pilgrimage to the place where a resistance movement had been born that stood in opposition to some of the very qualities and modes of being I was then fleeing. The Arts and Crafts Movement had arisen as a response to industrialization and bureaucratization. It wanted to create and sustain an alternative to the modes of production and the values that Max Weber had earlier identified: an emphasis on depersonalized control, efficient production, rationalization, and disenchantment. People could take greater charge of their lives, their relationships, and their time, it insisted, and their labor could be a fulfilling gift and a form of service, not just a way to "earn a living."

My time in London exposed me to this alternative vision. Some of this exposure came through reading and discussion, through museum visits and study. But mostly it came through experience. I lived a quieter, less dramatic, and less outwardly energetic life than I had lived in Palo Alto. Those many hundreds of hours sitting at a drawing board, using pencil, pen, and quill, were tranquil and even contemplative (although I wouldn't have used this word at the time). After the trauma of graduate school, this slower rhythm, these inner-centered practices, provided much-needed healing and rejuvenation.

So it was a great surprise when my inner momentum seemed to carry me back into the world of high tech. What carried me most directly was the love of writing, of written forms, of documents. I found myself not only wanting to luxuriate in the rhythms of earlier writing practices, but to study, come to further understand, and perhaps even influence, the newly emerging techniques and technologies. Most of all, though, without quite knowing what it could mean, I wanted somehow to carry the spirit of calligraphy — its values, not its specific practices — into the world of computers.

In the nearly twenty years since I returned from London, the distance between these two worlds — high tech and traditional crafts — seems only to have increased. We are more bureaucratic in our ways, not less. Industrial modes of production — efficient, calculated, impersonal — have an even stronger hold on us. And everything is speeding up. Many of us now find ourselves caught up in a frenzy of activity, both in our work lives and our personal lives. Borrowing a term usually reserved for children, Albert Borgmann, a philosopher of technology at the University of Montana, calls our entire culture "hyperactive."[1] Under such circumstances, some crucial dimension of life seems endangered, which the Arts and Crafts Movement took pains to support. As we rush faster and faster, we seem to have less time *to live*.

We can see the search for ever-greater speed and efficiency being played out in our documents and document-oriented practices. We've managed to create a technological infrastructure that allows us to produce digital forms in a flash and distribute them in unlimited quantities nearly anywhere in the world in an instant. And more than ever before, we think of these new, virtual documents as mere carriers of information, and information as the nutrients that need to be squeezed out of them and quickly ingested. In a fast-paced world in which fast food and caffeinated beverages have become the norm, we want (and have come to expect) that our new documents will deliver to us, as quickly as possible, just the information content we need to satisfy the next item on our agenda: to make a stock trade, to schedule a meeting, to respond to an urgent business or personal message.

In the early 1990s, while driving up Nineteenth Avenue in San Francisco, I saw a billboard advertising a local radio station painted on the wall of a building. "Don't Drive Around Empty-Headed!" the billboard declared in a bold typewriter font. A cartoon caricature of a man was shown lifting off the top of his skull; you could see that his head was filled with just the information the radio station could provide: sports, weather, recreation, and so on. Not only can we and should we fill up on the right information, the ad seemed to say, but we will be the worse for not having it: we will be *uninformed*.

At the same time that such messages flood our environment, other, albeit weaker, signals are also present. Other rhythms of living, other modes of being speak to us through our documents and our document practices. For some of us, books and libraries symbolize some of the very qualities and modes of being that are threatened in our fast-paced, instrumental lives. Books speak of time and depth and attention. They speak of a slower rhythm of life. And in their weighty physicality, they draw us back to our own materiality, and to the materiality of the world. Libraries are places not just where books can be found, but where people can temporarily remove themselves from the speed and busyness of life, where they can read and write and reflect. They are (or can be) shared, sacred spaces in a secular, common world — one of the only spaces outside places of worship where quiet and contemplation are not only sanctioned but enforced.[2]

A year or two ago, I was sitting in a café working on this book. A woman at the next table struck up a conversation with me, and asked me what I was writing. I gave her an overview, and this led to a discussion about the place of books in an increasingly digital world. She had recently visited a home that was empty of books, as far as she could tell: no bookcases, no books on coffee tables, none. What she said next has remained fixed in my memory. "I don't care if you don't read," she said, "but how can you live without books?" I know exactly what she meant; I feel much the same way. I don't know how

I could live without books. But the truth is, there are other things even more important to me than books or reading: certain views and values, states of mind and body, qualities of experience and attention.

Will books go away? Is a universal library just around the corner? Will e-mail supplant or revive the letter? Will digital technologies diminish, and perhaps abolish, paperwork and red tape? What are we really asking here? I suspect that these questions serve less as requests for information or insight than as expressions of concern for the character and quality of our lives. And I suspect that the artifacts, institutions, and practices we are inquiring about are largely functioning as symbols of qualities we want either to embrace or to avoid — qualities of time and attention, of intimate connection, of impersonal entanglement. Although I am concerned about the possible disappearance of books, for example, I am even more concerned about preserving and protecting these ways of being.

We make a mistake, I believe, when we fixate on particular forms and technologies, taking them, in and of themselves, to be the carriers of what we want either to embrace or resist. Not only do we fail to see the forms and technologies in their full complexity, but we use them, in their symbolic simplicity, as blunt instruments with which to beat one another over the head. We also make a mistake, we limit our possibilities, when we assume that one technology, or one form of activity, must necessarily replace another. It isn't a question, it needn't be a question, of books or the Web, of letters or e-mail, of digital libraries or the bricks-and-mortar variety, of paper or digital technologies. Nor need it be a question of speed and efficiency versus a slower pace of life. These modes of operation are only in conflict when we insist that one or the other is *the only way* to operate. Who would argue that speedy care is unimportant when someone's life is at stake? But equally, why should we have to justify the time — either in the workplace or in our personal lives — to think through the consequences of important decisions?

What we're most in need of, I believe, is balance. Depersonalized, disenchanted ways of being have increasingly come to dominate our lives. Melvil Dewey — obsessive, controlling, making order, and fearing death — is the symbol of our times. We see too little of Whitman — expansive, accepting, lingering, celebrating — even though he lives in us too. Ironically, though, to see this imbalance, and to stand a chance of correcting it, we need the very qualities of time, attention, and reflection that are so sorely lacking. It is almost as if the condition of modern life conspires to deprive us of that which would allow us to make the necessary adjustments.

Why, then, are we driving ourselves ever faster? On one level, the answer seems obvious enough. We are part of an economic system that defines success as progress, and progress as growth, and growth as productivity of a particular sort. Greater productivity means a higher standard of living, which means a better quality of life. From this standpoint, it is clear enough, *faster is better.* But from another point of view — the wear and tear on our bodies, the loss of "quality time," the narrowed perspectives on life — it is less obviously so. Yet the logic and momentum of our economic system take precedence over these other basic human needs.

What prompts us to ignore the needs of our bodies and psyches? There are many factors and reasons, I'm sure. Certainly, many of us feel we don't have a choice: we need to earn a living, to support our families, and we will do whatever it takes. We may well feel that *other people* — those with wealth and power — are setting the agenda, and deriving the greatest benefit. And while there may some truth in this, I suspect that we are all to some extent suffering from a system we didn't create. As I've tried to make sense of this picture, I have found some clues in examining the existential, or religious, dimension of our lives. Could it be that we are rushing ever faster, hoping to save ourselves, to liberate ourselves from our suffering and our sense of lack?

Max Weber believed that the roots of the capitalist system could be found in a displacement of the religious quest for salvation onto the economic sphere. Weber's thesis, as he presented it in *The Protestant Ethic and the Spirit of Capitalism,* was controversial in its time, and it remains controversial to this day. But others have continued to take up the spirit of his argument without fully adopting his specifics.

Certainly, Ernest Becker's story of the denial of death has a Weberian ring to it. David Loy's version, in which unexamined and unacknowledged lack drives us to seek a resolution we can never actually achieve, also points to the displacement of religious longing. "[A]lthough we think of the modern world as secularized," Loy says, "its values . . . are not only derived from religious ones . . . , they are largely the same values, albeit transformed by the loss of reference to an other-worldly dimension."[3]

I find this existential/religious perspective on our current circumstances useful in two ways. For one, it helps me make sense of the extreme claims, the hype and exaggeration, that are such a notable feature of our discussions of the new technologies. For some time now we have regularly heard that everything is revolutionary: that digital technologies are the biggest thing since Gutenberg (or are they bigger?); that digital books will fulfill the true (yet unfulfilled) promise of books; that we are on the verge of a universal library and a single, globally connected community; that digital technologies portend the arrival of global democracy; and even that the Internet is the infrastructure of Teilhard de Chardin's global consciousness, the noosphere.

Faced with such extreme and unsupported statements, I find myself wanting to turn away in frustration and disbelief. But in examining the claims more closely, I've come to see them as important expressions of something quite real, quite genuine. For what I now see in much of the current hype is a response to our existential plight: the longing to be freed from the confines of our earthly (and therefore mortal) conditions and our lack, the hope that information and knowledge will ultimately set us free, and that our new technological circumstances will provide the vehicles for achieving this. What is the long-standing dream of a complete, universal library about, if not the hope that knowledge will ease our burden, that it will ultimately save us?

I find the existential lens a useful one in another way as well: it serves as a reminder of the central questions of life. Especially when life is so busy, even frantic, when the claims on our time are impossible to meet, when we seem only to fall farther behind, and when the language of technology claims near-canonical status, it is useful to be reminded — at least I find it useful — that we are fragile creatures living uncertain lives, that the world is much bigger than any of our plans or projects. Looking through this lens, I see more clearly.

In the climax of Borges's story "The Aleph," which served as the basis for the calligraphic piece I mentioned earlier, the protagonist comes upon the point in the universe that contains all other points. Gazing into this point, the Aleph, he sees the entire universe. "And here begins my despair as a writer," he exclaims. How can he possibly describe what he has seen? For "[w]hat my eyes beheld was simultaneous, but what I shall now write down will be successive, because language is successive." He then launches into a description that owes much to Whitman, a catalog of the mundane and the miraculous:

> I saw the teeming sea; I saw daybreak and nightfall; I saw the multitudes of America; I saw a silvery cobweb in the center of a black pyramid; I saw a splintered labyrinth (it was London); I saw, close up, unending eyes watching themselves in me as in a mirror; I saw all the mirrors on earth and none of them reflected me; . . . I saw bunches of grapes, snow, tobacco, lodes of metal, steam; I saw convex equatorial deserts and each one of their grains of sand; . . . I saw horses with flowing manes on a shore of the Caspian sea at dawn; I saw the delicate bone structure of a hand; I saw the survivors of a battle sending out picture postcards. . . .

"And I felt dizzy and wept," he concludes, "for my eyes had seen that secret and conjectured object whose name is common to all men but which no man has looked upon — the unimaginable universe."

Borges is regularly invoked by commentators wanting to extol the virtues of the emerging digital age. A number of people have been quick to note the parallel between the Aleph and the Web. "The Aleph," says Douglas Wolk, "the portal through which one can see every point in the universe, is Netscape Navigator in all but name."[4]

In much the same vein, Douglas Davis observes that "Mac-and-Netscape is my personal Aleph, in an early T-model form. Already many of us harbor a tiny screen about the size of the one described by Borges that permits us instant access to deep space (cf. The Hubble telescope site) and to reams of information about any subject, including yourself. Can you doubt that within a decade you and I will be seeing countless eyes, hearing countless voices on this universal plate of glass?"[5]

I've come to wonder, though, if all points in the universe — and all things and all creatures — aren't alephs. Certainly anything closely observed has the potential to surprise, mystify, and enlighten us. Perhaps some of us are just more attuned to the portals present in particular kinds of things: some find God in the Web, while others see the divine in nature, or in the faces of men and women. My privileged route is through documents. At times, looking at a cash register receipt is enough for me to recall Whitman's words: "Why should I wish to see God better than this day?"

In the end, how can we separate hype from hope, and both of these from present reality? Through careful examination and reflection, through pointed questioning, through public discussion. By admitting our ignorance, our concerns, our fears. By looking at present instabilities to see what they have to show us. We may not be able to predict the future, but in looking at documents we can perhaps see something at least as important: ourselves. For to look at our written forms is to see something of our striving for meaning and order, as well as the mechanism by which we continually create meaning and order. It is to see the anxiety within and behind this order. And it is also, potentially, to peek at that which lies beyond all formulations — "the unimaginable universe" — not just as an object of fear and denial, but of wonder and celebration.

Notes

Preface

1. Quoted in Gillian Naylor, *The Arts and Crafts Movement: A Study of Its Sources, Ideals and Influence on Design Theory* (Cambridge, Mass.: MIT Press, 1971), 12.
2. Ibid., 26.

Chapter 1. Meditation on a Receipt

1. Lucien Febvre and Henri-Jean Martin, *The Coming of the Book: The Impact of Printing, 1450–1800,* translated by David Gerard (London: NLB, 1979). See in particular the chapter titled "Manuscripts" by Marcel Thomas and chapter 1, "Preliminaries: The Introduction of Paper into Europe."
2. Scott D. N. Cook, "Technological Revolutions and the Gutenberg Myth," in *Internet Dreams: Archetypes, Myths, and Metaphors,* edited by Mark Stefik (Cambridge, Mass.: MIT Press, 1996), 74.
3. Febvre and Martin, *The Coming of the Book,* 36.
4. Berthold L. Ullman, *Ancient Writing and Its Influence* (New York: Cooper Square Publishers, 1963), 64–65.
5. Denise Schmandt-Besserat, *How Writing Came About* (Austin: University of Texas Press, 1996).
6. George Kubler, *The Shape of Time: Remarks on the History of Things* (New Haven: Yale University Press, 1975), 2.
7. Chiang Yee, *Chinese Calligraphy: An Introduction to Its Aesthetic and Technique* (Cambridge: Harvard University Press, 1976), 5–6.
8. M. T. Clanchy, *From Memory to Written Record: England 1066–1307,* 2d ed. (Oxford: Blackwell, 1993).

Chapter 2. What Are Documents?

1. David Weinberger, "What's a Document?" *Wired,* August 1996, 112.
2. George Steiner, "The End of Bookishness?" *Times Literary Supplement,* 8–14 July 1988, 754.
3. Quoted in David R. Olson, *The World on Paper* (Cambridge, England: Cambridge University Press, 1994), 29–30.

4. Byron L. Sherwin, *The Golem Legend: Origins and Implications* (Lanham, Md.: University Press of America, 1985), 7.

5. Bruno Latour, "Where Are the Missing Masses? The Sociology of a Few Mundane Artifacts," in *Shaping Technology/Building Society: Studies in Technological Change,* edited by Weibe E. Bijker and John Law (Cambridge: MIT Press, 1992), 225–58.

6. Otto Jespersen, *Essentials of English Grammar* (University, Ala.: University of Alabama Press, 1969), 17. In the original, the phrase appears in bold-face for emphasis.

7. Geoffrey Sampson, quoted in *Writing Systems: A Linguistic Introduction* (Stanford, Calif.: Stanford University Press, 1985), 11.

8. Ibid.

9. Roy Harris, *The Origin of Writing* (London: Gerald Duckworth & Co., 1986), 29.

10. Nelson Goodman, *Languages of Art: An Approach to a Theory of Symbols* (Indianapolis: Bobbs-Merrill, 1968).

11. First published by the British Library, the lectures have been reissued by Cambridge University Press: D. F. McKenzie, *Bibliography and the Sociology of Texts* (Cambridge, England: Cambridge University Press, 1999).

12. Michael K. Buckland, "What Is a 'Document'?" *Journal of the American Society for Information Science* 48, no. 9 (1997): 804–9.

13. Both quotes are from Buckland's article, above.

14. Jay David Bolter, *Writing Space: The Computer, Hypertext, and the History of Writing* (Hillsdale, N.J.: Lawrence Erlbaum Associates, 1991), 31.

Chapter 3. Leaves of Grass

1. Stephen Mitchell, preface to *Song of Myself,* by Walt Whitman, edited by Stephen Mitchell (Boston: Shambhala, 1993), vii.

2. Paul Zweig, *Walt Whitman: The Making of the Poet* (New York: Basic Books, 1984).

3. Malcolm Cowley, introduction to *Leaves of Grass,* edited by Malcolm Cowley (New York: Penguin Books, 1986), xii–xiii.

4. Cowley is here quoting from the first edition. My childhood copy reads:

> Swiftly rose and spread around me the peace and joy and
> knowledge that pass all the argument of the earth;
> And I know that the hand of God is the promise of my own,
> And I know that the spirit of God is the brother of my own,
> And that all the men ever born are also my brothers, and the
> women my sisters and lovers . . .

5. Ibid., xxxii.

6. William Proctor Williams and Craig S. Abbott, *An Introduction to Bibliographical and Textual Studies,* 2d ed. (New York: The Modern Language Association of America, 1989), 4.
7. Cowley, introduction to *Leaves of Grass,* xv.
8. Mitchell, preface to *Song of Myself,* vii.
9. Charles Green, " 'I Sing the Body Electric': Walt Whitman on the Web," *Kairos* 2, no. 2 (1997). This is an online journal; its URL is english.ttu.edu/kairos/2.2.
10. Fortunately, scholarly online versions of Whitman's authorized editions can now be found in the Walt Whitman Hypertext Archive at jefferson.village.virginia.edu/whitman/.
11. E. E. Evans-Pritchard, introduction to *The Gift: Forms and Functions of Exchange in Archaic Societies,* by Marcel Mauss (New York: W. W. Norton and Company, 1967), ix.
12. Lewis Hyde, *The Gift: Imagination and the Erotic Life of Property* (New York: Vintage Books, 1983), 151.
13. Ibid.
14. Alfred Kazin, *God and the American Writer* (New York: Alfred A. Knopf, 1997), 113.

Chapter 4. The Dark Side of Documents

1. Denise Schmandt-Besserat, *How Writing Came About* (Austin: University of Texas Press, 1996).
2. C. M. Kelly, "Later Roman Bureaucracy: Going Through the Files," in *Literacy and Power in the Ancient World,* edited by Alan K. Bowman and Greg Wolf (Cambridge, England: Cambridge University Press, 1996), 167.
3. James R. Beniger, *The Control Revolution: Technological and Economic Origins of the Information Society* (Cambridge, Mass.: Harvard University Press, 1986), 219.
4. Ibid., 279.
5. Ibid., 14.
6. JoAnne Yates, *Control Through Communication* (Baltimore: Johns Hopkins University Press, 1989), 1–2.
7. Quoted in ibid., 9.
8. Ibid., 12.
9. Quoted in ibid., 5.
10. Quoted in ibid., 41.
11. Quoted in ibid., 61–62.
12. Ibid., 96.
13. Ibid., 15.

14. Quoted in Lawrence A. Scaff, *Fleeing the Iron Cage: Culture, Politics, and Modernity in the Thought of Max Weber* (Berkeley: University of California Press, 1989), 227.

15. Quoted in Rogers Brubaker, *The Limits of Rationality: An Essay on the Social and Moral Thought of Max Weber* (London: Allen & Unwin, 1984), 22.

16. Dorothy E. Smith, "The Active Text: A Textual Analysis of the Social Relations of Public Textual Discourse," in *Texts, Facts, and Femininity: Exploring the Relations of Ruling* (London: Routledge, 1990), 120–58.

17. Joseph Weizenbaum, *Computer Power and Human Reason: From Judgment to Calculation* (San Francisco: W. H. Freeman, 1976).

Chapter 5. Reach Out and Touch Someone

1. John L. Brown, "What Ever Happened to Mme. de Sévigné? Reflections on the Fate of the Epistolary Art in a Media Age," *World Literature Today* 64, no. 2 (1990): 215.

2. Leslie B. Mittleman, "The Twentieth-Century English Letter: A Dying Art?" *World Literature Today* 64, no. 2 (1990): 222.

3. Ibid., 226.

4. Martin Arnold, "Making Books," *The New York Times,* 21 January 1999.

5. Adam Gopnik, "The Return of the Word," *The New Yorker,* 6 December 1999, 49.

6. Ibid., 50.

7. Bill Harby, "Learning Our Letters," *Island Scene Online,* 2 April 1997. http://www.islandscene.com/internet/1997/970402/cybertalk_part1/index.html

8. "The Life of the Mind Goes Digital," *U.S. News Online,* 22 March 1999.

9. Howard Anderson and Irvin Ehrenpreis, "The Familiar Letter in the Eighteenth Century: Some Generalizations," in *The Familiar Letter in the Eighteenth Century,* edited by Howard Anderson, Philip B. Daghlian, and Irvin Ehrenpreis (Lawrence: University of Kansas Press, 1966), 274.

10. Ibid., 275.

11. Quoted in Stanley K. Stowers, *Letter Writing in Greco-Roman Antiquity* (Philadelphia: Westminster Press, 1986), 29.

12. Andrew Carroll, ed., *Letters of a Nation* (New York: Broadway Books, 1997).

13. Lisa Grunwald and Stephen J. Adler, eds., *Letters of the Century: America, 1900–1999* (New York: Dial Press, 1999).

14. Jennifer Williams, *The Pleasures of Staying in Touch* (New York: Hearst Books, 1998), ix.

15. Ibid., x.

16. See the Greeting Card Association's Web site: www.greetingcard.org.

17. Anderson and Ehrenpreis, "The Familiar Letter in the Eighteenth Century," 270.

18. Richard Carline, *Pictures in the Post: The Story of the Picture Postcard and Its Place in the History of Popular Art* (Philadelphia: Deltiologists of America, 1972), 57.

19. Ibid., 55.

20. Ibid., 57.

21. Ibid., 55.

22. Ibid., 57.

23. Ernest Dudley Chase, *The Romance of the Greeting Card* (Cambridge, England: Cambridge University Press, 1956), 5.

24. Ken Erickson, "Postal Modernism," *Anthropology Newsletter,* March 1999, 17–18.

25. The PRC approved the increase to 33 cents, and in November 2000 approved another one-cent increase.

26. Alan R. Swendiman, "Initial Brief of Greeting Card Association" (Washington, D.C.: Greeting Card Association, 1998), 1.

27. Customers engage in another card-buying practice as well. According to Marc Lesser, the founder of the greeting card publisher Brushdance, people will sometimes buy a number of cards at one time, creating their own private store of them, and choosing from these when they need a card for a specific occasion.

28. Ken C. Erickson, "Direct Testimony of Ken C. Erickson on Behalf of Greeting Card Association," 1997, 18.

29. Catherine C. Marshall, "Annotation: From Paper Books to the Digital Library," in *ACM Digital Libraries '97: Proceedings of the 2nd ACM International Conference on Digital Libraries* (New York: Association of Computing Machinery, 1997), 131–140.

30. Michael Warner, *The Letters of the Republic: Publication and the Public Sphere in Eighteenth-Century America* (Cambridge, Mass.: Harvard University Press, 1990).

31. Tamara Plakins Thornton, *Handwriting in America: A Cultural History* (New Haven: Yale University Press, 1996), 29–30.

32. Mauss, *The Gift,* 10.

33. Quoted in Marshall Sahlins, *Stone Age Economics* (Chicago: Aldine-Atherton, 1972), 153–54.

34. Erickson, "Direct Testimony," 21.

35. Ivan Illich, *In the Vineyard of the Text: A Commentary to Hugh's Didascalicon* (Chicago: University of Chicago Press, 1993), 35–36, n. 24.

36. M. T. Clanchy, *From Memory to Written Record: England 1066–1307,* 2d ed. (Oxford, England: Blackwell, 1993), 162.

37. Benedict Anderson, *Imagined Communities: Reflections on the Origin and Spread of Nationalism* (London: Verso, 1986).

Chapter 6. Reading and Attention

1. William James, *The Principles of Psychology* (New York: Dover Publications, 1950), 403–4.
2. Beatrice Ward, *The Crystal Goblet* (Cleveland: The World Publishing Company, 1956).
3. Roger Chartier, *Forms and Meanings: Texts, Performances, and Audiences from Codex to Computer* (Philadelphia: University of Pennsylvania Press, 1995), 18.
4. Robert Darnton, "What Is the History of Books?" in *The Kiss of Lamourette: Reflections in Cultural History* (New York: W. W. Norton, 1990), 107.
5. Robert Darnton, "How to Read a Book," *New York Review of Books*, 6 June 1996, 52.
6. Quoted in Nicholas Howe, "The Cultural Construction of Reading in Anglo-Saxon England," in *The Ethnography of Reading*, edited by Jonathan Boyarin (Berkeley: University of California Press, 1992), 61.
7. Jean Leclercq, O.S.B., *The Love of Learning and the Desire for God: A Study of Monastic Culture*, translated by Catharine Misrahi (New York: Fordham University Press, 1977), 19.
8. Illich, *In the Vineyard of the Text*, 54.
9. Daniel Boyarin, "Placing Reading: Ancient Israel and Medieval Europe," in Boyarin, *The Ethnography of Reading*, 13–14.
10. Quoted in Howe, "Cultural Construction," 59–60.
11. Illich, *In the Vineyard*, 82.
12. The distinction between intensive and extensive reading is controversial. Certainly it would be a mistake to think that extensive reading simply replaced intensive reading at one point in time (i.e., the second half of the eighteenth century).
13. George Steiner, "The End of Bookishness?" *Times Literary Supplement*, 8–14 July 1988, 754.
14. George Steiner, "Ex Libris: A Love Letter Written to Reading," *The New Yorker*, 17 March 1997, 27.
15. Illich, *In the Vineyard*, 3.
16. William Mitchell, *City of Bits: Space, Place, and the Infobahn* (Cambridge, Mass.: MIT Press, 1995).
17. Simon Jenkins, "Books Do Furnish a Mind," *The Times* (of London), 22 April 1998, 18.
18. Geoffrey Nunberg, ed., *The Future of the Book* (Berkeley: University of California Press, 1996).

19. Deborah Tannen, *The Argument Culture: Moving from Debate to Dialogue* (New York: Random House, 1998).

20. Carla Hesse, "Humanities and the Library in the Digital Age," in *What's Happened to the Humanities,* edited by Alvin Kernan (Princeton: Princeton University Press, 1997), 116.

21. Paul Duguid, "Material Matters: The Past and Futurology of the Book," in Nunberg, ed., *The Future of the Book,* 74.

22. Ibid., 73.

23. For an alternative conception of information, grounded in people and social reality, see John Seely Brown and Paul Duguid, *The Social Life of Information* (Boston: Harvard Business School Press, 2000).

24. Herbert Simon, "Rationality as Process and as Product of Thought," *American Economic Review* 68, no. 2 (1978): 13.

25. Richard A. Lanham, *The Electronic Word: Democracy, Technology and the Arts* (Chicago: University of Chicago Press, 1993), 227.

26. Warren Thorngate, "On Paying Attention," in *Recent Trends in Psychology,* edited by William J. Baker, Leendert P. Mos, Hans V. Rappard, and Henderikus J. Stam (New York: Springer-Verlag, 1988), 247–63.

27. Geoffrey Nunberg, "Farewell to the Information Age," in Nunberg, ed., *The Future of the Book,* 125.

28. Michael Joyce, "The Lingering Errantness of Place": A Talk Given at the ACRL/LITA Joint Presidents Program, American Library Association, 114 Annual Conference, Chicago, 26 June 1995.

29. Geoffrey Nunberg, "The Places of Books in the Age of Electronic Reproduction," *Representations* 42 (1993): 22.

Chapter 7. Libraries and the Anxiety of Order

1. Henry Petroski, *The Book on the Bookshelf* (New York: Alfred A. Knopf, 1999).

2. Geoffrey C. Bowker and Susan Leigh Star, *Sorting Things Out: Classification and Its Consequences* (Cambridge, Mass.: MIT Press, 1999), 1–2.

3. Luciano Canfora, *The Vanished Library: A Wonder of the Ancient World* (Berkeley: University of California Press, 1990), 20.

4. L. D. Reynolds and N. G. Wilson, *Scribes and Scholars: A Guide to the Transmission of Greek and Latin Literature,* 3d ed. (Oxford: Clarendon Press, 1991), 7.

5. Jack Goody, *The Domestication of the Savage Mind* (Cambridge, England: Cambridge University Press, 1977), 85–86.

6. James Westfall Thompson, *Ancient Libraries* (Hamden, Conn.: Archon Books, 1962), 3–8.

7. Reynolds and Wilson, *Scribes and Scholars,* 7.

8. Quoted in Patrick Williams, *The American Public Library and the Problem of Purpose* (New York: Greenwood Press, 1988), 4.
9. Francis L. Miksa, "Classification," in *The Encyclopedia of Library History*, edited by Wayne A. Wiegand and Donald G. Davis (New York: Garland Publishing, 1994), 145–46.
10. Dee Garrison, *Apostles of Culture: The Public Librarian and American Society, 1876–1920* (New York: Free Press, 1979), 114.
11. Ibid., 112–13.
12. Wayne A. Wiegand, *Irrepressible Reformer: A Biography of Melvil Dewey* (Chicago: American Library Association, 1996).
13. Francis L. Miksa, *The DDC, the Universe of Knowledge, and the Post-Modern Library* (Albany, N.Y.: Forest Press, 1998), 42.
14. *Library Catalog* (Boston: Library Bureau, 1909), 5.
15. Wiegand, *Irrepressible Reformer*, 377.
16. Quoted in Garrison, *Apostles of Culture*, 106.
17. Garrison, *Apostles of Culture*, 107.
18. Both quotes in ibid., 112.
19. Ibid., 115.
20. Bohdan S. Wynar, *Introduction to Cataloging and Classification*, 8th ed. (Englewood, Colorado: Libraries Unlimited, 1992), 332.
21. All quotes are from Francis Miksa, "The Cultural Legacy of the 'Modern Library' for the Future," *The Journal of Education for Library and Information Science* 37, no. 2 (1996): 100–119.
22. Roger Chartier, *The Order of Books*, translated by Lydia G. Cochrane (Stanford, Calif.: Stanford University Press, 1994), vii.

Chapter 8. A Bit of Digital History

1. Leila Avrin, *Scribes, Script and Books: The Book Arts from Antiquity to the Renaissance* (Chicago: American Library Association, 1991), 143.
2. Ibid., 328.
3. Ibid., 29.
4. Ibid., 329.
5. Ibid., 331.
6. Ibid., 329–30.
7. You would also have a great deal of trouble assuring consistency among the letters. Even a very skilled punchcutter would have difficulty making all the lowercase *e*'s look the same. This is more a consideration for us today than for the early printers. Because they were trying to replicate the look of handwritten manuscripts, they actually introduced variants in the letterforms to approximate the variability of handwritten text.

8. At roughly the same time, the designers of typesetting systems were beginning to use computers to further automate the work of setting type and printing documents. They were focused on the production of printed texts, and saw the computer as a tool in the service of this aim, not as a device in whose properties they were inherently interested. These two threads of development — from mathematics and computer science on the one hand, and from printing and typesetting on the other — would finally meet up in the 1970s.

9. Peter Deutsch and Butler Lampson, "An Online Editor," *Communications of the ACM* 10, no. 12 (1967): 793.

10. Theodor H. Nelson, *Dream Machines* (self-published, 1974), 21.

11. Bush published his vision of the Memex in Vannevar Bush, "As We May Think," *The Atlantic Monthly,* July 1945, 101–8. Earlier in the twentieth century, Paul Otlet, the Belgian lawyer and documentalist, envisioned hypertext-like systems. See W. Boyd Rayward, "Visions of Xanadu: Paul Otlet (1868–1944) and Hypertext," *Journal of the American Society for Information Science* 45, no. 4 (1994): 235–50.

12. www.lcweb.loc.gov/film/

Chapter 9. An Immense Effort

1. Mark Landler, "Now, Worse than Ever! Cynicism in Advertising," *The New York Times,* 17 August 1997.

2. Adrian Johns, *The Nature of the Book: Print and Knowledge in the Making* (Chicago: University of Chicago Press, 1998).

3. Susan Stellin, "Increasingly, E-Mail Users Find They Have Something to Hide," *The New York Times,* 10 February 2000.

4. Steven Shapin, *A Social History of Truth: Civility and Science in Seventeenth-Century England* (Chicago: University of Chicago Press, 1994), 8.

5. Peter Lyman and Stanley Chodorow, "The Future of Scholarly Communication," in *The Mirage of Continuity: Reconfiguring Academic Information Resources for the 21st Century,* edited by Brian L. Hawkins and Patricia Battin (Washington, D.C.: Council on Library and Information Resources and Association of American Universities, 1998), 95.

6. "As Publishers Perish, Libraries Feel the Pain," *The New York Times,* 3 November 2000.

7. Charles Bazerman, *Shaping Written Knowledge: The Genre and Activity of the Experimental Article in Science* (Madison: University of Wisconsin Press, 1988), 18.

8. Stanley Chodorow and Peter Lyman, "The Responsibilities of Universities in the New Information Environment," in *The Mirage of Continuity:*

Reconfiguring Academic Information Resources for the 21st Century, edited by Brian L. Hawkins and Patricia Battin (Washington, D.C.: Council on Library and Information Resources and Association of American Universities, 1998), 65.

9. Stevan Harnad, "The PostGutenberg Galaxy: How to Get There from Here," *The Information Society* 11, no. 4 (1995): 286.
10. Ibid., 289.
11. Stevan Harnad, "Sorting the Esoterica from the Exoterica: There's Plenty of Room in Cyberspace," *The Information Society* 11, no. 4 (1995): 320.
12. Ibid., 316.
13. Clifford Lynch, "The Scholarly Monograph's Descendants," in *The Specialized Scholarly Monograph in Crisis or How Can I Get Tenure If You Won't Publish My Book?,* edited by Mary M. Case (Washington, D.C.: Association of Research Libraries, 1999), 142–43.
14. Tom Bissell and Webster Younce, "All Is Vanity," *Harper's,* December 2000, 58.

Chapter 10. The Search for Stable Ground

1. George Steiner, "Our Homeland, the Text," *Salmagundi* 66 (1985): 4.
2. Ibid., 5.
3. Ernest Becker, *The Denial of Death* (New York: Free Press, 1973), 5.
4. David Loy, *Lack and Transcendence: The Problem of Death and Life in Psychotherapy, Existentialism, and Buddhism* (Atlantic Highlands, N.J.: Humanities Press, 1996), xiii–xiv.
5. Ibid., xiv.
6. Ibid., 14.
7. Jesper Svenbro, *Phrasikleia: An Anthropology of Reading in Ancient Greece,* translated by Janet Lloyd (Ithaca, N.Y.: Cornell University Press, 1993), 142.

Chapter 11. Scrolling Forward

1. Albert Borgmann, *Crossing the Postmodern Divide* (Chicago: University of Chicago Press, 1992).
2. Although this is changing — see Dean E. Murphy, "Moving Beyond 'Shh' (and Books) at Libraries," *The New York Times,* 7 March 2001.
3. David Loy, "Preparing for Something That Never Happens: The Means/End Problem in Modern Culture," *International Studies in Philosophy* 26, no. 4: 52.
4. Douglas Wolk, "Webmaster Borges," *salon.com,* 6 December 1999.
5. Douglas Davis, "Borges Is God (or, God Is Borgesian)," *New York Press,* vol. 11, issue 46, 18 November 1998.

Index